STRABO OF AMASIA

STRABO OF AMASIA

A Greek Man of Letters
in Augustan Rome

Daniela Dueck

London and New York

First published 2000
by Routledge
11 New Fetter Lane, London EC4P 4EE

Simultaneously published in the USA and Canada
by Routledge
29 West 35th Street, New York, NY 10001

Routledge is an imprint of the Taylor & Francis Group

Typeset in Garamond by
Florence Production Ltd, Stoodleigh, Devon
Printed and bound in Great Britain by
by MPG Books Ltd, Bodmin

British Library Cataloguing in Publication Data
A catalogue record for this book is available from the British Library

Library of Congress Cataloguing in Publication Data
Dueck, Daniela, 1965–
Strabo of Amasia : a Greek man of letters in
Augustan Rome / Daniela Dueck.
p. cm.
Includes bibliographical references (p.).
1. Strabo. 2. Geographers–Italy–Rome–Biography. 3. Strabo
Geography. 4. Geography, Ancient. 5. Augustus Emperor of Rome,
63 B.C.–14 A.D.–Influence. 6. Rome (Italy)–History–Augustus,
27 B.C.–14 A.D. I. Title.

G87.S95 D84 2000
937'.07'092–dc21   99–087661

ISBN 0–415–21672–9

CONTENTS

CONTENTS

PREFACE AND
ACKNOWLEDGEMENTS

This book is the offspring of a 1996 PhD dissertation on Strabo's *Geography* which I wrote as part of my studies at the Hebrew University of Jerusalem. Like an offspring it has some resemblance to its parent, but at the same time has a completely individual and separate character. Hence, many parts were added, others were omitted, and the rest was modified and freshly edited.

The key to the door leading into Strabo's world lies within his own writings. Therefore I often let the main character speak for himself. All quotations of Strabo's *Geography* and of his Greek and Latin contemporaries as well as of his predecessors are reprinted from the English translations of the Loeb Classical Library with few minor variations, with the kind permission of Harvard University Press. The individual translators are indicated in the proper places. Some epigrams of Crinagoras of Mytilene and Diodorus of Sardis are brought with the translation of Gow and Page (1968) *The Garland of Philip* with the kind permission of Cambridge University Press.

Many people have helped in various ways to promote the completion of this book. I would like to mention Hannah Cotton for her constant encouragement. Joseph Geiger has joined my Strabonian endeavour as my PhD adviser and was always prepared to read earlier versions of the present book and to give helpful comments. I am grateful to my teacher Margalit Finkelberg and to Benjamin Isaac for their true willingness to read versions and to give invaluable suggestions. Others discussed with me some points related to Strabo and shared their views. Among them were David Wasserstein, Hugh Lindsay, Sarah Pothecary, Katherine Clarke, Mira Reich and Johannes Engels. I am deeply thankful for the anonymous reader of two early chapters of this book who included in his favourable report some constructive suggestions. I am grateful to Ranon Katzoff and to the committee for the promotion of research of Bar Ilan University for consent to promote this book with financial aid. Finally, I thank all those who surrounded me during the time of writing, both family and friends, who helped me in more ways than they can imagine, such as an encouraging phone call or a homemade meal.

Daniela Dueck   Jerusalem, September 1999

ABBREVIATIONS

ABSA	*Annual of the British School at Athens*
ACD	*Acta Classica Universitatis Scientiarum Debreceniensis*
AFLPer	*Annali della Facoltà di Lettere e Filosofia. Università degli Studi, Perugia*
AIPHOS	*Annuaire de l'Institut de philologie et d'histoire orientales et slaves*
AJA	*American Journal of Archaeology*
AJPh	*American Journal of Philology*
ANRW	*Aufstieg und Niedergang der römischen Welt*
APA	*Acta Philologica Aenipontana*
AncSoc	*Ancient Society*
BAGB	*Bulletin de l'Association Guillaume Budé*
BRL	*Bulletin of the John Rylands University Library of Manchester*
CAH	*Cambridge Ancient History*
CIL	*Corpus Inscriptionum Latinarum*
ClAnt	*Classical Antiquity*
C&M	*Classica et Mediaevalia*
CPh	*Classical Philology*
CQ	*Classical Quarterly*
CR	*Classical Review*
DHA	*Dialogues d'histoire ancienne*
DNP	*Der Neue Pauly. Enzyklopädie der Antike*, ed. H. Cancik and H. Schneider, Stuttgart, 1996–
FGrH	*Fragmente der griechischen Historiker*, ed. F. Jacoby
FHG	*Fragmenta Historicorum Graecorum*, ed. C. Müller
GB	*Grazer Beiträge*
GGM	*Geographi Graeci Minores*, ed. C. Müller
GRBS	*Greek, Roman and Byzantine Studies*
HSCPh	*Harvard Studies in Classical Philology*
ICS	*Illinois Classical Studies*
IG	*Inscriptiones Graecae*
JHS	*Journal of Hellenic Studies*
JRS	*Journal of Roman Studies*

ABBREVIATIONS

LCL	Loeb Classical Library
LCM	Liverpool Classical Monthly
LEC	Les Études classiques
LS	Leipziger Studien zur classischen Philologie
LSJ	A Greek–English Lexicon, ed. H.G. Liddell, R. Scott, H.S. Jones, Oxford, 1953
MIL	Memoire dell' Instituto Lombardo
MUSJ	Mélanges de l'Université Saint Joseph, Beyrouth
OCD	Oxford Classical Dictionary, Oxford, 1996
OLD	Oxford Latin Dictionary, ed. P.G.W. Glare, Oxford, 1983
PBA	Proceedings of the British Academy
PEQ	Palestine Exploration Quarterly
PIR²	Prosopographia Imperii Romani, 2nd edn
P.Oxy.	The Oxyrhynchus Papyri
PRIA	Proceedings of the Royal Irish Academy
RE	Paulys Real-encyclopaedie der Classischen Altertumwissenschaft
REA	Revue des études anciennes
REG	Revue des études grecques
REL	Revue des études latines
RFIC	Rivista di filologia e d'istruzione classica
RhM	Rheinisches Museum
RIDA	Revue internationale des droits de l'Antiquité
RIL	Rendiconti dell' Instituto Lombardo
RSA	Rivista storica dell'Antichità
SVF	Stoicorum Veterum Fragmenta, ed. H. von Arnim
TAPhA	Transactions of the American Philological Association
ZPE	Zeitschrift für Papyrologie und Epigraphik
ZRGG	Zeitschrift für Religions- und Geistesgeschichte

1

STRABO'S BACKGROUND
AND ANTECEDENTS

AMASIA

Strabo of Amasia is known particularly for his geographical survey of the world of his time, the first century. But the work is more than the outcome of research and compilation of sources undertaken by a Greek scholar. It also supplies personal information about Strabo, being the only ancient source to throw light on his personality, which, as far as can be assessed, to some extent explains the nature of his writings. In this sense the man and his book are inseparable and present a mutual reflection, each of the other.

Strabo's intention was to survey the entire inhabited world. Dealing with northern Asia Minor, and describing the region of Pontus, he depicts Amasia, and mentions by the way that he was born in this city (12.3.15, C 547; 12.3.39, C 561), situated in central Pontus, about 75 km distant from the southern coast of the Black Sea.[1] This reticence is typical of all the biographical allusions and remarks scattered in the *Geography*, which are never part of a systematic self-presentation of the author, but appear somewhat sporadically throughout the work, to compose only an incomplete image. Thus, even Strabo's birth-date is no more than a conjecture and derives from what he chose to reveal in his work as we have it.

The Suda notes that Strabo 'lived at the time of Tiberius'[2] but this notion is too general and seems to refer to his prime as an active scholar. A better assessment of the birth-date was suggested by Niese who surveyed all the temporal phrases in the *Geography* such as 'a little before my time' (*mikron pro hemon*) and 'in my time' (*kath' hemas* or *eph' hemon*), interpreting them as literally referring to Strabo's lifetime since Strabo always refers to himself in the plural, the 'authorial we'. By collating these general temporal references with accurate dates derived from other sources, Niese tried to establish the period to which Strabo applies the term 'in my time'. Referring to the political situation in Paphlagonia Strabo says that 'this country . . . was governed by several rulers a little before my time, but . . . it is now in possession of the Romans' (12.3.41, C 562). It was Pompey who organized the region after subduing the Asian Iberians and the Albanians and before his campaign in Syria

1

and Judaea, that is, in the first half of 64 BCE. Since according to Strabo's phraseology these events occurred shortly before his time, meaning, as Niese understood it, shortly before he was born, Niese thought it possible to conclude that Strabo was born later that same year. This date is further made plausible by Strabo's comments on events occurring in the following year, which he already defines as happening in his lifetime, for instance, Galatia being governed by three rulers (12.5.1, C 567), a system ascribed to Pompey on his return from Syria at the end of 63 or the beginning of 62 BCE. It is true that Strabo applies the expression 'in my time' to his entire lifetime and to incidents covering a wide range of dates; still, Niese thought that the earliest events defined by these temporal expressions fix the year of birth in 64 BCE.[3]

In a recent article Sarah Pothecary has challenged Niese's conclusions, suggesting that these temporal clauses should not be taken as literally referring to Strabo's actual birth-date, for in order to thus understand them one would have to assume that every reader was indeed familiar with this exact date, otherwise the notion would not make any sense and would not serve any dating purpose. She therefore concludes that these clauses mean 'in our times' and differentiate between two historical periods, an earlier one when Pontus was an independent kingdom and a later one when the kingdom came under Roman domination, following Mithridates VI Eupator's defeat by the Romans and the reorganization of the region by Pompey roughly after 66–63 BCE. Hence, Strabo's exact date of birth cannot be discerned, though it is possible to put it between the years 64–50 BCE.[4] Pothecary's suggestion complies quite well with the chronological range deriving from the temporal clauses in Strabo, and although she challenges Niese's understanding of these clauses, the end result concerning the birth-date is still that it was probably not before 64 BCE.

The date of Strabo's death is also closely connected to his *Geography* and may be estimated in relation to the assumed date of composition of the work (chapter 6, p. 146), and the latest year alluded to in it. Strabo mentions the death of King Juba II of Mauretania and Libya, and the ascendance of his son Ptolemy to the throne (17.3.7, C 828), occurring in 23 CE.[5] Since this is the most recent event mentioned in the *Geography*, it indicates that Strabo was still alive at the time, and therefore that his death took place sometime after this year.

Suggestions as to the place where Strabo died also vary. This has again to do with the assumed place for the composition of the *Geography*, in Strabo's later years (below, p. 14), assuming that the place where he wrote the latest parts of the work is the place where he died shortly after he finished writing. Accordingly, the sites suggested are Amasia and Rome.[6] Strabo's notion of Naples is of interest in the present context:

> greater vogue is given to the Greek mode of life at Naples by the
> people who withdraw thither from Rome for the sake of rest,

2

meaning those who have made their livelihood by training the young, or still others who, because of old age or infirmity, long to live in relaxation.

(5.4.7, C 246)

This was taken by Honigmann as a hint at Strabo's own withdrawal in his last years from Rome to Naples where he may have died.[7] But as we shall see, Strabo's acquaintance with Rome after Augustus' death, and the probability that he composed the *Geography* in Rome at a later date, suggest that he also died there.

Amasia, and Pontus as a whole, require further attention, for the region underwent some political and geographical transformations which affected Strabo's family and possibly his approach to the politics of his adult life.[8] Prior to the Hellenistic era Pontus was one of the Asian satrapies of the Persian empire. The independent Pontic dynasty originated in the highest circles of the ruling Persian nobility in Cius. Mithridates III of Cius fled to Paphlagonia after his father was killed by Antigonus and after he defeated certain Seleucid forces. In 281 BCE he became the first king of the Pontic dynasty and thus acquired the name *Ktistes*, 'Founder'. His descendants continued the dynastic line until the reign of Mithridates VI Eupator.

The kings of the Pontic dynasty, each in turn, tried to extend the borders of the kingdom as well as to establish political relationships with neighbouring kingdoms through intermarriage. They tended to emphasize their local Iranian–Anatolian origins and at the same time in their courts and in their foreign relations they adopted the Hellenistic monarchical style. Thus Greek became the official language of Pontus. While a full account of the activities and policies of the Pontic kings down to the approximate time of Strabo's birth is out of order in this context, it will be useful to refer briefly to the ambitions of Mithridates VI Eupator who finally confronted Rome on Asian soil. Like his predecessors, Eupator extended the kingdom and in fact made it into the largest in existence. He also had some Roman contacts, such as Sertorius in Spain, and even bases in Greek territories in Athens and Boeotia. When the Romans finally decided to deal with his growing power, they challenged him in Greece and in Asia to a series of battles, during three 'Mithridatic' wars. Beginning in 97 BCE, these fierce struggles finally came to an end in 66 BCE with Eupator's refusal to surrender the kingdom to the Romans, and his death, perhaps by suicide. Pontus became part of the Roman province of Bithynia and Pontus. Under Antony some of the cities were ruled by native rulers, but in Augustus' time the west part of Pontus again became a Roman province, while the eastern part was governed by the dynasty of Polemon and Pythodoris.

The Roman domination of the Pontic region changed the political map not only by dividing it into parts of dissimilar political status, but also by joining areas of the Pontic kingdom of Mithridates to the adjacent Bithynia.

Thus Pompey subjected the regions around Colchis to local rulers and divided the rest into eleven political units comprising part of a new and larger province, Bithynia–Pontus.

Several times in his Pontic survey Strabo shows the complexity of the political situation in those years. The Roman governors following Pompey created new divisions, in some cases appointing rulers and kings, in others granting autonomy, even freedom, and in others keeping the cities under direct Roman control (12.3.1, C 541). The changes of rule in various cities also reflect the general fate of Pontus. For instance, Sinope was first subdued by Pharnaces, then by his successors in the Pontic dynasty down to Eupator, then by Lucullus, and 'now' has a colony of Romans who own part of the city (12.3.11, C 545–6). Again, Amisus, first possessed by the Pontic kings, was besieged by Lucullus, then by Pharnaces from the Bosporus, freed under Julius Caesar, handed over to local kings by Antony, later ruled by the tyrant Straton, and finally made independent by Augustus (12.3.14, C 547).

Due to these constant political permutations, the geographical borders of Pontus kept shifting. Pontus lies on the southern coast of the Black Sea, surrounded by Armenia Minor in the east, Bithynia in the west and Cappadocia in the south. The region is topographically divided into two large sections, the coastline and the mountainous inland region. Most of its cities were originally early Greek settlements founded along the sea-coast, such as Sinope, Amisus and Pharnacia, whose economy and character were determined by maritime commerce. Amasia was the largest inland urban centre. Most of the other settlements in the interior were villages, generally more affected by earlier Iranian–Anatolian culture.

The Pontic kings in general and Eupator in particular admired and fostered Hellenistic civilization. Eupator's court seems to have been full of Greek scholars, some of whom, such as Apellicon of Teos, also occupied political positions.[9] As we shall see, Strabo's family was among those who surrounded the kings, becoming part of an elite Hellenistic aristocracy.

The description in the *Geography* and some archaeological findings show that Amasia was a typical Hellenistic city in its monuments and culture (12.3.39, C 561). There were several temples, the main one devoted to *Zeus Stratios*, others to other divinities, some of them eastern, such as the Great Mother, Mithras and Serapis. The city possessed a theatre, a stadium and an aquaduct. The whole complex was surrounded by a wall, parts of which can still be seen on the ledge beside the mountain. Some Greek inscriptions from Amasia and the environs predating Augustus also indicate the Hellenization of the region.[10]

Strabo's interest in the affairs of Pontus and particularly his affiliation with its royal dynasty is apparent through his extensive survey of the military and political actions of Mithridates Eupator (for instance 12.3.2, C 541; 12.3.28; C 555; 12.3.40, C 562). He refers to his source for inside information as Neoptolemus, Mithridates' general (7.3.18, C 307), thus implying access to official documents or personal contact with a key personality in the Pontic court.

The constant border movements are reflected in the name of the region, called also 'Cappadocia near the Pontus' (12.1.4, C 534) or 'Cappadocia on the Euxine'.[11] This explains the various geographical apellations bestowed on Strabo, Josephus calling him 'Strabo the Cappadocian' (*ho Kappadox*) and the Suda 'Strabo the Amasian' (*Amaseus*).[12] Since these names are not contradictory it seems best to use the more specific rather than the more general one.

STRABO'S ANTECEDENTS

The political transformations in Pontus under Roman rule affected the behaviour and position of Strabo's family, which held a high position at the courts of Mithridates V Euergetes and VI Eupator. Three digressions in the *Geography* reveal some details about the author's ancestors.

Dorylaus of Amisus, Strabo's great-great-grandfather on his mother's side, was closely connected to Mithridates V Euergetes. In 121 BCE the king sent Dorylaus to recruit mercenaries from Greece, Thrace and Crete. During one of his sojourns in Crete Dorylaus became involved in a local feud between the people of Cnossos and the Gortynians, and helped to end the conflict. By the time he was ready to go back to Pontus he had heard of the king's assassination, the kingdom now being ruled by the queen and her young children. He therefore decided to remain in Cnossos where he established his own family by marrying a Macedonian woman named Sterope and begetting two sons – Lagetas and Stratarchas – and one daughter (10.4.10, C 477).

Meanwhile in Pontus, Mithridates VI Eupator, the eleven-year-old son of the murdered king, ascended to the throne. Dorylaus' nephew and homonym, Dorylaus son of Philetaerus, was adopted as the king's brother, and when both the king and his adopted brother grew up, Mithridates honoured Dorylaus by appointing him priest of Comana, second in rank to the king, and initiated the return of his kinsmen from Cnossos. Thus Lagetas, the son of Dorylaus the general, came to Pontus and established his family there. His daughter became the mother of Strabo's mother, making Lagetas Strabo's great-grandfather (figure 1). Strabo comments that as long as Dorylaus the priest prospered, his family enjoyed respect and prosperity, but when he was caught in an attempt to surrender the kingdom to the Romans, thinking that he might eventually become its ruler, the family lost its wealth and honour (10.4.10, C 477–8; 12.3.33, C 557).[13]

The family had another channel of relationship to the kings of Pontus, through Strabo's maternal grandfather. Mithridates Eupator was in the habit of appointing one of his friends to the governorship of Colchis. Among them was Moaphernes, the uncle of Strabo's mother on her father's side (11.2.18, C 499). But Moaphernes' brother, Strabo's grandfather, realizing

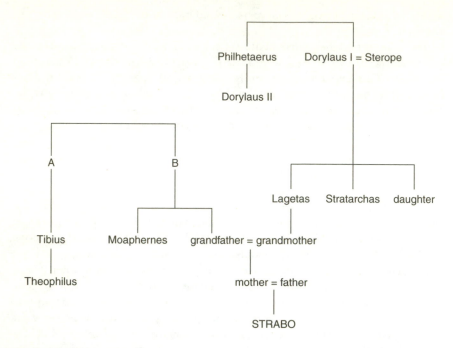

Figure 1 Strabo's genealogy

that the king could not succeed in his war against the Romans led by Lucullus, and troubled by the fate of his cousin Tibius and Tibius' son Theophilus, both executed by the king, caused fifteen fortresses to surrender to Lucullus. But the favours and honours promised him by the Romans were not granted and were not confirmed by the Senate, for the rivalry between Lucullus and Pompey caused the latter to consider all those who helped Lucullus as enemies (12.3.33, C 557–8).

These two stories are very similar. The two Dorylai as well as Moaphernes and his brother were of high rank in the kingdom and the closest intimates of the kings, but they betrayed Eupator by tending towards the Romans, thus humiliating and degrading their families. Strabo apparently decided to expose these intimate matters, perhaps to show his family's high rank and at the same time, in view of his personal connections with Rome (chapter 3), and the Roman-dominated political situation of his time (chapter 4), to accentuate its willingness to cooperate with the Romans.

The family information refers exclusively to the mother's side. Strabo's silence regarding his father's kin seems to imply the absence of any members worthy of mention, or perhaps a less elevated genealogy.[14]

Strabo's ancestors are known through sources other than the *Geography* though these do not specify the connection to Strabo. Appian, Plutarch and

Memnon all refer to the younger Dorylaus' military activities in the First Mithridatic War.[15] He was sent to help Archelaus, Eupator's general, and fought against Sulla near Orchomenus in Boeotia, later conquering Chios and expelling its inhabitants to Pontus. Plutarch recounts that Dorylaus was killed together with all Mithridates' friends during an army mutiny, for when the soldiers realized that the Pontic forces were in a bad situation *vis-à-vis* Lucullus, and that those who were close to the king were trying to save their property while denying the same right to the rest, they plundered their quarters and killed Dorylaus who 'had nothing else about him but his purple robe'.[16] This of course contradicts Strabo's version of Dorylaus' desertion of the king for the sake of the Roman cause.

Information on Strabo himself, as noted above, is confined to the few details he gives in the *Geography*. It seems especially strange that he does not introduce himself by name.[17] We attach the work to the author through later sources such as the Suda, which ascribes a *Geography* in seventeen books to 'Strabo of Amasia'; Plutarch, who identifies him as the composer of a historiographical work; and the medieval manuscripts of the geographical text entitled 'Strabo's *Geography*'.[18] 'Strabo', originally the Greek *strabon*, meaning 'a squinter', was a Roman *cognomen*, that is surname. The *cognomen* was chronologically the latest element in Latin nomenclature, and came after the *praenomen*, the *gentilicium* and the *tribus*. Roman *cognomina* referring to the human body and particularly those recording physical defects were very common among the nobility in the Republican period.[19] The fact that this Greek scholar bore a Roman name originates perhaps in his forefathers' relations with the Romans.

Several suggestions as to how the geographer acquired this Roman name have been offered, based on information given by Strabo about his family and about himself. The close relationship with Aelius Gallus, the governor of Egypt whom Strabo accompanied on his mission (chapter 3, p. 87), may suggest an association with names in his friend's and patron's family. Since Gallus had adopted Seianus whose biological father was Seius Strabo, perhaps when he made Strabo into a Roman citizen (if it was indeed Gallus who did this), he gave him a name associated with his adopted son, thus initiating him as Aelius Strabo.[20] Another suggestion derives from Strabo's social contact with Servilius Isauricus (12.6.2, C 568 and p. 88) who also had family connections with the name 'Strabo'. Apparently, in 51 BCE a certain Servilius Strabo sojourned in the neighbourhood of Nysa in Asia Minor. Since we know that the young geographer spent some time in that city studying with Aristodemus (below, p. 8), the meeting with Isauricus in Rome later in his life may imply an earlier contact with the family and a closer relationship which may have resulted in Roman citizenship and adoption of the name 'Strabo'.[21] A third proposal depends on the fact that Pompey's father was Pompeius Strabo. Perhaps, in spite of the tension between Lucullus and Pompey which caused the Romans to renege on their promises to Strabo's family, they got the citizenship from Pompey after all, and so the geographer became Strabo.[22]

All three suggestions thus assume that 'Strabo' is the Roman *cognomen* of a Roman citizen, but they are not supported by any hint of Strabo's *nomen*, whether Aelius, Servilius or Pompeius. Therefore we are left with this one part of a full Roman name and the supposition that it derives from a close relationship of Strabo or one of his ancestors with a Roman who granted one of them Roman citizenship together with the name. The circumstances of this event remain vague.

TEACHERS, FRIENDS AND EDUCATION

As the descendant of a highly ranked and formerly distinguished family in Pontus, belonging to the Hellenistic aristocracy nurtured by the Pontic kings, the young Strabo was educated by excellent Greek teachers and renowned scholars. These, as Strabo himself tells his readers, were Aristodemus of Nysa, Xenarchus of Seleucia and Tyrannion of Amisus. Such teachers evidently influenced him, and some of the details in his scholarly profile may be attributed to his early education. He mentions all three as famous natives of their cities, Nysa, Seleucia and Amisus.

Travelling to intellectual centres was part of usual scholarly activity in the Hellenistic age, facilitated by the peace prevailing at the time of Augustus. Strabo perceives the difference between the Tarsians who 'complete their education abroad and . . . but few go back home' and the Alexandrians who 'admit many foreigners and also send not a few of their own citizens abroad' (14.5.13, C 673–4). In these circumstances Rome became a major intellectual centre which turned into a meeting point for scholars from the entire Greek world (chapter 5). Strabo himself ended up in Rome (chapter 3) but he began his cycle of education in Asia Minor.

Aristodemus was 'extremely old' when Strabo came to study with him in the teacher's home, Carian Nysa (14.1.48, C 650). The city was at the time a great cultural centre with a large library and an intellectual circle known for its inclinations towards Homeric studies. Aristodemus himself was a grandson of Posidonius of Apameia, his mother being the daughter of the eminent historian and philosopher. His father was Menecrates who studied with Aristarchus, the great Homeric scholar, and he himself wrote a comparative study of the *Iliad* and the *Odyssey*. Aristodemus' brothers were Sostratus the grammarian who also wrote a geographical survey and Iason the philosopher who studied with his grandfather, Posidonius, and maintained his ideas. Aristodemus' cousin and homonym was also a grammarian, who taught Pompey.[23]

Aristodemus stood at the head of two schools of rhetoric, in Nysa and in Rhodes, where he lectured on rhetoric in the morning and on grammar in the evening, but when he instructed Pompey's children in Rome he focused on grammar alone (14.1.48, C 650). He wrote a *Histories* as an anthology of stories, engaged in Homeric studies, and produced commentaries and text amendments to the epics, claiming that Homer was originally a Roman.[24] Aristodemus' inclination towards Homeric studies and the particular intellectual character of Nysa as a centre of discussion on Homer, may have influenced and nourished Strabo's profound admiration of the ancient poet, to whom he ascribed extensive knowledge and erudite wisdom (chapter 2, p. 31). It is noteworthy that Aristodemus had lived in Rome, teaching Pompey's sons, a fact reflecting a wider phenomenon crystallizing in the latter half of the first century BCE, of interrelations between Greek intellectuals and Roman leaders (chapter 5). A similar connection emerged also in Strabo's personal biography, as we shall see. This may have influenced Aristodemus' writings as well, most apparently in his tracing of Homer's supposed Roman roots.

Xenarchus of Seleucia in Cilicia, a Peripatetic philosopher, was another mentor of Strabo's. He visited Alexandria and Athens, and finally came to Rome where he began to teach. He was one of Augustus' much-respected tutors and as such became a friend of Arius, another of Augustus' Greek professors of philosophy (chapter 3, p. 99). And 'shortly before the end he lost his sight, and then died of a disease' (14.5.4, C 670). It is possible that Strabo spent some time with Xenarchus as his disciple in Rome.[25] Xenarchus probably taught Strabo philosophy, thus completing another major part of the traditional education of the Greek aristocracy, consisting mainly of grammar, rhetoric and philosophy. Although Xenarchus was Peripatetic in his philosophical orientation, Strabo later seems to have developed his own inclinations, which were more Stoic (chapter 2, p. 62).

A third teacher was Tyrannion, the grammarian from Amisus. (12.3.16, C 548). Although originally from a town in Pontus near Amasia, Strabo's birthplace, Tyrannion taught Strabo in Rome, for, taken prisoner in the Mithridatic War in 70 BCE, he lived in that city from 67 BCE. There he became rich and famous for his scholarly skills, so much so that in 56 BCE he helped Cicero organize his library in Antium and even taught his nephew, the younger Quintus.[26] Strabo says that Tyrannion, 'who was fond of Aristotle (*philaristoteles on*)', also handled the books from Apellicon of Teos' library that had been transferred to Rome by Sulla (13.1.54, C 609).[27] This Greek scholar too was involved in the social milieu of the highest Roman circles.

A letter of Cicero to his friend Atticus implies Tyrannion's authority and perhaps interest in geography. In this letter, dated to the spring of 59 BCE, Cicero writes:

> The geographical work I had planned is a big undertaking. Eratosthenes, whom I had taken as my authority, is severely criticized by Serapion and Hipparchus, and, if I take Tyrannion's views too, there is no telling what the result would be.[28]

The geographers Serapion and Hipparchus disparaged Eratosthenes. In fact, Hipparchus' disapproval is the basis for Strabo's own assessment of Eratosthenes as it appears in the earlier parts of the *Geography* (chapter 2, p. 56). In this letter Cicero expresses his fear of similar criticism by Tyrannion which may be understood in this context as an indication of Tyrannion's particular authority in the subject. If this is so, the fact that Tyrannion was Strabo's teacher seems all the more significant since the student eventually himself composed a geographical work. Let us remember that Aristodemus of Nysa's brother Sostratus wrote a geographical treatise, which again shows that this subject matter came up in Strabo's more or less immediate intellectual surroundings. Cicero's plan was suggested eighty years before the probable date of Strabo's *Geography*, but it seems that this theme already had a special appeal for the Romans. Political developments under Augustus and the expansion of Rome by conquest added new horizons to the field. While Cicero's interest may reflect an adherence to a purely literary genre, geographical works in Augustus' time had an additional dimension of political relevance (chapter 4, p. 122).[29]

Strabo's friends and other people he met, particularly Greek scholars, probably also influenced his scholarly inclinations to some extent. The second-century scholar Athenaeus says that Strabo knew Posidonius of Apameia: 'he [Strabo] says in the seventh book . . . that he knew Posidonius, the philosopher from the Stoa'.[30] This inference is not entirely implausible since Posidonius died only in 50 BCE when Strabo may have been about thirteen or fourteen years of age. However, since we would expect Strabo to mention a meeting with such a renowned scholar, whereas he does not allude to it in his extant work, the comment in Athenaeus may derive from a misinterpretation of Strabo's remark on Posidonius, 'the Stoic, the most learned of all philosophers of my time' (16.2.10, C 753), understood as if Strabo said he knew him personally.[31] Still, even if no direct contact between the young Strabo and the great scholar occurred in reality, the influence of the latter is apparent throughout the *Geography* (chapter 2, p. 65), based on similar scholarly interests and perhaps enhanced by the fact that Aristodemus, Strabo's teacher, was Posidonius' grandson.

The persons whom Strabo names as his friends are mostly educated Greek men of letters although he had also relations with some Romans (chapter 3). Like other biographical and personal pieces of information in the *Geography*, the names of friends do not appear in the course of a particular digression, but as part of the lists of noted natives of famous cities.[32] Strabo's friends are Athenodorus of Tarsus, Posidonius' disciple (16.4.21, C 779); the philosophers Boethus and Diodotus of Sidon who were brothers (16.2.24, C 757); and the younger Diodorus of Sardis, an orator, historian and poet (13.4.9, C 628).

Athenodorus son of Sandon was a philosopher from Cana near Tarsus (14.5.14, C 674). Since 44 BCE he lived in Rome where he befriended

various Roman notables.[33] Cicero asked for his help while composing his
De Officiis, asking him to send a summary of Posidonius' opinion about
decision when duty contradicts utility. Like Arius, Xenarchus of Seleucia
and Apollodorus of Pergamon, Athenodorus, too, was Augustus' respected
teacher of philosophy (14.5.14, C 674). He even once came armed and
disguised to Augustus to warn him of a possible assassination. Leaving
Rome, he returned to Tarsus and became politically active, caused the fall
of the current undesirable government and ruled himself, supported by
Augustus. Strabo reports in detail the acts of the Tarsian opposition to
Athenodorus. Its members scribbled graffiti on the walls to express their
opinion of him and polluted the outside of his house, while he in turn
castigated them in the Tarsian assembly (14.5.14, C 674–5). Strabo's Tarsian
friend died at the age of eighty-two and was honoured annually like a hero.

Athenodorus, a Stoic, composed a philosophic treatise, an *On the Ocean*,
like Posidonius, and *On the Fatherland*, a description of Tarsus dedicated to
Octavia, Augustus' sister. Strabo made use of his friend's notions on low
and high tide, probably taking them from his *On the Ocean* (1.1.9, C 6;
1.3.12, C 55; 3.5.7, C 173). The details on the inner affairs of Tarsus
adduced in the *Geography* may derive from Athenodorus' *On the Fatherland*
or else from personal communications about political developments in the
city. Strabo also incorporated Athenodorus' impressions of his visit to Petra,
the capital of the Nabataeans.[34] Athenodorus was impressed by the justice
and peacefulness of the inhabitants and by the presence of many Romans
and foreigners in the city (16.4.21, C 799).

Strabo studied Aristotelian philosophy with Boethus of Sidon and probably
also met his brother Diodotus, likewise a philosopher (16.2.24, C 757).
Boethus, a Peripatetic, was a disciple of Andronicus of Rhodes and possibly of
Xenarchus of Seleucia whom he quotes in his writings. We may assume with
some caution that Strabo and Boethus studied together with Xenarchus, a
Peripatetic teacher. After his other teacher, Andronicus, died, Boethus moved
to Athens and became the head of the Peripatetic school in the city.[35]

Another friend was the younger Diodorus of Sardis. Strabo remarks that
Diodorus composed historical treatises and also lyric poetry and other poems
written in an ancient style (13.4.9, C 628). Diodorus lived for a while in
Rome where he probably met Strabo. This sojourn is apparent through the
contents of some of his epigrams, two of which glorify Tiberius and his
brother Drusus, thus reflecting the interest of Greek intellectuals living in
Rome in focusing on Roman affairs and society (chapter 5, p. 130).[36]

Strabo's travels, as far as we can trace their course (below), probably
enabled him to visit some of the most active scholarly centres of his times.
When he joined Aelius Gallus in his mission as governor of Egypt he spent
some years in Alexandria (2.5.12, C 118), in all likelihood enjoying its
great library, as his wide acquaintance with literature implies. Other great
cultural centres which also possessed libraries and concentrations of men of

letters, and to which Strabo had some access in the course of his life, were Nysa, where he was a disciple of Aristodemus, and Smyrna, which he may have visited.

Strabo's interest in the world of scholarship is apparent also through his allusions to scholarly centres of world-wide reputation in his time: Massilia which became a centre for philosophy and rhetoric so that Roman aristocrats prefer to go there rather than to Athens (4.1.5, C 180–1) and Tarsus whose people devote themselves to philosophy and to an encyclopaedic education (*paideia enkyklios*) so that their city functions as a well-known school surpassing even Athens and Alexandria (14.5.13, C 673–4). Strabo's extensive lists of scholars from the main fields of philosophy, rhetoric, grammar, poetry, history and so forth, who were born in various eastern cities (chapter 2, p. 79) may also be part of his respectful attitude towards the academic world. He stresses the influence of his own educational background on his tendencies as an author, saying that 'I am comparing present conditions with those described by Homer, for we must institute this comparison because of the fame of the poet and because of our familiarity with him from childhood' (8.3.3, C 337) and that he also feels he should quote 'legends that have been taught us from boyhood' (8.3.23, C 348).

With such teachers tutoring him and surrounded by friends who themselves had scholarly skills and interests, Strabo grew up to be a Greek man of letters with extensive knowledge in the celestial as well as the terrestrial sciences which he says a geographer would need (chapter 6, p. 186). The need for such wide and varied erudition is evident in order to enhance the perception of space, topography and ethnography. At the same time, Strabo's recommendation for a broad training is part of an approach common to Greek and Roman scholars, who stressed an encyclopaedic education and the acquisition of wide knowledge as necessary to anyone intending to become an expert in various fields such as history, rhetoric and even architecture. Polybius said that an historian has to be familiar with affairs of state and politics in order to be able to understand and describe historical events accurately. Cicero held that expertise in rhetoric requires from the orator-to-be skills of style, humour, acting, the understanding of emotions and knowledge of history, law and philosophy. Vitruvius, Strabo's Roman contemporary, contended that architecture requires graphic skill and proficiency in various and numerous fields which at first sight do not seem to pertain directly to architecture, like mathematics, history, philosophy, music, medicine, law and astronomy.[37] The polymath Varro, whose writings covered almost every field of knowledge and who influenced many Roman scholars, composed his *Disciplinae*, a work on the scholarly fields of knowledge befitting a free person, devoting one book to each of the nine *artes liberales*: grammar, dialectic, rhetoric, geometry, arithmetic, astronomy, music, medicine and architecture.[38] Varro's work is an indication of the importance of this canon of disciplines at the time, while its focus differs from the references of other scholars to a wider education. Each of these writers, as does Strabo, expands the variety of skills required in his profession in an attempt to emphasize its importance as a serious task suiting a philosopher.

The 'much learning' contributing to the utility of a *Geography*, and required from the ideal geographer, seems to be manifested in Strabo's own work, thus fulfilling his own ideal. True, he is far from being an expert in all scientific and philosophical realms and there are many inaccuracies throughout the *Geography*. However, the fact that he does touch on so many fields, from botany and zoology to history and philosophy, not only reflects the traditional Greek attitude to ethnography, but reveals his own interests and wide educational background, parts of which perhaps stem from his autodidactic inclinations.

Since Strabo's application of historiography, philosophy and science will be discussed at length in the following chapter, I shall briefly comment here on his reference to rhetoric and grammar as scholarly disciplines. Strabo was familiar with theories of rhetoric and literary definitions and also used rhetorical techniques in his own writing. He distinguishes between tragedy and comedy written in metric verse, and historiography and legal orations written in prose (1.2.6, C 17–18), and quotes Polybius' definition of the goal of oratory in comparison to other genres: 'the aim of history is truth . . . the aim of rhetorical composition is vividness . . . the aim of myth is pleasure and amazement' (1.2.17, C 25). In a reference which seems to imply techniques of legal oratory, Strabo says that it is possible to invalidate opinions of men who contradict themselves by showing that their own comments support the interest of their opponents (2.1.19, C 76).

Strabo does not include speeches in his work since he is not writing a *History*, but it may still be possible to evaluate his rhetorical skills. Several times he inserts imaginary dialogues with his predecessors, Polybius and Eratosthenes, adding energy and drama to the scientific discussion (chapter 2, pp. 49 and 57). He interweaves rhetorical questions, for instance 'Why should I speak of it?' (6.2.7, C 273), and uses irony, for instance against Zoilus the orator who tells a marvellous tale about a certain underground river while being 'the man who finds fault with Homer as a writer of myths' (6.2.4, C 271). At the same time Strabo admits that he cannot evaluate the rhetorical schools in his time, and especially the two main ones, those of Apollodorus of Pergamon and Theodorus of Gadara (13.4.3, C 625).

Grammatical discussions appear mostly in an Homeric context. These are numerous and are scattered throughout the *Geography*. To give only brief examples, Strabo adduces many poetic examples from Homer, Hesiod, Sophocles, Aratus and even pre-Socratic philosophers such as Empedocles, for the grammatical phenomenon of cutting off letters from a word (*apokope*) and using the shorter version to denote the whole word (8.5.3, C 364). Again in an Homeric context he elaborates on the question of the presence of a Dolopian army led by Phoenix in the Trojan War, and concludes that the fact that the poet does not mention them does not mean that there were no Dolopian soldiers present, this according to the principle of silence (*to siopomenon*) 'as the grammarians are wont to call it' (9.5.5, C 431).[39]

Even though our knowledge of Strabo's travels is limited (below), we have seen that he travelled to Nysa, Alexandria and Rome. These visits contributed to his scholarly activity. But where did Strabo write his works? This question should be in fact limited to the *Geography*, because this is his only extant composition and therefore may offer some hint at an answer. The issue is significant not only for the reconstruction of Strabo's whereabouts, but may also elucidate his intellectual and social surroundings at the time of writing.

As with most facts pertaining to Strabo, this too is not specified by the author and leaves scholars to conjecture. As with the question of the date of composition (chapter 6, p. 146), Niese took words indicating the place of writing such as 'here' (*enthade*) and 'hither' (*deuro*), and chose several excerpts from the *Geography* which point to Rome as that venue; for instance in referring to Maroboduus the leader of the Alpic tribes he says: 'as a youth he had been here (*enthade*) and had enjoyed the favour of Augustus' (7.1.3, C 290), thus clearly referring to Rome.[40]

This methodology was, however, proven inaccurate by Häbler who showed that Strabo's use of the local words is extensive and that these expressions refer to the place which is the subject of the sentence or passage and not necessarily to the place where the writer happens to be.[41] Thus he quotes excerpts which include such words, but refer to Iberia (3.5.5, C 170), or Gades (3.5.6, C 172) which we know Strabo never visited (below). Therefore perhaps these expressions originate in Strabo's sources and the passages cited as examples by Niese indeed refer to Rome but present only a partial picture. Häbler focused on refuting Niese's methodology and did not suggest another place, nor indeed did he show that Strabo had not written in Rome.

Pais added other considerations that exclude Rome as a possible writing place.[42] He used notions similar to those in his discussion on the date, mainly Strabo's silence about certain Roman affairs and his supposed ignorance of Augustan sources such as Agrippa's map. To this he added that Strabo does not reveal close familiarity with the environs of Rome and Italy in general and that the *Geography* seems to be unknown to Pliny and other Roman authors (chapter 6, p. 151). At the same time Pais showed that Strabo is well informed about later eastern events, mainly in Pontus, that his travels were more extensive in the east and that his work is known to eastern authors such as Josephus. Therefore he concluded that Strabo spent his last twenty-five years away from Rome, possibly in Asia Minor and probably in Amasia, his hometown.

Anderson ascribed Strabo's interest in the Pontic dynasty to the natural interest of a person born in the region.[43] Moreover, he showed that Strabo is not entirely updated about Pontic developments. Therefore he suggested that Strabo wrote in a provincial city in the eastern Mediterranean, away from both Roman and Pontic affairs.

It should be emphasized that Strabo's silence about certain events does not prove his ignorance. Thus the suggestions of both Pais and Anderson which rely on this 'silence' appear less valid. Anderson's suggestion is too impressionistic, for he does not prove Strabo's ignorance of eastern affairs, nor does he suggest any particular place other than a general notion about a provincial city. Strabo had no reason to return to Amasia after his family was no longer held in esteem there, and after the political situation had changed (above, p. 5).[44] Further, the diffusion of the *Geography* (chapter 6, p. 151) does not necessarily indicate the place of writing, for Strabo could write in Rome, intend his work for Roman readers and still not be read by Pliny. Pais contends that Pliny did not know the *Geography*, but we have no proof that Josephus did, for he quotes the *History* of Strabo and not the geographical treatise. Finally, it is probable that Strabo did know Agrippa's commentaries as well as the *Res Gestae* publicly displayed in Rome after Augustus' death in 14 CE (chapter 4, p. 129). He also knew Rome and to some extent several parts of Italy (below, p. 25), perhaps having passed through them during some of his earlier visits. Pais's notion of Strabo's ignorance of Italy becomes less convincing.

Therefore, although Häbler's reservations concerning Niese's methodology are to some extent persuasive, it seems that the suggestion that Strabo wrote in Rome is the one that best complies with the facts and with Strabo's character as it emerges from various directions. Whatever is extant of Strabo's writings and particularly the *Geography* should be viewed as a product not only of its author's time but also of his intellectual orientation. In his methods and interests Strabo reflects centuries of Greek scholarship and knowledge. As much as his own personality and the political and cultural developments of his time influenced the character of his survey, the core of its attitude derives from an old tradition transmitted to him through his cultural background and his education.

TRAVELS

In the second book of the *Geography* Strabo claims to have travelled further than all other geographers:

> I have travelled westward from Armenia as far as the regions of Tyrrhenia opposite Sardinia, and southward from the Black Sea as far as the frontiers of Ethiopia. And you could not find another person among the writers on geography who has travelled over much more of the distances just mentioned than I. Those who have travelled more than I in the western regions have not covered as

much ground in the east, and those who have travelled more in the eastern countries are behind me in the western, and the same holds true in regard to the regions towards the south and north.

(2.5.11, C 117)

Strabo emphasizes the extent of his journeys not by comparing himself to any traveller of whatever kind, but specifically to writers of geography. His predecessors may have visited other regions and sites where he never set foot, but as he makes clear, his achievement is the extent of his travels measured by the extreme points in each direction (see figure 2). Posidonius, for instance, visited Iberia and Gaul, places Strabo never saw, but this extensive acquaintance with the western parts of the Mediterranean does not compete with the entire territory covered by Strabo. The framework defining the extent of his journeyings is indeed wide if we take its four extreme points. This would imply a link between travel and competence as a geographer, assuming that the more one voyages the better one's descriptions of various regions. The importance of wide travel is also reflected in the pragmatic aspect of Strabo's work, influenced by the Polybian spirit (chapter 2, p. 47). Just as Polybius emphasized practical experience in politics and in military affairs as a requirement for an historian, so Strabo seems to indicate that extensive travel and acquaintance with distant regions are essential for a geographer.

The purpose of Strabo's travels however, was not always purely scientific,[45] and their extent was rather determined by several events in his personal biography. Thus, he went to Nysa to study with Aristodemus (14.1.48, C 560), and he joined his friend Aelius Gallus on his mission as governor of Egypt (2.5.12, C 118). Strabo incorporated into his work most of his personal experience that was relevant to the *Geography*, although at the time of some of his travels he had not yet thought of the literary project. The visit to Egypt is a good example. Having a social pretext, this visit, as Strabo describes it in detail, shows that he had the interests of a tourist and the wish to satisfy a broad curiosity. He went from site to site, perhaps not exactly with a notebook on his knee, but with his eyes wide open: his inquiry into the extent of the astronomic and philosophical knowledge of the priests in Heliopolis shows his inclination for philosophy; his indication of the exact place in Heliopolis where Plato spent thirteen years with the priests demonstrates his interest in the character of the great philosopher (17.1.29, C 806); and his detailed discussion of the round stones near the pyramids in Memphis shows his desire to understand natural phenomena (17.1.34, C 808–9). Some of his impressions were eventually inserted into his descriptions. He probably also used some of his visits for research, for instance to the great library in Alexandria. In this sense his earlier historiographical writings (chapter 2, p. 69) probably also contributed to the overall character of the *Geography*, in which he incorporated earlier research as well

16

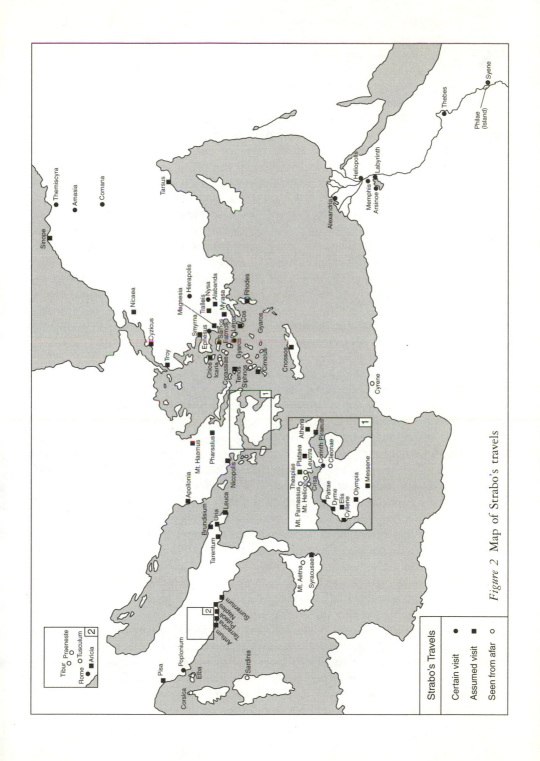

Figure 2 Map of Strabo's travels

Strabo's Travels

Certain visit ●

Assumed visit ■

Seen from afar ○

as earlier travelling impressions. Hence, it is very probable that quite large parts of the survey rely on Strabo's personal observations, even when he does not say so specifically.

The main problem concerning Strabo's travels, however, is that apart from his general declaration he does not tend to mention his visits in the course of the geographical survey. Even when he describes sites of which he had definite personal knowledge, such as Amasia, his birthplace, Rome and Alexandria, his presence is only indirectly implied. When he does choose to declare a direct acquaintance with a certain site he uses specific expressions of autopsy such as 'I saw' (4.5.2, C 200) and 'they showed me' (14.1.23, C 641) or other verbs indicating actual presence, like 'I heard' (16.2.25, C 758) or 'I threw' (13.4.14, C 630). All these places fall within the outline presented in the opening general statement. Surveying the few instances where Strabo specifically mentions a visit, Waddy concluded that the author alluded to his personal experience only in the case of exceptional matters or when he thought that his autopsy might add important information not found in written sources or derived from hearsay.[46] As we shall see, such an attempt to come up with any rules for Strabo's inserting or omitting to mention his visits to various places, does not seem to have strong enough foundations.

A survey of the places visited is therefore necessary, as well as a study of the nature of Strabo's personal impressions absorbed through autopsy. Our assessment of his character will perhaps be further enriched by joining him on his travels. I shall begin this survey with sites Strabo definitely visited, then go on to places where the probability of his visit is high, according to considerations specified below. The order within each category is determined by a combination of the biography and the geographical layout.

The city of Amasia, Strabo's birthplace, is described by the geographer in detail and with some emotion: 'My city ... both by human foresight and by nature it is an admirably devised city' (12.3.39, C 561). Naturally, Strabo also knew the regions around his city in the eastern part of Asia Minor, either in his early years as a child, or on the occasions of his journeys back home from his travels in the world as an adult.[47] He specifically informs his readers that he stayed in Cappadocian Comana, a city dominated by its temple of Enyo, which at the time of the visit had more than 6,000 temple servants, men and women, under the supervision of the high priest of the temple, second in rank to the king (12.2.3, C 535). This was a position once held by the younger Dorylaus, the nephew of Strabo's great-great-grandfather (above, p. 5). In this place Strabo watched the river Pyramus and its immense volume flowing through a narrow rocky channel; 'a noise like thunder strikes the ears of travellers long before they reach it' (12.2.4, C 536). Note the visitor's use of his senses of sight and hearing to express his personal experience. Strabo also uses terms from daily life to exemplify the narrowness of the channel: if one throws a javelin from above into the pit the force of the water resists it and the cleft is so narrow that a dog or hare could leap across. These impressions too seem to be based on his own associations, and together with the sensual reactions form a typical description based on direct experience. Identifying similar elements in descriptions of sites where the writer does not specify his presence may help to reconstruct his itinerary, as shall be shown below.

In Cappadocia Strabo saw the rites of the Magi: the sacrificial beasts slain with a wooden club and not with a sword, the constant fire and ashes on the altar and the special garb of the worshippers. At the end of the description he comments that he saw all these details but that there are others 'in the histories' which he intends to quote (15.3.15, C 733). This is a clear case of combination between eye-witness and written sources, the one not excluding the other.

Strabo came to study with Aristodemus in Nysa (14.1.48, C 650) and he elaborates on the position of many public monuments in the city, such as the amphitheatre, the gymnasiums, the agora, the river and the bridge (14.1.43, C 649). He also visited Hierapolis in Phrygia, not far from Nysa. In this city there were hot springs and a steaming underground cave named Plutonium. Strabo describes the appearance of the site, the density of the steam and its lethal nature, which he tested by throwing into the vapours live sparrows who fell dead into the depth of the cave. Even the priests of Cybele nearly choked with holding their breath while entering the obnoxious steam (13.4.14, C 629–30).

In the temple of Artemis in Ephesus, votive works of art were shown to him, among them a wax statue of Penelope and a statue of old Euryclea by Thrason (14.1.23, C 641). He saw the city itself, its dockyard and harbour, even if he does not specify this autopsy for every detail (14.1.23–4, C 641).

Leaving his native continent, Strabo had the opportunity to see other places, first in Europe and later in Africa. He arrived in the Italian peninsula on his various visits to Rome (chapter 3) specifically indicating his presence only at one point outside the capital. Standing in Poplonium in Tyrrhenia, Strabo saw 'from afar and with difficulty' (5.2.6, C 223) the islands of Sardinia, Corsica and Elba. He also saw some mines out in the country that had failed and the people who work the iron brought from Elba (5.2.6, C 223 and 15.2.8, C 225). In this case Strabo consciously challenges some notions of his predecessors, concluding, based on his own experience, that they were wrong:

> Neither is Eratosthenes correct, when he says that neither Corsica nor Sardinia can be seen from the mainland, nor Artemidorus, when he says that both islands lie in the high sea within twelve hundred stadia, for even supposing they were visible to some people at that distance, they could not have been so to me, at least, or else not to the extent of their being seen clearly . . .
>
> (5.2.6, C 224)

Poplonium would be the most westerly point of Strabo's travels, in agreement with the frame depicted in his general travel declaration.

Probably on his way to or from Italy, Strabo passed through Greece. From the highest hill in Corinth, the Acrocorinth, he observed the surroundings and described the entire region accordingly (8.6.19, C 377) and the city itself with its temples, springs and wells (8.6.21, C 379). The panoramic view from the Acrocorinth enabled Strabo to see also the town of Cleonae situated on a hill surrounded by houses on the road from Argus to Corinth (8.6.19, C 377), the snow-covered mountains Parnassus and Helicon, and the gulf of Crisa (8.6.21, C 379).[48] The case of Corinth is noteworthy because Strabo's treatment of the description once more demonstrates his method. Notwithstanding his personal presence at the site he quotes written sources such as Hieronymus of Rhodes and Eudoxus of Cnidus, mostly for measurements of the mountains and the hill and the circumference of the city.

Several Greek islands and coasts were seen by Strabo on his passage from Asia or Egypt to Rome. We know for certain that he was sailing among the Cyclades when Augustus was on his way to Rome to celebrate the victory of Actium. On this voyage in 29 BCE Strabo's ship anchored at the island of Gyaros where he saw a small fishermen's village and met one of the inhabitants sent on behalf of his island to greet Augustus (10.5.3, C 485–6).

Moving to Africa, we have ample evidence for Strabo's presence in the most famous sites of Egypt, one of the wider regions documented in the *Geography*. In about 29–26 BCE[49] Strabo joined Aelius Gallus as his companion on his mission as governor of Egypt, and as part of the entourage composed, as was customary in such cases, of officials, friends and soldiers (2.5.12, C 118; 11.11.5, C 518; 17.1.46, C 816). Gallus, accompanied by Strabo, sailed southward up the Nile (2.5.12, C 118; 17.1.29, C 806). In the course of this tour Strabo saw in Heliopolis the place where Eudoxus and Plato stayed on their visit to the city and the large houses of the priests whose inclinations towards philosophy and astronomy he tested, only to be disappointed by their meagre knowledge (17.1.29, C 806). He saw the sphinxes buried in the sand by the winds at Memphis (17.1.32, C 807), and the round stones near the pyramids (17.1.34, C 808–9).

Later Strabo came to the Heracleot Nome and documented in detail the architectural complex of the famous labyrinth (17.1.37, C 811).[50] The distinguished host of the group led the visitors to the lake in Arsinoe, also named Crocodilopolis, to see the sacred crocodile, Suchos, and to feed it. Strabo describes the animal's menu and its feeding by the priests:

> It is fed on grain and meat and wine, which are always being fed to it by the foreigners who go to see it. Our host, one of the officials . . . went with us to the lake, carrying from the dinner a kind of cookie and some roasted meat and a pitcher of wine mixed with honey. We found the animal lying on the edge of the lake, and

when the priests went up to it, some of them opened its mouth and another put in the cake, and again the meat, and then poured down the honey mixture. The animal then leaped into the lake and rushed across to the far side, but when another foreigner arrived, likewise carrying an offering of first-fruits, the priests took it, went around the lake in a run, took hold of the animal, and in the same manner fed it what had been brought.

(17.1.38, C 811–12)

Further up the Nile Strabo heard the strange whistle coming from the statues of Memnon in Thebes, and saw the kings' tombs and the inscribed obelisks posted near them (17.1.46, C 816). He then arrived at Syene at the Ethiopian border (2.5.12, C 118; 17.1.50, C 818). The embassy embarked on a light boat and sailed to the Nilotic isle of Philae (17.1.50, C 818) inhabited by a mixed population of Egyptians and Ethiopians, thus indicating the proximity of the Ethiopian border (1.2.32, C 40; 17.1.54, C 820). This was the southernmost point in Egypt, and according to Strabo's declaration, in the whole *oikoumene*, which he reached.

Strabo spent a few years in Alexandria (2.3.5, C 101), probably using the great library and writing one of his historiographical works before turning to the *Geography*. During this period he saw the flooding of Pelusium (1.3.17, C 58), observed the Roman security system at the entrance of the Alexandrian harbour (2.3.5, C 101) and became acquainted with the special plants of Egypt (3.5.10, C 175). He heard from the city glass blowers about their local production and design methods (16.2.25, C 758). He testifies how the summer inundation of the Nile moves the water in lake Mareotis in the city, thus counteracting the lake's unfavourable characteristics (5.1.7, C 214; 17.1.4, C 789). On his voyage back to Italy Strabo saw Cyrene from the sea and it seemed to him large and situated on a trapeze-shaped plain (17.3.20, C 837).

The list of sites Strabo professes to have actually seen is relatively short. This is surprising, if only for the simple reason that in order to arrive at these places he must have passed through others no less important or interesting. Pais, in his wish to prove that Strabo was more involved in the regions of Asia Minor than in some western areas, shows that Strabo probably knew places where his presence is not specified, but which are situated near or between sites he certainly visited.[51] This assumption, usually supported by particularly detailed descriptions of such places, could however apply also to other regions of the world, for instance Italy, and not be restricted to Asia Minor. Moreover, many descriptive features seem to display Strabo's direct acquaintance with certain places, even though he does not say so specifically. I shall therefore present these sites, together with the considerations for admitting them into Strabo's travel record.

There are hints of Strabo's presence in several locations, mostly in Asia, Greece and Italy. Concerning these presumed visits there is a spectrum of possible interpretations situated between two poles: the minimalist would accept as certain only the places Strabo specifically claims to have visited, and the maximalist would add all sites within the general frame of his travels. An intermediate approach may, however, be pertinent. Some sites may be added according to the nature of the description and the probability of a visit as far as we can assess it, but other places where Strabo's presence is insufficiently attested, for instance Berytus and Ascalon, let alone Judaea and Herod's court,[52] should be excluded from the 'map' of his travels.

Several criteria and clues may support the assumption of a visit to a certain location. First, the site should be located within the scope of Strabo's travels according to his declaration. If he had visited a place beyond this frame he would certainly not have suppressed the fact, especially since his declaration was intended to impress the reader and to make manifest the wide extent of his achievement. Second, Strabo sometimes includes sensual impressions of minute details which suggest that he is expressing a very personal and individual experience, such as his account of the fruits in the plain of Themiscyra lying beneath the fallen leaves (12.3.15, C 548) or his comment that the rocky coast of Sinope does not permit walking barefoot (12.3.11, C 545). Third, the description of the site of an assumed visit may be compared with accounts of places that Strabo certainly saw for himself and those of places he equally certainly did not see. Let us first take, for example, Amasia, his birthplace, and Corduba, which was beyond the scope of his travels.

Amasia is described thus:

> My city is situated in a large deep valley, through which flows the Iris river . . . it is a high and precipitous rock, which descends abruptly to the river, and has on one side the wall on the edge of the river where the city is settled and on the other the wall that runs up on either side to the peaks . . . within this circuit are both the palaces and monuments of the kings.
>
> (12.3.39, C 561)[53]

This is a model for a Strabonian description based on autopsy.

In contrast stands the description of Corduba, limited to some historical facts: its foundation by Marcellus and Sextus Pompeius' escape from the city (3.2.1, C 141); and to geographical information clearly not based on personal experience: the sailing distance to the city on the river Baetis (3.2.3, C 142), its distance from other sites and the road running through it (3.4.9, C 160). The descriptions of New Carthage (3.4.6, C 158), Tarraco (3.4.7, C 159), Massilia (4.1.4, C 179) and Lugdunum (4.3.2, C 192) are similar – all beyond the framework of Strabo's 'map' of travels, all limited to historical matters and to the importance of the cities as economic or administrative centres.

Now, let us examine a description of a city where we do not have a direct allusion to a visit, such as Smyrna. This city is thus delineated:

part of it is on a mountain and walled, but the greater part of it is in the plain near the harbour and near the Metroum and near the gymnasium. The division into streets is exceptionally good, in straight lines as far as possible, and the streets are paved with stone and there are large quadrangular porticoes with both lower and upper stories. There is also a library, and the Homereium, a quad-rangular portico containing a shrine and wooden statue of Homer . . . the river Meles flows near the walls . . . there is also a harbour that can be closed . . . when they paved the streets they did not give them underground drainage, but filth covers the surface, and particularly during rains . . .

(14.1.37, C 646)

The information is elaborate and essentially different from the account of Corduba. At the same time the references to some public monuments in the city, to the course of the river and to the topographical background are very similar to details in the description of Amasia.

Together with these two criteria, the position of the site within the decla-ration of travels and the personal character of the description, it seems that two linguistic features may also supply some clues to Strabo's possible acquaintance with a certain location. The verb 'to show' (*deiknymi*) in various forms may be interpreted as if someone did actually show Strabo some phenomena on the spot. It may derive from Strabo's sources, but sometimes the use seems genuinely his own, for example: 'the Pharsalians show . . . a city in ruins . . . and also two springs near it' (9.5.6, C 431–2). Although this verb has also the meaning of showing 'by words'[54] and not necessarily physically, the context helps to determine the meaning in each case. Strabo's use of superlatives in his references to certain places may also depend on his own impressions and may imply a comparison to places he knows, superlatives in their essence implying such a comparison, for instance refer-ring to Campania as 'a plain the most prosperous (*eudaimonetaton*) of all' (5.4.3, C 242).

Taking all these hints together, many other sites would join the few that Strabo specifically admits to have seen in person, and may possibly also be included in his itinerary.

Strabo describes in minute detail the plain of Themiscyra in Pontic Cappadocia which is 'always moist and covered with grass and can support herds of cattle and horses alike' and grows millet and sorghum, 'and the country along the mountain yields so much fruit . . . grapes and pears and apples and nuts . . . the fruits at one time still hanging on the trees and at another lying on the fallen leaves or beneath them' (12.3.15, C 547–8). All these details, especially the vivid allusion to the fruits hanging on the trees or lying under the leaves, give the impression of a personal and direct experience not likely to be derived from another written source.

Strabo's visit to Ephesus perhaps explains his knowledge of the roads from this city to the east as based on personal experience (14.2.29, C 663). He may have been to Tarsus, situated at the mouth of the Pyramus on the Mediterranean, for the city is on the road from the south to Amasia and the description may imply acquaintance: 'Tarsus lies in a plain ... the Cydnus river ... flows in the middle of the city past the gymnasium of the young men ... its discharge is both cold and swift,' (14.5.12, C 673).

As for the circumstances of an assumed visit to Tarsus, Sihler suggested that Strabo had studied philosophy there with Xenarchus of Seleucia and Pais thought that Strabo visited the place at a later date (7 BCE), coming back from Rome, for he is able to describe recent developments instigated by Athenodorus.[55] Neither assumption seems to have enough support. Strabo himself says that the best way to be brought up to date about Tarsus is to meet people in Rome (14.5.15, C 675).

Relying on the same methodology and based on Strabo's general declaration about the scope of his travels, other sites may be included in the line of his journeys. To the environs of Ephesus we may add Mylasa, Alabanda, Tralleis and Magnesia, each receiving brief but very particular descriptions focusing on special sights and using what seems to be Strabo's personal similes to illustrate certain traits. He mentions the marble quarries in Mylasa and the beauty of its colonnades and temples. He alludes to its topographical layout, a paved road leading to the temple and some statues decorating it (14.2.23, C 658–9). In Alabanda Strabo seem to have been impressed by the great number of scorpions and by the luxurious life of the inhabitants, among whom were many girls who played the harp (14.2.26, C 660–1). He describes a painted portrait of Anaxenor, a contemporary cithara player and singer, placed in the market of Magnesia and a bronze statue of the same performer with an inscription, in the theatre (14.1.41, C 648). As for Tralleis, he mentions its natural fortifications, the wealth of its inhabitants and the trapeze-like plain in which the city is situated (14.1.42, C 648). It is likely that Strabo also visited Smyrna for his general notion that this city is 'now the most beautiful of all' (14.1.37, C 646) seems to imply autopsy, as does also the detailed description (above, p. 22).

Sinope, 'the most noteworthy of the cities in that part of the world' (12.3.11, C 545), is a place to catch tunny-fish, to be salted later. It is situated on a promontory naturally protected by its rocky shores. The rocks on the beach hurt the feet and do not permit walking barefoot. The city itself is surrounded by a wall and adorned with a gymnasium, an agora, colonnades and on its outskirts there are fertile fields and olive trees (2.1.15, C 73; 7.6.2, C 320; 12.3.11, C 545–6). Would we expect a written source to record the unpleasant effect of a barefoot walk on sharp rocks, and if so, why would Strabo choose to include this impression in his scientific and practical work? This case is a good example of a possible personal experience of the geographer walking on the beach, even if he does not say plainly that he was there.

The description of Nicaea may also imply autopsy. Strabo says that the city is square, situated in a plain and has four gates. The streets lie in straight and parallel lines so that the four gates are visible to a person standing on a stone situated in the centre of the gymnasium (12.4.7, C 565–6). Did Strabo himself stand there? We may assume that he did. Strabo mentions Cyzicus too as a special city, exceptional for its beauty and its administration. He is familiar with the government and describes marble monuments in the city (13.1.16, C 589).

A Strabonian visit to the surroundings of Troy would seem natural for a person so involved in the contents and spirit of the Homeric epics (chapter 2, p. 31), but some topographical inaccuracies in the description of the Troad and some misinterpretations of Demetrius of Scepsis' discussions would seem to dismiss such an assumption.[56] Still, Strabo's constant use of the verb *deiknymi*, along with the mention of several specific phenomena in the region – a place called Gargarum on the upper parts of Mount Ida (13.1.5, C 583); a temple on a hill near Lampsacus (13.1.17, C 589); three craters near Mysia (13.4.11, C 628) – all increase the probability of his visit there. Of course, the verbs as well as the descriptions may be derived directly from the writings of Demetrius who was born in this region and inspected it thoroughly, but we have already seen that Strabo's own visit does not necessarily preclude his use of written sources.

Visits to Rome and a long sojourn in the city (chapter 3) enabled Strabo to see, or at least to pass by, several other places in Italy. He indicates that 'between the fifth and the sixth of those stones which indicate the miles from Rome there is a place called Festi, and this, it is declared, is a boundary of what was then the Romans' territory' (5.3.2, C 230). Similarly, he may have observed the outlets of the springs in the lake near the temple of Artemis at Aricia (5.3.12, C 240). Strabo twice defines the nearby lakes as similar in size to an open sea (5.3.12, C 239; 5.3.13, C 240), a view perhaps based on his own impression.

Strabo says that for those who sail from Greece or from Asia to Italy, the shortest and straightest route is to Brundisium (6.3.7, C 282), a contention possibly based on general knowledge of sea routes but perhaps indicating that Strabo himself landed there. He also knows other sea routes from Greece to Italy and back (6.3.8, C 283; 7.7.5, C 324; 8.6.20, C 378), and enumerates in detail the various land routes to Rome, indicating their quality and their length in Roman miles and also in terms of time (6.3.10, C 285). It is likely that he passed through them himself, although at the same time the information on their exact course and length may derive from other sources, mainly Artemidorus and the Chorographer, i.e. Agrippa in his commentaries (chapter 4, p. 127).

Near Brundisium Strabo may have visited Tarentum for he describes in detail the special features of its harbour and bridge, the wall of the city and the general layout. He also says that 'it has a very beautiful gymnasium, and also a spacious market-place, in which is situated the bronze colossus of Zeus' (6.3.1, C 278).

Referring to two sites near Tarentum Strabo uses the verb *deiknytai* ('it is to be seen'), once in connection with a foul-smelling spring in Leuca (6.3.5, C 281) and again in referring to a palace of one of the Roman officials in Uria (6.3.6, C 282). This verb may indicate some kind of tourist guidance from the local inhabitants who point out interesting sites for visitors to see.

The exports from Alexandria exceed the imports, this being clearly apparent from an inspection of the cargo loaded by the ships both in Alexandria and in the target harbour, Dicaearchea, that is Puteoli (17.1.7, C 793).[57] Did Strabo himself see the ships come and go in both harbours? He certainly did in Alexandria and probably also in Puteoli. Moreover, he tells us that in Puteoli there is a tunnel leading to Naples and he elaborates on the topography of the city and the sulphurous odours in it, clearly a sensual impression (5.4.5–6, C 245–6). We may therefore assume that Strabo landed in Puteoli, probably when he came back from Egypt after escorting his friend Aelius Gallus, or that he sailed from that port after one of his visits to Rome.

Strabo seems to have some knowledge of the coast in the gulf of Naples. He describes the city itself and its gymnasiums, a tunnel with windows admitting daylight, a wide road and hot springs (5.4.7, C 246). The whole coast line is covered with houses and plantations which 'present the appearance of a single city' (5.4.8, C 247). He then goes on to indicate the extravagant palaces of the Romans in Antium and says that near Tarracina there is a place where people show a sort of bowl and say that it belonged to Odysseus (5.3.5–6, C 232). He describes the sight revealed to a person going towards Rome, the canal by the Via Appia along which boats are pulled by mules (5.3.6, C 233). The repeated allusions to the luxurious and expensive palaces of the Romans in Tarracina (5.3.6, C 233), Tusculum (5.3.12, C 239) and Baiae (5.4.7, C 246) may also suggest Strabo's personal impression.

Tibur and Praeneste are said to be visible from Rome and the description of both places yields some minor details which could very probably derive from autopsy, such as the waterfall in Tibur and other monuments and the topographical surroundings of Praeneste and its subterranean passages (5.3.11, C 238–9).

A textual discussion of a piece of commentary on Homer suggests that Strabo visited the neighbourhood of Surrentum. One commentator identified the place of the Sirens as a three-peaked rock called the Sirenussae separating the gulf of Naples from the gulf of Salerno. Strabo reports that this rock has no peak at all and describes the topography and the shape of the place (1.2.12, C 22 partly quoted on chapter 2, p. 38).

In another place he describes the region of Campania, situated above a wide gulf, and possessing fertile hills and mountains which grow excellent wheat (5.4.3, C 242). The description of the rivers near Pisa also implies autopsy, for Strabo says that when the two rivers, Ausar and Arnus, unite, the current becomes so wide that people standing on either bank cannot see each other (5.2.5, C 222), even if such an impression is hardly accurate.

Strabo may have passed by Sicily and perhaps even landed on the island. Next to Syracuse 'is at the present time a bridge which connects it with the mainland, whereas formerly there was a mole, as Ibycus says' (1.3.18, C 59). If this information is not derived from a personal visit, it is nevertheless based on the testimony of an eye-witness who came to the island shortly before Strabo wrote this passage, thus providing the geographer with an updated piece of information. The comment that the water of Arethusa is potable may also imply personal experience (6.2.4, C 271).

The detailed description of the volcano Aetna may be based on the sight perhaps revealed to Strabo from his ship passing through the Straits of Messina on its way to or from Puteoli. The highest parts of the mountain are grey and in winter they are shrouded in snow, and the lower parts are covered with forests and plantations. The peak is transformed whenever a volcanic eruption occurs. At night a bright light shines from within its mouth and during the day the top of the mountain is veiled in smoke and steam (6.2.8, C 273–4). This testimony relates to various times and seasons: night and day, summer and winter, and thus may make it somewhat doubtful that Strabo saw the mountain so often. This may be a case of combining autopsy on the occasion of a journey to or from Italy with other evidence. The details given can evidently be seen from a distance, but the testimony of people who visited the mountain 'recently' and came very close to its mouth is also cited.[58]

There are some signs of Strabo's direct acquaintance with certain sites in the Peloponnese, all based on minor and specific details creating the impression of a personal experience. In Elis the river passes near the gymnasium (8.3.2, C 337). In Cyllene there is a statue of Asclepius, 'an ivory image that is wonderful to behold' (8.3.4, C 337). In Olympia there is an olive grove in front of the temple of Zeus, a stadium and a river, and inside the temple many works of art (8.3.30, C 353). Messene is similar to Corinth because near it too there is a high mountain (8.4.8, C 361) and we know for sure that Strabo was in Corinth. The ability to make such a comparison may derive from acquaintance with both places. Again, Strabo says that between Patrae and Dyme traces of an old settlement are shown (*deiknutai*) and there is also a temple (8.7.4, C 386); perhaps the local people showed him the sites.

As for central Greece, Strabo says that Leuctra 'is to be seen (*deiknutai*) on the road that leads from Plataeae to Thespiae' (9.2.39, C 414). Even if he did not visit Leuctra the phraseology may indicate that he travelled along this road himself and saw Leuctra from a distance, thus passing both Plataeae and Thespiae on his way to the northern parts of Greece. Wallace widens this presumed visited area and suggests that Strabo's depiction of Boeotia as impoverished and desolated in his times (9.2.5, C 403; 9.2.25, C 410) probably reflects the actual situation towards the end of the first century BCE, and thus implies Strabo's presence in Boeotia.[59]

The people of Pharsalus show (*deiknyousin*) a ruined site called Hellas 60 stadia distant from their city and near it two springs (9.5.6, C 431–2). Referring to the mountain Haemus in Thrace, Strabo says that Polybius is wrong in his contention that it is possible to see both the Black Sea and the Aegean from it, because the distance is too great and there are obstacles in the way (7.5.1, C 313). This may imply that Strabo actually stood there and inspected the matter personally.

He perhaps also knew Apollonia near Epidamnus, for he can tell that in it there is a fountain called Cephisus near the gymnasium (9.3.16, C 424), and that the road from the city to Macedonia is marked by milestones and there are various sites to its 'right' and to its 'left' (7.7.4, C 323). Although Polybius is mentioned in this context as a specific source, and the terminology of 'right' and 'left' may derive from Strabo's use of a map or an itinerary, it is still possible that he saw the layout himself.

The general issue of the extent of Strabo's travels stands in the background of modern studies focusing on the particular question of the author's acquaintance with various parts of Greece. The problem centres specifically on the question whether or not Strabo visited Athens, the city which was and still is a first priority site at the top of the travel list, so to speak, of any scholar with historiographical inclinations and certainly of all those educated in Hellenic values.

There are two opposing approaches to the question. Weller adopted a critical attitude, suggesting that Strabo's descriptions of Greece are based entirely on oral and literary sources, mainly the Homeric 'Catalogue of Ships' (chapter 2, p. 36). Thus, Strabo did not visit the Greek sites and did not spend time in Athens. The only place he did see was Corinth, and his acquaintance with the islands is based merely on a quick sailing passage.[60]

In sharp contrast stands Waddy who systematically showed that the fact that there is no specific allusion to Strabo's visit to Athens is insignificant. Strabo's silence on this point is consistent with his silence about his almost certain visits to other sites. He says specifically that he will not expand the description because there is no place for so much detail in a universal survey such as his *Geography* (9.1.16, C 396), as is the case, in his opinion, also with Sparta and Argos (8.6.18, C 376; 9.1.19, C 397). Finally, it is unlikely that Strabo passed through Greece, probably saw the Piraeus and did not enter Athens. Waddy concludes therefore that he did visit the city even though he does not say so explicitly.[61] Strabo indeed describes the statues and paintings in the temple of Zeus in the Piraeus (9.1.15, C 396), thus implying his presence there and making the assumption for his visit to Athens all the more likely.

Strabo had a special connection with Cnossos, where his ancestor Dorylaus lived for some time and founded his family (above, p. 5). Therefore he defines it as 'a city to which I myself am not alien, although . . . the bonds which at first connected me with this city have disappeared' (10.4.10, C 477). He says specifically that Lagetas, the oldest son and Strabo's great-grandfather, came back to Pontus, but at the same time he refers to Lagetas' brother, Stratarchas, whom 'I myself saw when he was an extremely old man' (10.4.10, C 477). It is therefore possible that Strabo met the old man in his birthplace, that is Cnossos. This assumption is supported by the description of the island: 'mountainous and thickly wooded, and it has fruitful glens' (10.4.4, C 475). Strabo's allusion to the length of the journey from Cyrenaica to Crete and from Crete to Egypt in terms of time – respectively two days and nights and four days and nights (10.4.5, C 475) – may indicate personal experience, although such usage is common in the genre of *periploi* (chapter 2, p. 40).[62]

As for other Greek islands, although there is no specific indication for Strabo's presence in them, his references do not exclude at least the possibility of a remote view from his passing ship. He describes Chios and its various harbours and ports (14.1.35, C 645). The details about Rhodes may also be based on autopsy, for Strabo describes monuments such as the Colossus of Helius, one of the seven wonders of the world, which 'now lies on the ground, having been thrown down by an earthquake and broken at the knees'; some paintings of Protogenes, 'his Ialysus and also his Satyr, the latter standing by a pillar, and on top of the pillar stands a partridge' (14.2.5, C 652); and says that 'as one sails from the city, with the island on the right, one comes first to Lindus' (14.2.11, C 655), that is, a description of a circumnavigation of the island.

Strabo evidently visited Cos for he testifies that 'the city is not large, but it is the most beautifully settled of all, and is most pleasing to behold as one sails from the high sea to its shore', and elaborates on its appearance (14.2.19, C 657–8). He claims that from the island of Cimolus it is possible to see Siphnos (10.5.1, C 484) and that in Tenos there is no big city but a temple of Poseidon including large banquet halls, 'a spectacle worth seeing' (10.5.11, C 487). He mentions the neighbouring islands of Patmos, the Corassiae, Icaria and Leros and their position in relation to one another (10.5.13, C 488), but elaborates particularly on the description of Samos. On it there is a harbour city, a river and a temple to Poseidon. A temple to Hera functions 'now' as a library, containing dedicatory inscriptions and rooms full of ancient works of art. The temple is open to the sky and possesses many beautiful statues. The island does not produce wine although its neighbours have wines of high quality (14.1.14–15, C 637).

Pais holds that on his way to Rome Strabo may have visited Nicopolis and Patrae, for the two are situated on the sea route from Corinth to Brundisium.[63] The description of both cities could well support this assumption for Strabo says that in Nicopolis, founded after the Actian victory, there is a sacred grove, a gymnasium and a stadium (7.7.6, C 325) and in Patrae, 'a noteworthy city', there is a comfortable harbouring spot (8.7.5, C 387).

The relatively few places where Strabo openly allows himself to mention his presence verify his general declaration on the extent of his travels, which is therefore not to be regarded as an exaggeration. Accordingly, the most extreme points marking the frame of his travels are: in the east – Armenia in his general statement, and more specifically the border between Pontus and Armenia; in the west – Tyrrhenia, and specifically Poplonium; in the north – the region of the Black Sea, that is Sinope and Cyzicus; and in the south – the border of Ethiopia, that is Syene and the island of Philae.

We have seen that Strabo is on the whole proud of the extent of his travels, but at the same time is not keen to mark his presence frequently in the course of his geographical survey. Waddy's conclusion that a conscious method and systematic rules lie behind Strabo's decisions to omit or to mention his visits seems too rigid. Strabo, however, as in many other contexts, seems to supply the answer himself: 'Everybody who tells the story of his own travels is a braggart' (1.2.23, C 30).

2

STRABO AND THE GREEK TRADITION

HOMER

The time and place of Strabo's birth, and, naturally, his education, helped to determine his character as a man of letters. His extant writings, both the major geographical opus and, to a lesser degree, the fragments of the historiographical works, show him as a Greek scholar in terms of his interests and views. This orientation is manifested principally through the traditions of a literary nature, from Homer to Polybius, which influenced both the framework and the contents of his work. Strabo was also well grounded in geographical discussions by earlier Greek scholars who had scientific tendencies and he constantly confronts them in his survey. At the same time, his work, particularly the *Geography*, reveals its Greek basis through typical Hellenic concepts parallel to some Stoic ideas or demonstrated in the perception of Greeks vs. Barbarians.

The earliest geographer and the unchallenged founder and luminary of geography is, says Strabo, Homer. This opinion is introduced at the beginning of the *Geography*:

> both I and my predecessors, one of whom was Hipparchus himself, are right in regarding Homer as the founder (*archegetes*) of the science of geography. For Homer has surpassed all men, both of ancient and modern times, not only in the excellence of his poetry, but also . . . in his acquaintance with all that pertains to public life. And this acquaintance made him busy himself not only about public activities . . . but also about the geography both of the individual countries and of the inhabited world at large, both land and sea; for otherwise he would not have gone to the uttermost bounds of the inhabited world, encompassing the whole of it in his description.
>
> (1.1.2, C 2)

Strabo not only admires Homer, but points out the special connection of the ancient poet to the main theme of his own work, that is, to geography. These opening remarks present several aspects of Strabo's great reverence

31

towards Homer, which figure many times throughout the *Geography*. These are Homer's chronological priority; his knowledge and his supposed ignorance; and the attitude of Strabo's predecessors to the poet.

To begin with, Strabo defines Homer as 'the first geographer' (1.1.11, C 7), thus assigning to him chronological priority over all other geographers. This point is further elaborated in the course of the description of Greece:

> In general, it is the most famous, the oldest, and the most experienced men who are believed, and since it is Homer who has surpassed all others in these respects, I must likewise both inquire into his words and compare them with things as they now are . . .
>
> (8.3.23, C 348–9)

However, Homer's superiority does not depend merely on chronology, but chiefly on the contents of his poems, which reveal an educated and well-informed geographer even by the standards of Strabo's time. Moreover, Strabo argues that even when Homer did not mention sites or did not refer to certain phenomena, he could have known them, or else was unable to know them because they had not yet occurred. Strabo concludes: 'it is not well for us to accuse him of ignorance' (1.1.6, C 3). He strongly rejects such accusations by claiming that 'Homer both knows and expressly says what is to be said, and . . . he keeps silent about what is too obvious to mention, or else alludes to it by an epithet' (1.2.29, C 36).

In the course of his discussion on the extent of Homer's knowledge, Strabo blames those who find faults in the poet, naming them as men who are wilfully deaf (1.2.30, C 36). However, at the same time he admits that 'Homer . . . leaves us to guess about most things. And it is necessary to arbitrate between his statements and those of the others' (13.1.1, C 581).

Strabo observes that omission of detail is normal even in writings more scientific than poetry, and therefore one should not look for absolute accuracy in the poems of Homer:

> If between these countries there are some countries which he leaves out, one might pardon him, for the professed geographer himself omits many details. And we might pardon the poet even if he inserted things of a mythical nature in his historical and didactic narrative. That deserves no censure.
>
> (1.1.10, C 6–7)

It is against nature for any man to be aware of every detail and to be an expert in all fields of knowledge. Therefore, Homer is exceptionally remarkable:

> The desire to invest Homer with all knowledge might be regarded as characteristic of a man whose zeal exceeds the proper limit, just

as would be the case if a man – to use a comparison of Hipparchus – should hang apples and pears, or anything else that it cannot bear, on an Attic wreath of olive or laurel. So absurd would it be to invest Homer with all knowledge and with every art.

(1.2.3, C 16)

Strabo goes a step further and compares poetry to philosophy, thus endowing the former with a much higher value: 'the wisest of the writers on poetry say . . . that poetry is a kind of elementary philosophy (*prote philosophia*)' (1.1.10, C 7). The basic difference between philosophy and poetry is their respective audience. While philosophy is aimed at a minority of people capable of grasping it, poetry, and especially Homeric poetry, is more popular, because it mixes mythology and truth, and ordinary people enjoy myths and legends (1.2.8, C 20). Nevertheless, this combination of fiction and fact does not alter Strabo's opinion that in poetry there is still some historical truth. Further, Strabo is so eager to attribute philosophical qualities of truth and knowledge to Homer, finding these abundantly in the poems, that he ascribes outright philosophical intentions to the poet: 'Homer's object was not to indulge in empty talk, but to do useful service' (1.2.19, C 26).

In addition to the title 'founder of geography', Strabo refers to Homer as 'The Poet, man of many voices (*polyphonos*) . . . and of wide information (*polyhistor*)' (3.2.12, C 149). Moreover, relating what seems to be an historical anecdote, he shows the impact of the poet on Alexander, who loved Homer and treasured his poetry, so much so that his political actions were affected, for he favoured the people of Ilium (13.1.27, C 594).[1]

The principal discussion on poetry, and especially Strabo's own view, is evidently influenced by Stoic notions of poetry and particularly the Homeric epics.[2] The Stoic philosophers argued for didactic qualities in poetry, and considered Homer very learned. To them, poetry was a means for expressing philosophical ideas and they often quoted verse, especially the Homeric. Strabo expresses the same idea in referring to the Stoics and at the same time he reveals his Stoic inclinations (below, p. 62):

Our men (*hoi hemeteroi*) contend that the wise man alone is a poet. That is the reason why in Greece the various states educate the young, at the very beginning of their education, by means of poetry, not for the mere sake of entertainment, of course, but for the sake of moral discipline.

(1.2.3, C 16)

True, here Strabo is referring to poetry in general as an instructive channel, but this certainly applies to Homeric poetry as well.

Strabo's admiration of the poet and his discussion of the qualities of his poems are obviously a part neither of a philosophical study nor of a literary

33

analysis. He associates Homer particularly with geographical proficiency. Homer's geographical knowledge and the value of his poems for geographical matters had preoccupied earlier geographers and historians. The predecessors of Strabo had tried to see to what extent there was a correlation between Homeric toponyms and site-descriptions and geographical and topographic realities. They also attempted to determine whether the absence of certain geographical details in Homer implied his ignorance.[3] Strabo's crowning of Homer as the unchallenged king of geography as well as of other fields of knowledge, is part of this general debate on the role and purpose of poetry in general and of the Homeric epics in particular.

In the *Geography* the shape of this debate is obviously connected to the question of the epics as a source of information on geographical matters. Thus, although Strabo deals with the general didactic qualities of poetry, he refers particularly to the opinions of certain geographers about the Homeric poems. Among earlier writers some did not consider the epics to be a valuable source for geography but merely saw their pleasurable qualities. One of these was Eratosthenes, who is a target for criticism while his contentions offer Strabo an excellent pretext to express his views on Homer. Eratosthenes saw pleasure and entertainment as the sole purposes of poetry, and accordingly did not consider Homer as a reliable source of information (1.2.3, C 15–16). Strabo declares that Eratosthenes 'is wrong in his contention that the aim of every poet is to entertain, not to instruct' (1.1.10, C 7), and that he himself considers the Homeric epics to be a treasure of facts and details based on the poet's experience (1.2.5, C 17).[4]

In the present context, Eratosthenes seems to be the exception among earlier geographers, for three other important predecessors of Strabo did rely on Homer for geographical issues. Among supporters of the poet's geographical value, Strabo mentions Hipparchus, Polybius and Posidonius. Hipparchus, who investigated the scientific aspects of geography, apparently relied on Homer in certain matters, and his arguments for the poet's proficiency serve Strabo's position, as is evident in two of the excerpts quoted above (1.1.2, C 2 and 1.2.3, C 16). Polybius, though an historian, also exploited the Homeric epics in the geographical discussions which were an integral part of his *History*. And, finally, Posidonius wrote about poets who had touched upon scientific matters, referring extensively to Homer. Posidonius was also accustomed to rely on Homer for support in his geographical arguments and Strabo does the same, both when he uses Posidonius' discussions directly and when he applies the same method by addressing the epics in various contexts. For instance, he quotes Posidonius' discussion of the extent of Homer's knowledge of low and high tide (1.1.7, C 4).[5]

In accordance with his conviction of Homer's geographical knowledge, Strabo bases large parts of his work on Homeric foundations. The epics are quoted many times throughout the entire *Geography*. Only in Book 4 of the seventeen are there no Homeric citations, almost certainly because its subject, the northern parts of Britain and Gaul, was unknown to Homer. Since Strabo uses Homer extensively and for various pieces of information, I shall illustrate this variety by random references chosen from each book of the *Geography*. The range of topics that impel Strabo to consult Homer shows his practical use of the poems for many details.

Book 1 – Homer indicated that the Ocean surrounds the earth (1.1.7, C 4).
Book 2 – He divided the Ethiopians into two groups, thus implying his knowledge of the Indians (2.3.7, C 103).
Book 3 – He knew a lot about Iberia, and the far west and north (3.2.12–14, C 149–51).
Book 5 – He mentioned the wild mules in the land of the Heneti in northern Italy (5.1.4, C 212).
Book 6 – Identification of the islands of Aeolus mentioned by Homer (6.1.5, C 256).
Book 7 – Homer described the habits of the Scythians accurately (7.3.9, C 302).
Book 8 – He distinguished between homonyms by using different adjectives, for instance, Arcadian Orchomenus and Boeotian Orchomenus (8.3.6, C 338–9).
Book 9 – He divided Thessaly into ten parts and ten dynasties (9.5.4, C 430).
Book 10 – He named some of the Sporades (10.5.14, C 488).
Book 11 – He referred to the fertile earth of Caucasian Albania (11.4.3, C 502).
Book 12 – He was well-informed about the regions of the Black Sea (12.3.26, C 553).
Book 13 – He alluded to the hot and cold springs of the Scamander (13.1.43, C 602).
Book 14 – He mentioned the Carians (14.2.28, C 661).
Book 15 – He referred to the association of Dionysus with Nysa (15.1.7, C 678).
Book 16 – He pointed out the artistic skills of the Sidonians (16.2.24, C 757).
Book 17 – He spoke of the size and wealth of Egyptian Thebes (17.1.46, C 815).

Apart from such general references to Homer in a wide range of topics, Strabo also uses Homer extensively in some principal matters. Following the first two chapters of the *Geography*, Strabo begins his survey with a summary of Homer's view of the *oikoumene*, its shape and its various countries (1.1.3–7, C 2–5; 1.1.10–11, C 6–7 and below, p. 43). In the course of the general survey of the inhabited world, beginning in Book 3, Strabo exploits the *Odyssey* and the *Iliad* for information about various regions of the *oikoumene*. As one could expect, the different natures of the two epics and their geographical settings determine the character and the extent of their use by Strabo. Citations from the *Odyssey* abound in descriptions of the western parts of the Mediterranean (Book 3), whereas the *Iliad* is the obvious basis for information on the Troad (Book 13).

Strabo also makes particular use of the 'Catalogue of Ships' as a geographical frame for his description of the Greek regions. This 'Catalogue' in the second book of the *Iliad* presents the united Greek forces arranged against the Trojans according to their geographical origins.[6] The list covered the major Greek territories, mentioning various towns and places. This was Strabo's guideline for the description of the Greek regions, with reference also to the discussions of Homer commentators, mainly Apollodorus of Athens, who wrote specifically about the 'Catalogue' (below, p. 39). Strabo also uses other geographical units treated in the Homeric poetic narrative, writing of the seven cities that Agamemnon gave to Achilles (for instance 8.4.5, C 360) and also of other cities according to their leaders, such as the cities subjected to Protesilaus, to Eumelus, to Philoctetes and so forth (9.5.14–22, C 435–43), and the islands subjected to Odysseus (10.2.18, C 457). That is, Strabo uses the Homeric narrative as a tool to create some order in the survey of the different regions. The lists form a reference framework for the position of other sites which are not mentioned in the 'Catalogue' or in any other enumeration in Homer. They thus help Strabo especially in descriptions of inner parts of the land and in this way complement the coastline descriptions the order of which was determined by accounts in the form of *Periploi* (below, p. 40). Given that these Homeric 'political' units reflect a pre-historic situation, Strabo's use of them for an 'updated' survey of the geography of the world is significant for the understanding of his whole orientation.

The Homeric presence is very obvious in the description of Greece, the Aegean islands and the western regions of Asia Minor (chapter 6, p. 175), all of them famous settings of the Trojan Saga including the later wanderings of Odysseus. Homer is in fact mentioned in almost every section of Book 8 of the *Geography*, that which describes western Greece and specifically the Peloponnese. Strabo explains the significance of Homeric poetry for the methodology of his descriptions:

> I am comparing present conditions with those described by Homer . . . since all of us believe that we have not successfully treated any subject which we may have in hand until there remains in our treatment nothing that conflicts with what the poet says on the same subject, such confidence do we have in his words. Accordingly, I must give conditions as they now are, and then, citing the words of the poet, in so far as they bear on the matter, take them also into consideration.
>
> (8.3.3, C 337)

He accordingly identifies various sites by consulting the epics (for instance 8.3.1–11, C 336–42); refers to the Homeric commentaries of Demetrius of Scepsis (8.6.15, C 375) and Apollodorus (8.3.6, C 338–9) and discusses broadly poetical and textual problems, for example the various ways in which Homer used the term 'Argos' (8.6.5–6, C 369–70).

Similarly, Book 9, on Attica, Boeotia, Phocis, Locris and Thessaly, is based on the outline of the 'Catalogue', as Strabo explicitly reminds his readers again and again (chapter 6, p. 175) Thus, the order of the various regions as well as the toponyms are discussed in relation to Homeric knowledge, also consulting writers who have written about the 'Catalogue' 'when they say things appropriate to the purpose of our work' (9.2.42, C 416).

Similar Homeric orientation is also apparent in Book 10, on the islands around Greece, Crete, the Sporades, the Aegean and the islands in the Ionian Gulf. The poems help Strabo identify sites, for instance: 'Geraestus is not named in the "Catalogue of Ships", but still the poet mentions it elsewhere' (10.1.7, C 446), and are the focus of some textual inquiries like the one referring to the Homeric epithets (10.2.10–12, C 452–5). Book 12 includes two principal Homeric discussions, one on the 'Catalogue' (12.3.20–7, C 549–54) and the other on the definition of boundaries between regions according to Homer (12.4.5–6, C 565). In Book 14, which surveys the western parts of Asia Minor and the large islands at its shores, Strabo similarly relies on Homer for the prosperity of the Rhodians (14.2.10, C 654) and analyses Apollodorus' commentary on the Homeric 'Catalogue' (14.5.22–9, C 677–81). Since the regions described in these three books are relatively marginal to the poetic narrative, the Homeric references in them are scantier, particularly in comparison with Books 9 and 13.

Book 13 of the *Geography* surveys the regions near Troy, Lydia and the adjacent islands. The description of the Trojan vicinity is clearly based on the *Iliad*. Strabo relies on the epic for the identification of various points including Troy itself (13.1.25, C 592–3) and also draws on some topographical features in order to understand certain details in Homer. This book abounds in long discussions of the course of battles during the Trojan War, their topographical settings and other textual problems. Strabo further expands the relation between geography and Homer. In addition to his use of the epics as a source for geographical information, trying to understand the topography according to the poetry, he also reverses the process by trying to understand parts of the epic through the geographical layout. This is especially apparent in the detailed references to battles fought during the Trojan War. For example in 13.1.35, C 597–8, confronting the topography and the inhabited points with Homeric expressions; in 13.1.36, C 598, identifying the exact position of the naval station of the Greeks in accordance with the poetic narrative; and in 13.1.43, C 602, comparing the allusions of the poet to the Scamander with current conditions.

Elsewhere Strabo challenges geographical commentaries on Homer. While in Surrentum, he tried to assess the hypothetical location of the Sirens (chapter 1, p. 26). One suggestion put them in Sicily, while another on the Sirenussae, a three-peaked rock near Surrentum.

But neither does this rock have three peaks, nor does it run up into a peak at all; instead it is a sort of elbow that juts out, long and narrow ... with the sanctuary of the Sirens on one side ... while on the other side ... lie three uninhabited rocky little islands, called the Sirens ...

(1.2.12, C 22)

This method was used by Demetrius of Scepsis and later by Apollodorus. Demetrius was the first to examine geographical information in Homer in relation to the known facts. Strabo uses Demetrius directly in these matters and applies his method to other regions as well. In this way the Homeric epics explain geographical matters and geographical conditions clarify poetic matters.

Strabo's interest in Homer is of course quite traditional. However, it may gain an additional dimension if we bear in mind the inclination of his personal teachers for Homeric studies (chapter 1). He openly professes that he devotes so much attention to the information in the epics 'because of the fame of the poet and because of our familiarity with him from our childhood' (8.3.3, C 337). More specifically, his teacher Aristodemus of Nysa was engaged in Homeric research, possibly following his father Menecrates who studied with Aristarchus of Samothrace, a central Homeric commentator. Menecrates himself had written a comparison between the *Iliad* and the *Odyssey*[7] and his son Aristodemus was a commentator and editor of the Homeric text. Strabo also alludes to a local tradition (*'phasi'*) in Nysa, Aristodemus' birthplace, concerning Homeric interpretation (14.1.45, C 650).

Part of Strabo's interest in the epics is due to his acquaintance with famous Homeric commentators. He not only alludes to their works but quotes some of them extensively and even disputes their views in some geographical and ethnographical matters. Thus, he refers to Demetrius of Scepsis, the Stoic Crates of Mallus, Aristarchus of Samothrace, Apollodorus of Athens and Aristonicus of Alexandria.

Demetrius of Scepsis wrote 'thirty books of commentary on a little more than sixty lines of Homer, that is on the *Catalogue of the Trojans*' (13.1.45, C 603) and 'was born at about the same time as Crates and Aristarchus' (13.1.55, C 609). He is a primary source for Strabo's discussion of the Trojan region. Demetrius is especially reliable, says Strabo, since he was born in Scepsis, not far from Ilium, and his acquaintance with the region from childhood increases his credibility (13.1.43, C 602; 13.1.45, C 605).[8] In sixteen contexts Strabo alludes to him simply as 'The Scepsian', demonstrating his importance in the eyes of the geographer.

Aristarchus of Samothrace[9] was a contemporary of Demetrius of Scepsis and Crates of Mallus (13.1.55, C 609). He taught Menecrates the father of Aristodemus who was Strabo's teacher (14.1.48, C 650). Strabo refers to him together with Crates as 'the leading lights in the science of criticism' (1.2.24, C 30), although he also alludes to Aristarchus' misinterpretation of the Homeric text which caused him wrongly to accuse Homer of ignorance (1.2.27, C 33).

Crates of Mallus[10] was another contemporary of Demetrius and Aristarchus (13.1.55, C 609). He was a grammarian, born in Mallus in Cilicia, the teacher of Panaetius who became the head of the Stoic school in Athens (14.5.16, C 676). Crates was interested in science and made a globe of the earth (2.5.10, C 116). He also used Homeric poetry as a basis for his scientific investigations (3.4.4, C 157). Strabo refers to his interpretation of the tides according to Homer (1.1.7, C 4) and also points out that Crates approached the problem of the 'double' Ethiopians 'as an astronomer' (1.2.24, C 31), and emended the Homeric text to avoid astronomic inconsistencies (1.1.6, C 3).

Apollodorus of Athens[11] composed a work on the *Marshalling of the Trojan Forces* (12.3.24, C 552) and another on the 'Catalogue of Ships' in which he tried to assess the truth in the descriptions of the regions mentioned by Homer in the 'Catalogue' (1.2.24, C 31). His geographical inclinations determined the nature of his Homeric analysis, and he also composed a description of the earth (*ges periodos*), which was, according to Strabo, 'a work on chorography in metre of comedy'. Strabo relies on his geographical analysis of the text yet accuses him of ignorance of chorography (14.5.22, C 677).[12]

It is evident that both Crates and Apollodorus combined science with Homeric studies, and both did this in sciences affiliated to geography, Crates dealing with astronomy and Apollodorus with chorography. Their works must have had a special appeal for Strabo, who in fact does the same by using the epics in a geographical context.

Strabo refers also to Aristonicus of Alexandria[13] but only once (1.2.31, C 38). He calls him a 'grammarian of my time' and mentions his work on the wanderings of Menelaus. In it Aristonicus 'recorded opinions of many men' concerning the specific question of the nations Menelaus visited in his travels. The pretext is an Homeric allusion, but the implications of the discussion are purely geographical and ethnographic and involve attempts to identify the Erembrians and to define the course of Menelaus' journey.

Why does Strabo devote so much of his work to Homer and to poetical discussions? First, his scholarly orientation, based on his personal education, is deeply rooted in traditional Greek culture. Specifically, there may have been a direct influence on Strabo from his teacher Aristodemus who was engaged in Homeric studies. Second, his Stoic background (below, p. 62) probably also encouraged him in the attribution of extensive knowledge to Homer. Finally, the discussions of preceding geographers on these matters caused him to confront the problem, deciding to refute Eratosthenes and to accept Hipparchus' view.[14] All in all, it is clear that

Strabo does not merely pay lip service to a traditional topic in geography, but turns Homer into his guide for purely geographical descriptions.

PERIPLOI AND THE CONCEPT OF THE OIKOUMENE

The earliest sailors and explorers tended to circumnavigate (*periplein*) continents and islands while keeping the coastline in sight. What was determined by considerations of safety adapted to uncertain weather conditions and primitive vessels, also established the character of the first geographical descriptions in Greek. In these accounts of 'a coasting voyage' or 'circumnavigation' (*periploi*) early travellers described distant and strange peoples. Such earlier surveys were arranged according to coast lines and thus focused on the documentation of harbours, ports and islands. They also mentioned towns and tribes according to their habitation by the seashore or on the banks of navigable rivers.[15]

The marks of a survey based on a *periplous* are apparent in Strabo's *Geography* in the terminology and the method of description. He sometimes specifies a voyage by boat or describes regions following the order of the coastline before going on to a description of the hinterland. There are also references to distances in terms of days of sailing. Since this was the method of reckoning early sea journeys,[16] similar information in the *Geography* may imply an ancient source, especially since Strabo usually gives distances by stadia.[17]

The typically Greek *periploi* figure repeatedly in the *Geography*. Though Strabo does not always cite them as such, their terminology and arrangement is apparent in every book. Naturally, the background existence of *periploi* is more evident in the parts of the *Geography* describing islands, gulfs and promontories, or regions with large and navigable rivers, where it is always possible to find some hints of *periplous* terminology.

Strabo claims that in using *periploi* as his sources he follows Ephorus: 'just as Ephorus, using the sea-coast as his measuring-line . . . so it is proper that I too, following the natural character of the regions, should make the sea my counsellor (*symboulon*)' (8.1.3, C 334).

The basic advantage of the sea as a 'counsellor' is that it 'more readily suggests the order of places' (9.2.21, C 408), but rivers can also serve as a reference line for geographical description: 'the rivers in particular, being a kind of natural boundary for both size and shape of countries, are very convenient for the purposes of the whole of our present subject' (15.1.26, C 696).

The basic advantage of the descriptions in the *periploi* is thus the linear order created either by a coastline or a river channel. These lines serve as a reference basis for topographic and ethnographic features situated near them.[18]

How does Strabo apply this general method to particular sites? In some books the application is more apparent and the references are numerous, their number and nature determined by the character of the region described, that is, the quantity of navigable parts.

In Book 3 of the *Geography* the survey begins with Iberia. Strabo describes this region with specific emphasis on strategic information, manifested also through details of navigation routes and harbours (chapter 6, p. 170). The book abounds with records of rivers in the Iberian peninsula, their length, the extent to which they are navigable and their nature. For instance:

> The Baetis . . . is navigable for approximately one thousand two hundred stadia from the sea up to Corduba and the regions a little higher up . . . up to Hispalis, the river is navigable for merchant vessels of considerable size, that is, for a distance not much short of five hundred stadia, to the cities higher up the stream . . . for the smaller vessels, and, as far as Corduba, for the river boats . . . but above Corduba . . . the river is not navigable
>
> (3.2.3, C 142)

The rivers and the coastline serve as the 'counsellor' or 'ruler' under whose guidance Strabo mentions sites and describes the land. For instance, he furnishes lists of harbours on the coastline in 3.4.7, C 159. These details undoubtedly both derive from and contribute to commercial and military expediency. At the same time it is clear that the descriptive basis is a *periplous*. For instance: 'when you sail from Our Sea into the exterior sea, you have this mountain on your right hand' (3.1.7, C 140) and 'on your left, as you sail up the river, are these mountains, while on your right is a large plain' (3.2.3, C 142).

In Book 4 the parts of the survey pertaining to the Mediterranean coastline of Gaul, past Massilia, and the sailing distance to Britain, imply a *periplous*. A distinction is made between descriptions of the sea-coast (*paraplous*), for instance in 4.1.6, C 181, and surveys of the inner parts of the land (*mesogaia*), for instance in 4.1.11, C 185. In Book 5 on Italy, Strabo gives a clear sailing-description with reference to the distance by sea between Iapygia and the Sicilian Strait (5.1.3, C 211), and again in the survey of the islands of Sardinia and Corsica (5.2.8, C 225). Book 6 continues the Italian survey, where the contexts suited to descriptions of navigation are the Lipariean islands, Sicily and the sea routes to the Italian peninsula (6.1.11, C 261 and many more). In Book 7 the sailing routes are, as in Iberia, rivers, the Ister (Danube) and the Borysthenes, and the region of the Chersonessus including the Pontic seaboard. Strabo describes the regions with reference to the course of the Ister and speaks of voyages along the sea coast (*paraploi*) (for instance 7.1.1, C 289; 7.1.3, C 290 and many more).

The descriptive framework of Book 8, on western Greece and mainly the Peloponnesian peninsula, is a *periplous*.[19] Strabo constantly refers to a sailor's point of view: 'this would be the voyage for one who is sailing towards the south from Eleian Pylus, whereas one who is sailing towards the north, where Ithaca is, leaves all these parts behind him' (8.3.27, C 351).

Book 9, as far as *periploi* are concerned, surveys the coasts of Attica, Locris and Thessaly (9.1.3, C 391) and Book 10 refers in terms of navigation to Euboea, being an island, to the islands near Aetolia and Acarnania and the Cyclades (for instance in 10.1.2, C 445). Book 11 contains suggestions of a coastal voyage in the description of the river Tanais (Don) and the coasts of the lake next to it and the Caspian Sea (11.2.2, C 492 for example). Book 12, on central Asia Minor, includes a description of the southern coasts of the Black Sea and the harbours and cities situated along them, for instance in 12.3.2, C 541. In the survey of the Troad, in Book 13, a sailing voyage is less apparent though there are a few allusions as in 13.1.6, C 584; 13.1.16, C 588; and 13.1.23, C 591.

The background *periplous* is, however, strongly felt in the survey of the western coast of Asia Minor in Book 14 as only two out of many examples show:

> The coasting voyage round Ionia is about three thousand four hundred and thirty stadia, this distance being so great because of the gulfs and the fact that the country forms a peninsula of unusual extent; but the distance in a straight line across the isthmus is not great.
>
> (14.1.2, C 632)

and also

> The voyage from Miletus to Heracleia, including the sinuosities of the gulfs, is a little more than one hundred stadia, though that from Miletus to Pyrrha, in a straight course, is only thirty – so much longer is the journey along the coast.
>
> (14.1.9, C 636)

Book 15 on India relies primarily on the writings of Alexander's historians who visited its northern parts. Strabo refers specifically to the sailing experience of Nearchus (for instance 15.2.12–13, C 725–6) and that of contemporary sailors, and the description of India includes sailing vocabulary (see for example 15.1.15, C 691). The Euphrates and the Tigris, the coastline of Phoenicia and the Persian Gulf are the geographical contexts calling for a use of navigation terminology in Book 16, for instance in 16.1.27, C 747–8 and many more. Finally, the last book of the geographical survey of the world describes Egypt and obviously devotes large sections to the Nile. Sailing up the Nile, personally experienced by Strabo (chapter 1, p. 20), calls for an account of the regions as they are seen from the point of view of a tourist on a boat. Here personal experience may have supplanted reliance on an earlier *periplous*.[20]

It is thus clear that Strabo based his work to some extent on traditional foundations in the form of *periploi*. Since this method of geographical description, which indeed cannot be defined as a literary genre, was very early, it is hard to identify the original *periplous* behind the description. We know, however, that two of Strabo's main authorities, Artemidorus and Posidonius, wrote a *periplous*.[21] Strabo himself alludes only in a very general way to 'the writers of the *periploi*' as his source (8.3.20, C 347).[22]

While *periploi* are indeed Strabo's guiding principle for descriptions of regions with navigable features, they seem also to have determined the ancient concept of the inhabited world, the *oikoumene*, which he wholly adopts. The very definition of the *oikoumene* as an island surrounded by the Ocean disregards the size of the Ocean itself; it is based on a continental concept in which the coastline is the defining contour of all parts of the world.[23] Strabo shows that Homer already comprehended the *oikoumene* as an island (1.1.3–7, C 2–5) and he himself accepts this idea but at the same time supports this view of the inhabited world by experience, by the senses and by logical inferences. Even though no one has made an entire circum-navigation of the inhabited world, it is still possible to infer from logic that the Ocean surrounds it (1.1.8, C 5; 2.5.5, C 112–13).

Strabo explains: 'we call '*oikoumene*' the world which we inhabit and know' (1.4.6, C 65). This world is vast but has borders. It is an enormous island surrounded by the Ocean which forms its ultimate limits. On it are various countries and peoples, some of them dwelling at the edges of the *oikoumene* or very close to them, since there are also limitations to the inhabited parts of the island itself. These are deserts, or regions otherwise not suitable for habitation, or unknown regions. Strabo is aware of the inadequacies of infor-mation about regions beyond the boundaries of the inhabited world.

At the edges of the world there are countries beyond which there are unknown regions. On the eastern edge lies India, in the west – Iberia and Mauretania, in the north – Scythia and Celtica, in the south – Ethiopia.[24] No one has travelled beyond these edges. The farther regions are unknown and information about them is obscure and interwoven with rumours and legends. Thus the island of Thule (probably the Shetlands)[25] is outside the *oikoumene* in the north (1.4.4, C 63; 4.5.5, C 201). And the island of Taprobane (Sri Lanka), being uninhabited, is outside the *oikoumene* in the south-east (2.5.14, C 119). Furthermore, information on the southern parts of Libya and North Africa is based on conjecture since it is impossible to reach these places (17.3.1, C 824).

This image of the *oikoumene* is very similar to the ancient concept of nations or tribes who dwell at the edges of the world. Strabo does not use names of nations but rather names of regions. In fact he criticizes the ancients' habit of using general ethnonyms, such as Iberians or Ethiopians, without distinguishing the ethnic differences among them (1.2.27, C 33 and 1.2.28, C 35). However, the definition of the boundaries of the world in the form of four fixed entities, whether nations or countries, is basically the same. This similarity, which again indicates Strabo's traditionalism, is very apparent in light of the earlier division of Ephorus who defined the four edges of the *oikoumene* according to the border nations: the Indians who dwell in the part from which the wind *Apeliotes* blows, the Ethiopians in the part of *Notos*, the Celts in the part of *Zephyros* and the Scythians in the part of the northern wind, the *Borras* (1.2.28, C 34).[26]

During hundreds of years of geographical tradition this ancient definition made use of the same typical nations to indicate the boundaries of the world, although the names were applied to different peoples. Thus, the Scythians, for example, were always the barbarians of the north even when geographical knowledge expanded and the boundaries of the *oikoumene* moved farther north. Strabo does not adopt this ethnological picture because he is aware of ethnic pluralism, but the countries he mentions as border regions of the world are clearly parallel to the traditional concept. This goes hand in hand with another traditional feature of this picture, which he also echos, that of the fixed characteristics of the border peoples who are always unsocial, wild, very rich and live under extreme weather conditions (3.1.1, C 137 and 11.8.7, C 513).

Strabo likens the shape of the enormous island, the *oikoumene*, to a cloak (*chlamys*) which lies in the northern quarter of the globe.[27] To measure it one must measure the distance between two longitudes, one at the westernmost point of the *oikoumene* and the other at the easternmost, and then calculate its extent. As for the width of the inhabited world, the measure is between two latitudes, one at the northernmost point and the other at the southernmost (2.1.3, C 285; 2.4.7, C 108). The line of the greatest width passes through the Nile from the Cinnamon country (Somalia) to Ireland, and of the greatest length from the Pillars of Heracles (Straits of Gibraltar) to the eastern sea between India and the Scythians (2.5.14, C 118–19). The result is 30,000 stadia for the width of the world and 70,000 stadia for its maximum length.[28] Accordingly Strabo defines Delphi as the centre of the *oikoumene,* since it lies at an equal distance from the ends in the east and in the west (9.3.6, C 419–20). Strabo's notions and calculations here are based on the ideas of his predecessors Eratosthenes and Posidonius, but as we shall see, by transmitting them Strabo made a significant contribution to the history of geography and exploration (chapter 6, p. 153).

Strabo accepts the traditional division of the *oikoumene* into three continents, Europe, Asia and Libya. The three are not equal in size since Libya is much smaller than the other two (17.3.11, C 824). He mentions several methods of defining the boundaries between the continents. One is by using rivers and thus the Nile separates Libya from Asia and the Don separates Asia from Europe. This might reflect a concept similar to the one underlying the idea of *periploi*. Another method uses isthmuses, such as the isthmus between the Caspian and the Pontic seas and the isthmi between the Red Sea and the outlet of Lake Sirbonis (1.4.7, C 65–6). A third method, that of Posidonius, defines the continents according to zones of latitude (2.3.7,

C 102–3). Strabo criticizes two out of these three methods, that of rivers (1.2.25, C 32; 1.2.28, C 35) and that of zones (2.3.7, C 102–3), yet his own preferred method is not clearly specified. Nevertheless, he thinks that the division between the continents has practical and political consequences, for the primary definition of the continents by the Greeks determined the self-definition of Greece in relation to the rest of the world (1.4.7, C 65) and similarly the attachment of Egypt to Asia or to Libya is politically significant (1.4.8, C 66).[29]

Finally, Strabo also adopts the traditional division of the globe into climatic latitudinal zones. According to this division the torrid zone lies in the centre of the globe on both sides of the equator, two temperate zones lie parallel to each other on both sides of the torrid zone, and an arctic zone lies at either pole. Therefore, the *oikoumene* also straddles different zones of climate which affect the extent of habitation. In the coldest or hottest regions, that is, towards the northern pole, and closer to the equator, habitation is very sparse. The climate affects the fauna and the flora as well as the water sources and the entire nature of the various countries, and also the ability of the inhabitants to rule. Strabo relies on the teachings of Aristotle, Polybius and Posidonius on these matters although he prefers the Posidonian division into five zones to the Polybian six (2.2.1, C 94; 2.3.2, C 96–7).[30]

To sum up, Strabo bases his concept of the *oikoumene* and his geographical survey on ancient ideas and on very early foundations such as voyages of exploration. At the same time he is well aware of political and social changes which affect the ethnic structure of the *oikoumene* although the physical foundation is still unchanged. This would be the explanation for his criticism of the ancients who used general ethnic titles without understanding that the picture is much more diverse, and also for his implication that the division of continents has political significance.

This human change within the rigid framework of the *oikoumene* is in fact what the whole *Geography* is about. As I hope to show also later on, Strabo's primary intention in his geographical work was indeed to produce an updated representation of the geographical information about the *oikoumene*. He does not spare words in order to describe both accurately and simply the topographical layout of the world and the boundaries of the various countries within it, usually presenting first the natural limits of each region which are constant and unchanged, that is, coastlines, rivers and mountains. But at the same time he is very much aware of other sorts of boundaries which are changeable and pertain to political and ethnographic factors. The final product is not a 'dry' topographical survey which is purely scientific, but rather a combination of several layers of maps, so to speak, the topographic, the ethnic and the political. If we imagine these three conceptual maps as overlying transparencies, the overall representation emerges as complex and yet clear. This seems to be Strabo's original intention, which I believe he successfully attained in the *Geography*.

POLYBIUS

Our knowledge of Strabo as an author is prejudiced, because only his geographical work has survived.[31] However, he was well versed in the historiographical discipline and this is apparent not merely through allusions to his earlier career as an historian, but also in his tendencies towards earlier historiographical methodologies within the geographical contents of the later work. The nature of the *Geography* obliged Strabo to rely on scientific foundations, but at the same time he was clearly influenced by earlier historians also in his approach to geography.

Herodotus, the 'Father of History', was the first author to insert geographical and ethnographical information into his survey of the historical developments of the first decades of the fifth century BCE. Thus, he thoroughly discussed nations who were part of the historical narrative, referring to their origins, their marriage customs and nourishment, their clothes and their weapons, and their country, with its climate, fauna and flora. His well-known digressions on the habits and the country of the Persians (1.131–40), the Egyptians (2.4–98), the Indians (3.99–106) and the Scythians (4.17–75), became an important landmark on the road to later and more elaborate geographical descriptions. Nevertheless, his methods and his approach did not impress Strabo, to say the least, and it is in fact very difficult to refer to any direct influence of Herodotus on the *Geography*. Surprising as it may seem, such an influence is simply non-existent.[32] On the other hand, Strabo's scholarly orientation is deeply rooted in the writings and methods of another Greek historian, Polybius.

Writing in the second century BCE, Polybius personally experienced the political developments of the age in the eastern Mediterranean, being deported to Rome by the conquerors of his native land, Achaea. Despite this experience, he became associated with Scipio Aemilianus and soon decided to record and explain what he saw to be the meteoric ascendance of Rome to the position of a world power.[33]

At first glance, both the relative chronological proximity to Strabo of Polybius compared to Herodotus, and his historiographic theme which focused on the central role of Rome in world politics seem to explain our geographer's inclinations to the ideas of the historian, especially as compared to his neglect of Herodotus. But there is much more to it.

According to Strabo's own testimony, he began his writing career with historiography (below, p. 69). One of his major projects was a chronological continuation to Polybius (11.9.3, C 515). The idea of producing a work which is a chronological sequel to an existing composition was not an invention of Strabo's. We know of several other historians who did this before him: Xenophon in his *Hellenica* after Thucydides, Theopompus of Chios after Thucydides, Polybius after Timaeus and Posidonius after Polybius.[34] However, Strabo declared that the *History* he had written was not only a

46

chronological continuation of Polybius, but also an ideological continuation of his approach, for like Polybius Strabo stressed the benefit 'for moral and political philosophy'. Polybius, whom Strabo considers a philosopher worthy of intellectual discussion (1.1.1, C 1; 1.2.1, C 14), was thus Strabo's forerunner in many respects.

Some details from Polybius' writings, and to a much larger extent his views and ideas, can be clearly identified in the *Geography*. The Polybian fingerprints are not just simple quotations from the *Histories*. The more striking influence is on Strabo's ideas. These refer to Polybius' methodology and purposes in writing and to his political attitudes, and are manifested in the methods and goals of Strabo's work.

Polybius is famous for his notion of pragmatic history intended to instruct any future readers, ideally military men and statesmen, living in historical circumstances similar to those he describes. He assumes the role of a teacher who intends to help men avoid error in the future and aim at success. This pragmatic orientation determined the character and scope of his work: 'men have no more ready corrective of conduct than knowledge of the past . . . the soundest education and training for a life of active politics is the study of History' (1.1.1–2).[35] and

> In speaking at such length on this matter, my object has been
> . . . to rectify the ideas of students. For of what use to the sick is
> a physician who is ignorant of the causes of certain conditions of
> the body? And of what use is a statesman who cannot reckon how,
> why and whence each event has originated? The former will scarcely
> be likely to recommend proper treatment for the body and it will
> be impossible for the latter without such knowledge to deal properly
> with circumstances. Nothing, therefore, should be more carefully
> guarded against and more diligently sought out than the first causes
> of each event.
>
> (3.7.4–7)[36]

Strabo clearly approaches his task in the *Geography* along the same lines of pragmatic thought. First, he defines the advantage of the geography he aims at as one which 'has to do with practice (*pros tas praxeis*)' (1.1.18, C 11), that is, intended for practical application. This idea may be phrased synonymously as *pragmatike geographia*, parallel to Polybius' *pragmatike historia*, even if this exact wording does not appear in the text.[37] Carrying out this purpose, Strabo includes various details and excludes others according to what he thinks beneficial for his audience (chapter 6, p. 157). These pragmatic considerations function as filters for both authors. Polybius observes that 'in the case of unknown lands such citation of names is just of as much value as if they were unintelligible and inarticulate sounds' (3.36.3), and Strabo announces that he will avoid giving too many names, because they are unpleasant to hear and to write and have no significance (3.3.7, C 155).

In the course of his work, Strabo on several occasions reverts to his intentions in determining when to elaborate on a subject in order to enhance the knowledge of leaders, and when to abbreviate where information does not contribute to this task. His choice of themes for inclusion reflects pieces of information useful to an army commander, for example, strategic information for military and commercial navigation in Books 3 and 4; on the system of Roman roads in Italy and central Europe in Books 5 and 6; on contemporary political developments and balance of power in the world in Books 7, 11 and 12 (chapter 6, p. 170). Besides these, various facts and details about plants, animals, landscapes and natural phenomena, contribute to the reader's general knowledge and often to his practical information as well.

The Roman atmosphere in which Strabo wrote, which generally favoured practical undertakings, possibly also played some part in his orientation.[38] Thus, Strabo responded to 'market demand', so to speak, and provided the Romans with useful geographical material, such as travel instructions, records of distances, description of foreign countries and their economic and military advantages, and various kinds of travellers' information. In reality, however, his writings, and particularly the *Geography*, were not widely read (chapter 6, p. 151).

Another Polybian attribute was the universalistic approach to history. While his predecessors focused on regional matters, Polybius tried to show a more complete historical picture by describing events occurring simultaneously in several places around the Mediterranean. Polybius intended to compose a universal history, encompassing people, countries and events throughout the *oikoumene*. He noted that Ephorus was indeed the first universal historian (5.33.2), but he himself expanded this tendency to achieve a more general picture. He tried 'to inquire critically when and whence the general and comprehensive scheme of events originated' (1.4.3) and declared that 'I am not, like former historians, dealing with the history of one nation, such as Greece or Persia, but have undertaken to describe the events occurring in all known parts of the world' (2.37.4).[39]

In this sense, Strabo's *Geography* is universal in its definition and goal, for his intention is to describe the entire *oikoumene* known at his time. While earlier geographical works usually focused on certain regions, mainly as excursuses in an historiographical context, Strabo proposes to devote his attention equally to every region of the world. Hecataeus of Miletus in his *periodos ges* indeed attempted to describe the entire world as it was known in the middle of the sixth century BCE, with its two continents, Europe and Asia. But his approach was unusual and was meant to accompany a map he had made. Thus, Strabo presented a new concept of universalistic geography.

Strabo seems to have applied a similar universalistic approach also in his earlier historical survey which was meant to continue Polybius' *Histories* (below, p. 69). Here, however, he was not unique at his time, since we know of several other Augustan authors who composed universal histories, such as Diodorus of Sicily and Nicolaus of Damascus who wrote in Greek and Pompeius Trogus in Latin.[40]

Owing to their universalistic approach, both Polybius and Strabo stress the general picture and not particular points. Therefore both ask their readers to forgive them their mistakes and inaccuracies of detail.

Polybius:

> I may be justly pardoned ... should I happen to be mistaken in the names of mountains and rivers or in my statements about the characteristics of places. For in all such matters the large scale of my work is a sufficient excuse.
>
> (29.12.10–11)

and Strabo:

> Just as in my *Historical Notes* only the incidents in the lives of distinguished men are recorded, while deeds that are petty and ignoble are omitted, so in this work also I must leave untouched what is petty and inconspicuous, and devote my attention to what is noble and great, and to what contains the practically useful, or memorable, or entertaining.
>
> (1.1.23, C 13)

Strabo's involvement in the ideas of Polybius is evident through the lively discussions he has with his predecessor as if he were present in the flesh: 'But, my dear Polybius (*o phile Polybie*), one might reply, just as the test based upon your own words makes evident the error of these false reckonings ... so also those other reckonings are both false' (2.4.3, C 105). And again when arguing with Polybius he offers his reasonings in the first person and addresses him directly '*o Polybie*' (10.3.5, C 465). In this way Strabo gives the discussion the form of a dialogue, possibly influenced by Platonic conventions (below, p. 68).

Apart from the influence of Polybius on Strabo in some general ideas and methodologies, both writers discuss similar and specific topics pertaining to geography. Polybius admired Homer and drew geographical information from the *Iliad* and the *Odyssey*. In his thirty-fourth book he apparently discussed the journeys of Odysseus in detail and tried to identify the various points at which the hero landed.[41] According to Strabo, Polybius claimed that Homer had surrounded historical facts with myths. This point contradicted Eratosthenes' view that there were no factual details at all in the

Homeric epics (above, p. 34) and might have been the basis for Strabo's discussion on the matter (1.2.15–18, C 23–6). At the same time, Strabo accuses Polybius of using unsatisfactory arguments in his discussion of Homer's credibility (1.2.18, C 26).

Polybius wrote of latitudal climatic zones and their influence on the character of their human inhabitants and on animals and plants (4.21); Strabo does the same (for instance 2.1.14, C 72 and further). In this case Polybius is not the only precedent, for Strabo was influenced also by Posidonius and his discussions of climatic zones. Strabo indeed does not accept Polybius' conclusions, and rejects his division of the globe into six zones, preferring Posidonius' five-zone division (2.3.1, C 96 and above, p. 45).

On other matters too Strabo censures Polybius quite sharply and comprehensively. He criticizes Polybius' carelessness in recording distances, especially in regions he himself had visited (2.4.2–5, C 104–7; 8.8.5, C 389); he does not accept Polybius' astronomical methods for measuring the length of the *oikoumene* (2.4.7, C 108); and he indicates that Polybius is wrong in his opinion that it is possible to see both the Adriatic and the Black Seas from the Balkan mountains (7.5.1, C 313 and chapter 1, p. 28). Strabo also points out that before him Posidonius had also noted some problems in the distances given by Polybius for Greece and for other regions (10.3.5, C 564).

Thus, notwithstanding Polybius' significant influence on his work, Strabo defines one of his missions as the correction of Polybius' mistakes: 'In my detailed account I shall make the suitable corrections, not only of these mistakes, but also of all the other serious mistakes that Polybius has made, both in the matter of Europe and in his circuit of Libya' (2.4.8, C 109).

Polybius' universal and pragmatic views obviously influenced Strabo to a large extent, but the *Geography* as a whole presents an approach essentially differing from previous methods.[42] Geographical and ethnographical digressions were, traditionally, an integral part of historiography, but they served as a mere background to historical matters. Herodotus expanded his main historiographical line by inserting detailed digressions with descriptions of nations who played a role in the course of events. Polybius, too, saw geography as an aid to understanding historical developments, and accordingly included short descriptions of sites in his record of certain occurrences. When speaking of the struggle between the Carthaginians and the Italian Celts, he surveyed the regions of northern Italy, the Apennines and the Po valley (2.14–16). In referring to the time when Rhodes waged war on Byzantion, he described the latter and the Black Sea (4.38–45). In so doing Polybius was aware of his advantage over his predecessors:

In our own times since, owing to Alexander's empire in Asia and that of the Romans in other parts of the world, nearly all regions have become approachable by sea or land, since our men of action

50

in Greece are relieved from the ambitions of a military or political career and have therefore ample means for inquiry and study, we ought to be able to arrive at a better knowledge and something more like the truth about lands which were formerly little known. This is what I myself will attempt to do ... mostly for this very purpose of correcting the errors of former writers and making those parts of the world also known to the Greeks.

(3.59.3–8)[43]

Polybius indeed followed this principal line, but his expansion of the role of geography took place within the historiographical context. Unlike his predecessors, who always used the literary form of an excursus inserted in the narrative, Polybius presented a new approach, by treating geography in a separate section of his *Histories*: 'I decided not to make scattered and casual allusions to such matters [sc. geographical], but assigning the proper place and time to their special treatment to give as true an account of all as is in my power' (3.57.5).[44]

Thus, his now lost thirty-fourth book had a purely geographical character and was devoted to descriptions of regions in which the historical events occurred.[45] Polybius thus proposed devoting a larger stage to descriptive geography, but for all that it remained an appendix to history, playing a secondary, though important, role.

In this respect too Ephorus preceded Polybius, for Strabo indicates that Ephorus devoted a separate part of his history to geography (8.1.1, C 332 quoted below p. 165). As we have seen, Ephorus preceded Polybius also in his universalistic approach to history, and although the Polybian influence on Strabo seems to be much more extensive and significant, it is clear that Strabo appreciated the historian from Cyme.[46] He defines him, with others, as a philosopher engaged in geography (1.1.1, C 1), and refers also to Polybius' praise of the man, as 'better than others' (10.3.5, C 465) and 'indisputably noteworthy' (13.3.6, C 622). Strabo tells us that Ephorus was a disciple of Isocrates the orator and that he wrote a *History* and a work on *Inventions* (13.3.6, C 622). The fourth book of his historical treatise was on Europe (1.2.28, C 34; 7.3.9, C 302) and was probably the separate section devoted to geography. Although Strabo censures Ephorus several times (for instance 6.1.7, C 259; 9.3.11–13, C 422–3), his respect for his early predecessor is apparent, and is clearly influenced by Polybius' attitude: 'I am using [Ephorus] more than any other authority because ... he exercises great care in such matters' (9.3.11, C 422).[47]

To come back to Polybius, Strabo refers briefly to the content of the thirty-fourth book, which apparently included a detailed description (*chorographia*) of Europe (2.4.1, C 104) and Africa (2.4.8, C 109), and the topography of the continents (8.1.1, C 332).[48] In his geographical descriptions Polybius was also guided by pragmatic considerations. He was not interested in scientific

51

and theoretical discussions on geography and topography, but preferred to furnish his readers with new information and to increase their knowledge of remote and less-known regions, all of which had had a role in historical events.[49] In this sense, the pragmatic geography of Strabo seems to continue these goals and achievements. Nevertheless, his *Geography* is different from Polybius' geographical section in two principal ways. First, Strabo's work is much larger not only in volume but mainly in its scope, which covers the entire *oikoumene*. Second, his central theme is geography, without the pretext of providing a background to historical developments. Geography is the focus and not an appendix to history.

While Polybius, or probably Ephorus before him, made the first step towards expanding the role of geography, Strabo completed the move by making geography the centre of his interest and his motivation. In fact, in the *Geography* he reversed the interrelation between geography and history by turning history into the servant of geography.

Another similarity between the two writers, and a possible influence, is the political context of their works. Polybius focused on the growth of the Roman empire, its organization and its increasing power. He tried to explain its might and stability by analysing its political institutions and military organization.[50] Strabo, too, writing at the end of the Augustan age (chapter 6, p. 151), refers to Roman power and to the progress it brought to many barbaric nations (below, p. 75). Although Strabo does not refrain from criticizing the Romans (chapter 4, p. 115), he is well aware of their position and he also dwells briefly on the causes for their superiority, clearly in 6.4.1–2, C 285–8.

However, there is a difference in tone and in focus between the two authors. Each of them lived in a different epoch in Roman history, which circumstance also affected their political views. Whereas Polybius is very much interested in the causes for the increase of Roman power and tries to understand what lay behind them, Strabo cares less about the causes and more about the current situation of peace and prosperity. Polybius wrote after the second Punic war, when Roman power was in the ascendant and he was astounded by the fact that 'in less than fifty-three years' (6.1.3) it had become so dominant. Strabo, on the other hand, wrote at the end of the Augustan age, which marked the end of a century of enormous territorial expansion almost equivalent in size to what Polybius had discussed but also creating the atmosphere of a completed process. He seems to have absorbed the Roman sense of the age as a golden one in all respects, and accordingly he focused on the benefits created by the new situation. Besides, it is important to bear in mind that Polybius wrote a *History* and therefore dealt with causes, while Strabo wrote a *Geography* and was less interested in processes and causes.[51]

Finally, there seems to be some similarity between the personal biographies of Polybius and Strabo. Both lived in Rome; both were on friendly terms with Roman generals, Polybius with Scipio, Strabo with Aelius Gallus; and both escorted their Roman friends on their missions. But whereas Polybius was forcibly taken to Rome as a representative of a conquered nation, Strabo came there freely, as did many other Greek scholars who gathered in the city (chapter 5). All in all, both writers showed their admiration of the Romans, Strabo, at least, fully identifying with Rome.

SCIENTIFIC GEOGRAPHY

To evaluate the position and character of Strabo as a geographer we must confront his work with earlier geographical writings. Such a comparison may show the extent of Strabo's reliance on traditions of writing while defining his own approach to the description of the geographical and ethnographical situation in the world.[52]

Geography as a research discipline developed in two directions differing in focus, terms and methodology. Scientific geography, which also contributed to cartography, used astronomy, arithmetic and geometry to establish coordinates of sites, distances between points, shapes and sizes of regions in terms of length, width or circumference. Descriptive geography on the other hand did not apply exact calculations and empirical research at all, but dealt with descriptions of regions and sites according to the writer's tendencies and goals. The basis was usually a description of the appearance of the site, its nature, and topographical, botanical and zoological characteristics. Descriptive geography could sometimes include mathematical details but never engaged in calculating them. The Greeks thus developed two styles of written geography. One was descriptive and usually formed an appendix to historiographical discussions in the tradition initiated by Herodotus. The other was scientific and dealt with various mathematical and astronomical aspects of geography such as zones of latitude, measurements of the circumference of the earth, and definition of sites according to coordinates of longitude and latitude.

Strabo himself seems to have made a clear distinction between what he calls 'geography' and 'mathematics'. On several occasions he explains what subjects pertain to geography and therefore should be included and what subjects should be left out. The latter are often scientific matters, which, he feels, have no place in his work. The compromise between excluding scientific investigations, but still using scientific data and terminology, is expressed in 1.1.14, C 8:

> even if it be impossible in a treatise of this nature because of its having a greater bearing on affairs of state, to make everything scientifically accurate, it will naturally be appropriate to do so, at least in so far as the man in public life is able to follow the thought.

and again:

> The geographer need not busy himself with what lies outside of
> our inhabited world, and even in the case of the parts of the inhab-
> ited world the man of affairs need not be taught the nature and
> number of the different aspects of the celestial bodies, because this
> is dry reading for him.
>
> (2.5.34, C 132)

That is, the factors determining inclusion or omission of scientific details
are the scope of the work, i.e. the boundaries of the *oikoumene*, and the
intended readers of Strabo, men of affairs to whom an interesting survey is
also important (chapter 6, p. 161).

Strabo observes that ordinary people and even military commanders get
the impression that the world is flat and find their way by using fixed signs
on the surface of the earth. Usually they are not aware of the differences in
astronomy between various points on the globe and are not interested in the
principles of the movements of the constellations. But his intended readers
should have some basic mathematical understanding (2.5.1, C 109–10). At
the same time Strabo sees no need to adduce all the detailed mathematical
calculations in a geographical work. That is, knowledge is necessary but
practical considerations dictate brevity in these matters (chapter 6, p. 157).

Strabo declares that in general the geographer does not need to form
mathematical or physical rules nor to do research in these fields, but that
he should be familiar with the terms and the principles in order to be able
to use them as far as the description of the *oikoumene* is concerned. In this
sense he shows himself familiar with the world of science, while always
elucidating its contribution to geography. There is an internal grading in
the sciences so that various branches rely on conclusions from others. At
the top of this conceptual pyramid stands physics and from it spring
astronomy, geometry and geography, each one resulting from the former:[53]
'The geographer must rely upon the geometricians who have measured the
earth as a whole; and in their turn the geometricians must rely upon the
astronomers; and again the astronomers upon the physicists' (2.5.2, C 110).

Most of the scientific discussions in the *Geography* appear in the first two
books of the work, in which Strabo presents his plan and argues with his
predecessors about basic geographical principles. He summarizes the physical doctrines which contribute to the science of geography (2.5.2, C 110)
and explains astronomical phenomena in so far as they pertain to geographical
matters, that is, to the description of the face of the earth (2.3.1–2, C 96–7;
2.5.3, C 111). Next, following his general pyramid-like scheme, comes
geometry. The task of the man engaged in this field is to measure areas.[54]
To this end he uses physical and astronomical principles, particularly latitudes and longitudes and the angles between the rays of the sun and the

surface of the earth (2.5.4, C 111–12). The geographer exploits the results of these inquiries and calculations, adopting the conclusions which contribute best to the description of the world.

The branch of science most commonly used by Strabo is geometry and measurement. In his scheme of sciences, geography derives directly from geometry. Thus, he consistently gives measures of territories, distances between various points and descriptions of shapes of regions (see for instance 2.1.30–31, C 83–4; 4.1.3, C 178; 5.1.2, C 210; 9.3.1, C 417). In the case of Italy, for example, he has difficulty in defining the geometrical outline of the peninsula and concludes that 'it is better to confess that the representation of non-geometrical figures is not easy to describe' (5.1.2, C 210). He also exploits geometrical terminology in his attempts to reject the views of his predecessors concerning the shape of the *oikoumene* (2.1.22, C 78; 2.1.28–9, C 81–3). Furthermore, he applies geometrical axioms: lines are parallel when they do not meet (2.1.10, C 70) and 'a line has no angle when its parts do not converge towards one another' (5.1.2, C 210).

In addition to these general discussions Strabo alludes to specific scientific matters throughout the entire work. Thus, he refers to kinetic energy by contending that when circles of different sizes move at the same time, the larger circle will move faster (2.3.2, C 97). He speaks of scientific methodology, declaring that it is impossible to measure something permanent which does not change, such as a continent, by using changeable and impermanent things such as the angle between the sun's rays and the surface of the earth (2.4.7, C 108). He is aware of volcanic phenomena and of changes occurring in the shape of continents and islands (1.3.16–20, C 57–61). He knows of the connection between the moon and the tides (3.5.8–9, C 173–5). And he speaks of springs and wells which fill up and produce water irregularly (3.5.7, C 172–3). Strabo even refers to the empirical aspect of science. He favours the use of the senses as a method to know the world and elaborates on an experiment he himself performed. When he visited the Plutonium in Hierapolis (chapter 1, p. 19) he sent sparrows into the poisonous hot vapours in order to test their effect on the birds (13.4.14, C 629–30).

Physics, astronomy and geometry belong, according to Strabo, to '*meteorologia*' that is, they pertain to the heavenly bodies. In addition to them there are 'earthly' sciences which a geographer also needs to know (1.1.15–16, C 8). Thus, Strabo is interested in zoology and botany and includes many references, often very detailed, particularly to exceptional animals or plants.[55] These, however, were a traditional part of descriptive geography ever since the work of Herodotus and are not considered as science proper. Nevertheless, sometimes Strabo applies a sort of scientific explanation to zoological obscurities, based on logical inferences. For instance, while describing the grasshoppers in south Italy and Sicily he wonders why the insects on the Locrian bank sing and those on the side of Rhegium remain mute. The explanation he, or his source, offers is that 'on the latter side the region is so densely shaded that the grasshoppers, being wet with dew, cannot expand their membranes, whereas those on the sunny side have dry and hornlike membranes and therefore can easily produce their song' (6.1.9, C 260).

Although Strabo does not include medicine as a discipline required from the ideal geographer, he does show familiarity with various medicinal materials including olive oil and wine;[56] he knows of healing resorts beside springs and rivers;[57] he elaborates the symptoms of the scurvy among the army of Gallus in Arabia (16.4.24, C 781); and he uses a chirurgical metaphor to explain the nature of the writing of geography (2.1.30, C 83 quoted in chapter 6, p. 156). All these may be part of general popular knowledge transmitted by word of mouth as travellers' information and therefore should not necessarily be considered as scientific. In the case of the scurvy, it is probable that Gallus himself, being Strabo's friend (chapter 3, p. 87), described the details to the geographer.

Thus, Strabo alludes extensively and elaborately to scientific matters and to authors and works that dealt with these aspects before him. In referring to his sources he usually briefly indicates the name of the author or the work he has consulted. However, he singles out four scholars whom he defines as geographers and considers better than all others:

> It is not my purpose to contradict every individual geographer, but rather to leave the most of them out of consideration, men whose arguments it is unseemly even to follow ... to engage in philo-sophical discussion with everybody is unseemly, but it is honourable to do so with Eratosthenes, Hipparchus, Posidonius, Polybius and others of their type.
>
> (1.2.1, C 14)

These four are not mere sources of information used in a random quotation, like dozens of other sources he uses, but much more: they are Strabo's model for writing geography. By imitating them or opposing their views Strabo forms his work and his character as a geographer.

According to Strabo, Eratosthenes of Cyrene had knowledge of poetry, grammar, philosophy and mathematics and was much respected by the kings of Egypt. (17.3.22, C 838).[58] He discussed geography in its two aspects and styles, that is, the descriptive and the scientific, while elaborating on mathematical matters and calculations, the most famous of which is his almost accurate figure of the circumference of the earth. At the same time, he was engaged in some methodological questions pertaining to descriptive geography, and also described specific regions. Strabo is aware of this duality in Eratosthenes' character and phrases it nicely, if rather coolly, by defining Eratosthenes as 'a mathematician among geographers, and a geographer among mathematicians' (2.1.41, C 94). This definition implies Eratosthenes' dual interest in mathematical geography – like Hipparchus and Claudius Ptolemy after him – and descriptive geography – like Ephorus, Polybius and Strabo.

Despite Strabo's appreciation of Eratosthenes' many talents, he still points out that Eratosthenes is not 'so trustworthy as some have been taught to believe that he is, notwithstanding the fact that he had been associated with many eminent men' and that he had the tendencies

> of a man who is constantly vacillating between his desire to be a philosopher and his reluctance to devote himself entirely to his profession, and who therefore succeeds in advancing only far enough to have the appearance of being a philosopher; or of a man who has provided himself with this as a diversion from his regular work, either for his pastime or even amusement; and in a sense Eratosthenes displays this tendency in his other writings, too.

Therefore, Strabo concludes, 'I must correct Eratosthenes' geography as far as possible' (1.2.2, C 15).[59]

Strabo evaluates his predecessors according to the standards he sets for the ideal geographer, concluding that Homer, Polybius, Hipparchus and Posidonius were philosophers and thus excellent scholars and geographers (1.1.1, C 1), whereas Eratosthenes who wavered between his wish to become a philosopher and his other interests only seemed a philosopher but in fact was not a serious and profound scholar (1.2.2, C 15).

Strabo thus approaches the writings of his predecessor from a critical point of view though at the same time with explicit respect. His critical attitude to Eratosthenes is based largely on Hipparchus' work *Against Eratosthenes*.[60] One of the major points of discussion is the question of the Homeric epics as a source for geographical information. As we have seen, Strabo admires Homer and accepts the epics as a geographical source and indeed as a source for various kinds of information. Eratosthenes, on the other hand, claimed that poetry was meant solely for pleasure and could not instruct, contending that Homer should not be a source for scientific matters (1.1.10, C 7; 1.2.3, C 15–17; 1.2.12, C 22). The debate is so urgent in Strabo's eyes that, as he does with Polybius (above, p. 49), he addresses Eratosthenes directly as if the third-century scholar was present at his side: 'You may be right, *o Eratosthenes*, on that point, but you are wrong when you deny to Homer the possession of vast learning' (1.2.3, C 16).

Eratosthenes of course enjoyed direct access to the library at Alexandria and to various kinds of sources (2.1.5, C 69), but Strabo attacks his uncritical use of bad sources (1.3.1, C 47). He explains that Eratosthenes had the habit of alluding to unreliable and marginal sources and exploiting them to some extent, whereas one should use only the works of famous men who have proved their credibility on many occasions. Strabo also does not accept

Eratosthenes' view on the division of mankind according to moral qualities. While he himself holds to the traditional Greek view of Barbarians
vs. Greeks (below, p. 75), Eratosthenes defined the differences according to
bad or good moral qualities and not according to 'nationality', arguing that
there are bad Greeks and good Barbarians (1.4.9, C 66–7).

Notwithstanding this thorough and sometimes harsh criticism, Strabo in
a way continues Eratosthenes' line of descriptive geography, at least by
discussing the same topics, such as the position of Homer and some other
methodological matters. For instance, he uses Eratosthenes' method for
dividing regions and their descriptions according to their natural borders.
Eratosthenes divided the *oikoumene* according to its nature and so Strabo
does with Asia, that is, divide it and describe it first according to its natural
boundaries (11.1.1, C 490).

Hipparchus, a native of Nicaea (12.4.9, C 566) and a scholar worthy of
citation (1.2.1, C 14), dealt with astronomy and mathematical calculations.[61]
Strabo defines him as a writer of 'mathematical' and not 'geographical' works
(2.1.41, C 94). Hipparchus tried to apply mathematical accuracy to geography, making astronomical observations from Rhodes over a long period
of time and recording his impressions in writing. These observations enabled
him to predict the movements of stars and foretell weather changes. The
majority of his fourteen known works deal with astronomical and astro-
logical matters and with physical geography (8.1.1, C 332). Among them
were works on the zodiac, the size of the sun and the moon and their
distance from the earth, the planetary system, the length of the year and,
as noted, an extensive treatise against Eratosthenes.[62]

Most of the surviving fragments of this work are known to us from the
Geography since Strabo reviews its major points in discussing his predecessors.
He presents the arguments in the form of an indirect dialogue between
Eratosthenes and Hipparchus, even though they did not live at the same
time (1.3.14, C 56). Hipparchus, unlike Eratosthenes and like Strabo, considered Homer the founder of geography (1.1.2, C 2; 1.2.20, C 27). Apparently,
Hipparchus also challenged some calculations of longitude and latitude
made by Eratosthenes and presented his own (2.1.38, C 90; 2.5.7, C 113;
2.5.34, C 132). Further, he disagreed with Eratosthenes on matters such
as the connection between various seas and the water level in each of them
(1.3.13–14, C 55–6); credibility of sources (2.1.7, C 69–70; 2.1.19, C 76);
and distances between sites (2.1.21–2, C 77–8). In several instances Strabo
forms an opinion on the matter under discussion, not always in favour of
Hipparchus (see for instance 2.1.5, C 69). But he generally supports the
critical comments Hipparchus addressed to Eratosthenes and concludes that
there is nothing one can add to them (2.1.41, C 94).

Strabo does not argue with Hipparchus on matters of science and mathematics, which are not his field. However, he does present his disagreement
with Hipparchus on methodological matters which involve inferences from

logic. Accordingly, Strabo does not accept Hipparchus' opinion that the Ocean does not surround the *oikoumene* (1.1.9, C 5–6) and he amends Hipparchus' claim that the Danube flows into both the Black Sea and the Mediterranean (1.3.15, C 57). Strabo criticizes Hipparchus on some other matters as well: his contradictory arguments on Eratosthenes' sources (2.1.5, C 69); his erroneous understanding of sources and acceptance of false declarations (2.1.19–20, C 77); and his false assumptions and wrong conclusions (2.1.21, C 77–8; 2.1.36, C 88). Strabo rather harshly ascribes the flaws in Hipparchus' writing and methodology to his feelings of envy towards Eratosthenes, to a hidden rivalry with his predecessor (2.1.23, C 790) and to 'childish ignorance (*paidike amathia*)' (2.1.29, C 83). The root of the problem, says Strabo, is that Hipparchus judged Eratosthenes according to geometrical accuracy as if Eratosthenes had made his observations using measuring tools, whereas in fact he only made approximate observations according to the traditional methods of geography (2.1.34–5, C 86–7; 2.1.39, C 91).

Hipparchus was the first geographer to apply the theory of zones of latitude scientifically. He presented his conclusions, based on astronomical theory and scientific calculations, in a chart on which he defined each zone according to its typical climatic and astronomical phenomena.[63] Strabo used this information (1.4.4, C 63) and his discussions on zones of latitude are based on Hipparchus' calculations (2.5.34, C 131–2).

Since Hipparchus' approach to geography was mathematical and astronomical, his writings do not function as a literary precedent for Strabo, who was engaged in descriptive geography. Thus, Strabo does not look for new empirical and scientific research, accepts the information gained by Hipparchus and refers the reader to the writings of his predecessor:

> If any one wishes to learn about these regions also, and about all the other astronomical matters that are treated by Hipparchus, but omitted by me as being already too clearly treated to be discussed in the present treatise, let him get them from Hipparchus.
>
> (2.5.43, C 135)

Artemidorus of Ephesus is not specifically included in the group of four great geographers with whom it is proper, according to Strabo, to have philosophical discussions (1.2.1, C 14). Strabo also defines him as a layman (*idiotes*) in certain matters (3.5.7, C 172). However, he often refers to him as an authority especially for distances, measurement of islands and geographical coordinates.[64] Although he does not allude to it specifically, it is possible that Strabo consulted the *periplous* written by Artemidorus. Thus Artemidorus, like Hipparchus, is a source that spares Strabo the need to form new measurements and observations. Strabo accepts some of Artemidorus' amendments to Polybian distances (8.8.5, C 389), and ascribes to him ethnographical and zoological information such as the barbaric customs of the women in Iberia (3.4.17, C 164) and the size of the Ethiopian rhinoceros (16.4.15, C 774). Still, Strabo points out misinformation and real distortions of distances in Artemidorus (14.5.22, C 677; 17.1.18, C 801; 17.3.8, C 829).

Strabo refers to one significant advantage of Artemidorus: he visited the most western point in the *oikoumene*, the 'Sacred Cape' in western Iberia. As an eye-witness of the site Artemidorus described it as looking like the prow of a ship and documented the religious customs of the inhabitants (3.1.4, C 137). However, Strabo criticizes this testimony, using logical inferences and presenting the contradictory observations made by Posidonius. Accordingly, he cannot accept Artemidorus' claim that the setting sun at this point is a hundred times bigger than usual and that night falls there instantaneously (3.1.5, C 138).

Once again Strabo announces that he is not going to consider scientific discussions, this time alluding to Posidonius of Apameia:[65]

> In my detailed discussions many of his views will meet with fitting criticism, so far as they relate to geography, but so far as they relate to physics, I must inspect them elsewhere or else not consider them at all.
>
> (2.3.8, C 104)

Thus, Strabo limits his interest in the work of Posidonius to its purely geographical aspect.[66]

Posidonius apparently composed three geographical works. One discussed poets whose poems related to scientific matters although they themselves had no scientific knowledge. The focus was Aratus, who had written astronomical poetry. Posidonius criticized Aratus' non-professional attitude to science and compared his mathematic skills with those of Homer. Although there is no indication of Strabo's acquaintance with this work, we may assume that the discussion on the scientific qualities of Homer would have been of special interest to him.

Strabo knew and summarized another work by Posidonius, *On the Ocean*, which had some scientific and geographical inclinations (2.2.1, C 94). First, he defines it as mostly a geographical work which is in part mathematical (2.2.1, C 94), and this of course suits his own purposes, which are not scientific. He refers his readers to Posidonius' discussions of the tide in the Ocean (1.1.9, C 6; 1.3.12, C 55). He also refers to Posidonius' discussion of zones of latitude.[67] Posidonius, he says, thought that there were five climatic zones in the *oikoumene*, unlike Polybius who made a division of six (above, p. 50). These zones were different from each other in the shape of the shadows, that is, the angle of the sun, in the extent of habitation, in their nature and in their climate (2.2.1–3.8, C 94–104). Posidonius alluded to attempts to circumnavigate Africa, to expeditions to India and to the length of the *oikoumene* and its boundaries. He himself also visited the western parts of the Mediterranean such as Massilia, Gades and Iberia, and recorded his impressions in his work on the Ocean (for instance 3.1.5, C 138; 3.2.5, C 144 and more). Thus, he is one of Strabo's main sources for the description of these regions. A third Posidonian composition alluding to geographical matters was a *Periplous*, that is, a description of coast voyages. It is not clear whether Strabo knew this work or not, even though a background *periplous* is quite evident throughout his own work, as we have seen (above, p. 40).

In one case Strabo cites the ideas of Posidonius in direct speech, as if his predecessor was talking directly to him or to the reader. Thus, in the story about Eudoxus of Cyzicus who tried to circumnavigate Africa he puts the words in Posidonius' mouth: 'Well, I for my part, he says . . .' (2.3.5, C 100).

Pédech argues that Posidonius presented several new approaches to geography, apparent in both content and methodology.[68] First, he added ethnographical, zoological and botanical considerations to the traditional division of the *oikoumene* according to climate which was based on astronomical calculations of latitude, thus creating more detailed divisions based on these factors. Second, Posidonius tried to find explanations for geographical phenomena, referring to factors of space and time. He recognized the role of time in geographical changes and extensively discussed geological upheavals caused by time and also social and political turbulence which resulted in the immigration of nations. His third innovation was the use of generalizations and models in order to explain similar phenomena in different places, such as low and high tide and volcanic eruptions.

Strabo seems to have absorbed these Posidonian approaches in various contexts and matters: in his discussions of latitude zones (for instance 1.1.12–13, C 7; 2.1.14, C 72–3); by applying considerations of time and political change to the description of geographical sites (for instance 6.1.2, C 253); and in his attempts to find parallels and general explanations for repeated phenomena, for instance the tides (3.5.8, C 173–4).

Despite Strabo's affinity to the ideas of Posidonius he does not spare him criticism. He does not accept Posidonius' commentary on Homer (1.1.7, C 4), and he points out inaccuracies in the descriptions of north and west Europe which are especially disappointing because Posidonius visited these regions (2.4.2, C 104). Strabo criticizes Posidonius' story about the attempt of Eudoxus of Cyzicus to circumnavigate Africa (2.3.4, C 98–100) and locates contradictions in it which do not comply with geographical conditions and with logic. He therefore assumes that Posidonius might have invented it (2.3.5, C 100–2). Strabo goes on to say that there is not much of a difference between this story and the stories and inventions of Pytheas of Massilia, Euhemerus and Antiphanes: 'those men, however, we can pardon for their fabrications . . . just as we pardon jugglers, but who could pardon the master of demonstration (*apodeiktikos*) and the philosopher, whom we may almost call the claimant for first honours?' (2.3.5, C 102).

On the whole, despite Strabo's disapproval of various details included in the works of his predecessors, the fact that he engages in such thorough and extensive discussions of their ideas, and his particular focus on Eratosthenes, Hipparchus and Posidonius, proves that not only do they stand behind his own notions on scientific matters, but they are the basis for entire sets of scientific premises which Strabo is not interested in reproducing in his own treatise. Thus, Strabo cannot be understood without reference to the Greek tradition of scientific and mathematical geography.

STOIC PHILOSOPHY

The very first sentence of the *Geography* reveals much about Strabo's scholarly convictions: 'The science of geography, which I now propose to investigate, is, I think, quite as much as any other science, a concern of the philosopher' (1.1.1, C 1). He goes on to point out that the geographers who preceded him, from Homer to Posidonius, were philosophers, in the sense that they had a broad education (*polymatheia*) and proficiency in many subjects.

Later writers in fact called Strabo a philosopher. Plutarch in his *Lives* refers twice to 'Strabo the philosopher (*ho philosophos*)'.[69] The Suda, similarly, alludes to Strabo as '*philosophos*'[70] while Stephanus of Byzantion is more specific in his definition of Strabo as 'the Stoic philosopher'.[71] A study of Strabo's background and his treatment of various topics in the *Geography* shows that Strabo was indeed deeply embedded in the world of philosophy and had special tendencies towards Stoicism.[72]

Four allusions in the *Geography* clearly indicate Strabo's leaning towards the Stoic school. Twice he ascribes a textual amendment of an Homeric verse to 'our Zenon' or 'my Zenon' (*Zenon ho hemeteros*) (1.2.34, C 41 and 16.4.27, C 784). Another time, again in an Homeric context, he contends that 'our men (*hoi hemeteroi*)[73] said that the wise man alone is a poet' (1.2.3, C 15), thus referring to the Stoic appreciation of Homer. And he also adduces the Stoic avoidance of searching for causes: 'in Posidonius there is much inquiry into causes and much imitating of Aristotle (*to Aristotelizon*), precisely what our men (*hoi hemeteroi*) avoid, on account of the obscurity of the causes' (2.3.8, C 104).[74] Strabo's affiliation to the Stoic school is evident in the personal turn of these phrases.

In addition to these specific expressions of affinity, Strabo's treatment of various matters tends to reveal his use of Stoic terminology and concepts. First, his pragmatic intentions (chapter 6, p. 157) depend particularly on the principles of the new Stoa in Rome, which favoured discussions of philosophical topics with pragmatic implications. Second, some particular notions disclose the Stoic background. For instance, Strabo considers physics an *arete* (2.5.2, C 110), following the Stoic concept of three philosophical *aretai*: physics, ethics and logic.[75] As we have seen, Strabo's attitude to Homer

and his epics also had roots in the Stoics' respect for poetry and their particular use of Homer (1.2.3, C 15 and above, p. 33). He also refers to a central
literary genre found in some Stoic discussions, when he tells how he read
about self-filling wells 'in the *Paradoxes*' (3.5.7, C 172), thus suggesting
his interest in paradoxical phenomena.[76]

In the field of science, Strabo suggests the existence of three additional
worlds situated on the globe besides the *oikoumene* (1.4.6, C 65). Although
there were no scientific proofs for this hypothesis at the time when Strabo
composed his *Geography*, he shows his loyalty to traditional Stoic concepts
of geography by inserting it.[77] Another typical Stoic concept is that of
providence (*pronoia*), which is responsible for the order in the world.[78]
When describing the general geographical layout of the world, Strabo often
uses the term *pronoia*. Providence complemented nature by creating living
creatures, the most noble of which were gods and humans. It then added
everything else for the sake of man's benefit and utility, thus creating earth,
water, air and light. In this way the deeds of both nature and providence
contributed to one end, the existence of the world (17.1.36, C 809–10).
Since all these components are in constant movement and change, topography changes: land becomes sea and sea becomes land. These unceasing
shifts of boundary between dry land and sea, influenced by inundations,
excite in Strabo feelings of admiration towards this order (*taxis*): 'all these
instances must needs contribute to fix strong our belief (*pistis*) in the works
of nature' (1.3.17, C 58 and 16.2.26, C 758). He refers to geographical order in three specific locations by applying similar Stoic concepts.
The rivers and the sea near Tolossa contribute to the agricultural fertility
and the convenience of transportation in that area. This harmony (*homologia*)
is a proof of the actions of providence, for the regions are not laid out
by mere chance but as if according to a plan (*logismos*) (4.1.14, C 189).
Sinope also 'is beautifully equipped both by nature and by providence'
(12.3.11, C 545), and so is Amasia, the city where Strabo was born (12.3.39,
C 561).

Notwithstanding the central and beneficial role that Strabo ascribes to
providence in matters of geographical and topographical organization, he
also shows that in some cases providence and fate have failed. He presents
examples where it would have been better had other developments taken
place. Therefore, it would have been better for Egypt to be watered by rain,
and it would have been better if Paris had drowned and had not abducted
Helen (4.1.7, C 183). Moreover, *contra* Posidonius, Strabo holds that while
providence determines order in the natural sphere, it does not determine
human character and the nature of various races. Therefore he thinks that
the distribution of races and languages in the *oikoumene* is accidental, and
human character is not natural but is based on habit and custom (2.3.7,
C 102–3), thus reducing the role of providence and increasing the role of
human freedom and control.

Strabo's political views and his attitude towards the Roman empire, its power, its ascendance and its flaws (chapter 4), also seem to be influenced by the political concepts of the Stoa. The picture of a world empire bringing peace and progress to the Barbarians and led by one leader echoes the Stoic ideal of the unification of mankind under one power and the formation of a world citizenship.[79] Strabo writes: 'the greatest generals are without exception men who are able to hold sway over land and sea, and to unite nations and cities under one government and political administration' (1.1.16, C 9). The author does not refer specifically to Rome in this context, but it is rather obvious that the Roman empire at the time of Augustus, as Strabo himself presents it, fits this definition.

The implied criticism of Roman luxury and extravagance (chapter 4, p. 115) is basically Stoic, for the Stoics considered the wise man as he who is free of desires and does not look for pleasure.[80] On this particular point Strabo indeed reflects some Stoic terminology and ideas, but at the same time he also uses a Platonic explanation for corruption, ascribing the debasement of morals to money and proximity to the sea (7.3.8, C 302). His entire view on culture vs. savagery, and his definition of 'Barbaric' deeds, are based on his ethical concepts, but while the Stoics spoke of a universal union of mankind, Strabo makes a clear distinction between Greeks and Barbarians (below, p. 75).

The Stoic ideal of a peaceful and stable mind which is not easily shaken is further implied in the *Geography* by Strabo's aspiration to *athaumastia*, the state of 'marvelling at nothing' (1.3.16, C 57); he remarks that this virtue was praised by Democritus and by all other philosophers, thus also implying the central Epicurean idea of *ataraxia*. Strabo adds to this other virtues: *athambes* – 'being fearless'; *atarachos* – 'not being disturbed'; and *anekplektos* – 'being intrepid' (1.3.21, C 61).[81] To fortify this virtue of 'marvelling at nothing', Strabo tries to provide his readers with many examples of unusual phenomena in the world such as strange animals and plants, inundations and volcanic eruptions, 'for if a large number of such instances are placed in view, they will put a stop to one's amazement (*ekplexis*)' (1.3.16, C 57). Moreover, he thinks that descriptions of demographical changes based on movements of nations and tribes contribute to enhance the serenity of the soul (1.3.21, C 61). In fact, the entire *Geography* and its encyclopaedic approach could be related to Strabo's Stoic orientation. He describes the *oikoumene* with so much detail about the variety of animal and plant species and behaviours of different kinds of people, that a man acquainted with all these phenomena would be less amazed and would learn not to marvel.

The way in which Strabo understands and interprets the deeds of Alexander and the events occurring in his expeditions perhaps reveals some Stoic overtones. Pédech has pointed out the presentation of Alexander's expedition as an adventurous journey of exploration and discovery of new regions and strange nations, with an emphasis on human qualities of effort, will, courage and endurance, qualities that may be related to the moral ideas of the Stoa. He showed, however, that the Stoics, unlike Strabo, presented Alexander as a corrupt tyrant. Nevertheless, there may be an ethical tendency behind Strabo's harsh criticism of the flattery of Alexander's historians, who distorted geographical facts in order to glorify the king and enhance his political achievement (chapter 4, p. 111).[82]

The reference to Judaism under the guidance of Moses presents some Stoic ideas possibly derived from Posidonius. Thus Strabo identifies the Deity (*to theion*) with the sea, the land, nature and the entire universe, and ascribes to Moses the teaching to live 'self restrained (*sophronos*) and righteous (*meta dikaiosynes*) lives' (16.2.35, C 760–1).[83]

Strabo's teachers Tyrannion and Xenarchus were Peripatetics (chapter 1, p. 9), and according to Strabo's own testimony he also studied Aristotelian philosophy with Boethus from Sidon (16.2.24, C 757). All these were not Stoics, which may suggest an explanation other than early education for the origin of Strabo's Stoic tendencies. Perhaps another teacher not mentioned in the *Geography* influenced him, or a friend, such as Athenodorus of Tarsus who had Stoic inclinations, or else sojourn in Rome at a time when Stoicism was widespread and popular.[84]

One possible inspiration for Strabo in his Stoic tendencies could be Posidonius. Strabo's admiration of the scholar who was the head of the Stoic school in Rhodes might have been a product of his Stoic inclinations, or the other way around: it might have been the influential factor behind Strabo as a Stoic geographer. Posidonius' influence probably derived from his fame as a great scholar and philosopher. Strabo was also the disciple of Posidonius' grandson, Aristodemus, and may have met Posidonius personally, though this is not proven (chapter 1, p. 10).

Posidonius dealt with ethics and logic from a Stoic point of view; he was interested in history, he looked into physical and astronomical phenomena and he wrote geographical works (above, p. 60). Strabo respects him as a philosopher, as well as a geographer like Eratosthenes and Polybius (1.1.1, C 2). Moreover, he calls him 'Posidonius, the Stoic, the most learned (*polymathestatos*) of all philosophers of my time' (16.2.10, C 753). It is thus possible that Posidonius' approach to history and to geography may be behind Strabo's Stoic inclinations, and more specifically his combination of Stoic ideas with geography and history that Strabo imitated. For instance, Posidonius held that the Roman conquerors were bearers of progress and culture but at the same time also cruel rulers. This concept of duality in the Roman character combined Stoic concepts of human peace and fraternity with a realistic recognition of the devastation created by the conquests.[85] Strabo similarly presents the Romans as bearers of progress and culture to Barbaric nations and draws a detailed picture of a world ruled by one person. At the same time he also shows negative aspects of Roman dominance, although he does not specifically mention violence and cruelty (chapter 4, p. 115).

The idea that philosophy is an essential requirement for a geographer is closely connected to the pragmatic goal of the *Geography* and the proposed utility (*opheleia*) of a geographical survey encompassing various pieces of information (chapter 6, p. 154). Strabo explains this connection by philosophical expressions and concepts:

> The utility of geography – and its utility is manifold, not only as regards the activities of statesmen and commanders but also as regards knowledge both of the heavens and of things on land and sea, animals, fruits, and everything else to be seen in various regions – the utility of geography presupposes in the geographer the same philosopher, the man who busies himself with the investigation of the art of life, that is, of happiness (*eudaimonia*).
>
> (1.1.1, C 2)

A work referring to various fields of knowledge which both appeal to and derive from human life is useful and therefore brings happiness, which is also the ultimate goal of philosophy. Only a philosopher can fulfil these requirements, but, unlike poetry, philosophy is acquired by only a few (1.2.8, C 20).

Several philosophical discussions are interwoven in the geographical description, and Strabo shows acquaintance with many philosophers whom he mentions according to their native cities (below, p. 79), some of them his contemporaries who spent some time in Rome (chapter 5). He further sheds light on his tendencies by bringing philosophical ideas into typical geographical descriptions.[86] These ideas are various and allude to different branches of philosophy such as political theory, ethics, logic and epistemology. Strabo displays an eclectic approach in the field of political theory by using Plato's *Republic* (6.1.8, C 260) alongside Aristotle's comparative studies on various polities (7.7.2, C 321–2). He discusses the essence of monarchy, aristocracy and democracy (1.1.18, C 10–11) and alludes to the ideal mixed constitution while describing the Roman republican regime. After the fall of the kings the Romans 'constituted a constitution mixed of monarchy and aristocracy' (6.4.2, C 286). Although the mixed constitution as a philosophical ideal was an idea already extant in the fifth century and formed one of the political ideals of the later Stoa, the first to apply it to current political developments was Polybius. Strabo in fact follows him in this notion, although he does not include democracy in his scheme, probably owing to the different epoch in which he lived. While Polybius worked at the peak of the republican era, Strabo wrote at the end of the age of Augustus, when the principate had already gained power. What he sees in the Roman state are the monarchic and aristocratic aspects of the constitution, whereas the democratic aspect had already been put aside.[87]

In this area of philosophical political discussion Strabo also alludes to the natural tendency, common to Greeks and Barbarians, to live under common mandates (*prostagmata*) originating either from the gods or from men. The ancients, he explains, held those of the gods in greater honour (16.2.38, C 761–6). This assumption of a natural tendency to form or accept mandates may be behind Strabo's notions about the Barbarians who are too savage to have social or political organizations (below, p. 78).

Strabo uses the phraseology of logic in parts of his survey. For example, he says: 'it is not possible for a man to leave the whole and still be in the whole' (1.1.7, C 5). Or, he says that political philosophy deals mainly with rulers, and geography is aimed at rulers, therefore geography has an advantage over political theory (1.1.18, C 11). Occasionally, when certain matters do not comply with logic, Strabo expresses scepticism. Thus, he carries out a rational analysis of legends and myths (below, p. 73) and he does not accept the stories about the the wooden image of the Trojan Athene that closed its eyes (6.1.14, C 264) and about the whistling sculptures of Memnon in Egypt (17.1.46, C 816).

Strabo reveals his epistemological opinion in his discussions of the senses as a means to grasp the truth about various natural and geographical phenomena. The senses, particularly the sense of sight, help us to grasp and understand some facts about the universe. It might occasionally be that sight is more reliable than a technical scientific measurement (2.1.11, C 71). Thus, the senses tell us that the *oikoumene* is an island (1.1.8, C 5). They also help us to understand that the world is round, for sailors can see harbour lights only when they approach them because of the roundness of the globe (1.1.20, C 11–12). And they assist in determining the distance of the sun from various points on the earth (15.1.24, C 696). It is enough to experience the length of the day in the far north and there is no need for mathematical calculations (2.1.18, C 76). Strabo himself uses his senses, looking at various phenomena for the sake of learning: he looks at the breaking of the waves on the beach (1.3.8, C 53) and watches the influence of the poisonous vapours in Hierapolis on men and birds (13.4.14, C 629–30). But in some cases the senses are not sufficient to inform us and there is also need of logic or of measuring tools (1.1.8, C 5). For example, it is possible to discern major differences between various latitudes by observing sensory factors such as temperature and crops, but milder differences can be inspected only by using a *gnomon* or other measuring tools (2.1.35, C 87).

Pythagoras and his teachings also figure in the *Geography*. Strabo presents some biographical information about Pythagoras (14.1.16, C 638) and mentions several of his ideas. Among these are the influence of music – instrument-playing or singing – on the moral character of men (1.2.3, C 16);[88] the concept of four spherical elements (1.3.12, C 55); the doctrine of vegetarianism (7.3.5, C 298); and the concept of the universe in terms of harmonies, with a comparison to Plato's concept of philosophy as music (10.3.10, C 468).

Stylistically, Strabo uses expressions based on the Platonic dialogues. These occur in the first two books of the *Geography* in his argumentation with his predecessors, where he sometimes composes an imaginary dialogue on controversial matters. For example, when he discusses the question of the didactic value of the Homeric epics, he presents the arguments with the help of typical Platonic expressions. The interlocutor might be the reader or any other person who does not accept Strabo's view. In the discussion on Homer, this opponent might be Eratosthenes who, unlike Strabo, thought that Homeric epic did not have any educational value.

> — Well then (*poteron oun*), is the poet who makes use of these epithets like a person engaged in entertaining, or in instructing?
> — Yes, by Zeus (*ne Dia*), the latter, you reply . . .
>
> (1.2.3, C 16)

We find the same in other contexts as well:

> — . . . What is so much a part of rhetoric as style? . . . And who has surpassed Homer in style?
> — Yes, by Zeus (*ne Dia*), you answer, but the style of poetry is different from that of rhetoric . . .
>
> (1.2.6, C 18)

And once more:

> — . . . there is no great store of any of these things [gold, amber, silver] among those people . . .
> — Yes, by Zeus (*ne Dia*), you say, but Arabia and the regions as far as India belonged to them . . .
>
> (1.2.32, C 39)[89]

Another way in which we can see Strabo's interest and acquaintance with the world of philosophy is his knowledge of philosophers from various schools, both in his days and before his time. Among his contemporaries he mentions the Peripatetics Athenaeus from Seleucia (14.5.4, C 670) and Ariston from Alexandria (17.1.5, C 790); the Academic Nestor from Tarsus (14.5.14, C 675); the Stoic Antipater of Tyre (16.2.24, C 757); and Eudorus of Alexandria (17.1.5, C 790) – the Eclectic (chapter 5). In addition, the Stoic Athenodorus of Tarsus, a disciple of Posidonius, was a friend of Strabo's (16.4.21, C 779). Strabo also says that he studied Aristotelian philosophy with Boethus of Sidon (16.2.24, C 757), later head of the Peripatetic school in Athens. His brother Diodotus was also a philosopher and Strabo probably met him (16.2.24, C 757 and chapter 1, p. 11). He is also particularly interested in the fate of Aristotle's library that finally ended up in Rome.[90]

Strabo also shows familiarity with several philosophical schools throughout the Roman world, such as the school of Massilia which attracts Romans and competes with Athens (4.1.5, C 181) and the philosophical schools of Megara, Elea and Eretria and their founders and philosophical tendencies (9.1.8, C 393). In Cyrene, he relates, there were two schools: the Cyrenaean led for a while by a woman called Arete, and the Annicerian (17.3.22, C 837–8). He alludes to the philosophical preoccupations of the Egyptian priests (17.1.3, C 787), and the schools in Heliopolis (17.1.29, C 806) and Thebes (17.1.46, C 816).

To sum up, Strabo not only demands philosophical qualities from the ideal geographer, but also exercises them himself. His philosophical orientation is evident through the ideas and terminologies interwoven in his geographical survey. His particular inclination to Stoicism is apparent mostly in his ethical inferences and in his political views.

THE *HISTORY*

Strabo presents his scholarly activity and orientation prior to the writing of the *Geography*: 'After I had written my *Historical Notes (hypomnemata historika)*, which have been useful, I suppose, for moral and political philosophy, I determined to write the present treatise also' (1.1.23, C 13). That is, he was engaged in a kind of historiography which, like his later geographical work, had pragmatic tendencies.

From two other references in the *Geography* to his historical work, we learn that Strabo discussed the reliability of the historians of Alexander in his *Deeds of Alexander (Hai Alexandrou praxeis)* (2.1.9, C 70), and dealt with the customs of the Parthians in the sixth book of his *Hypomnemata historika*, and in the second book of the *Sequel to Polybius (Ta meta Polybiou)* (11.9.3, C 515). That is, Strabo refers to three different historiographical excerpts: (1) *Hai Alexandrou praxeis*, (2) *Hypomnemata historika*, (3) *Ta meta Polybiou*. To this we should add the reference in the Suda:[91] 'Strabo of Amasia too wrote *Ta meta Polybiou* in forty-three books.' It has been suggested[92] that all three excerpts are parts of one whole, presenting different topics in one work. Accordingly, the first part of the work, the *Notes*, surveyed ancient history briefly and generally in four books, including the deeds of Alexander, whereas the main part of the work, the 43-book-long *History*, discussed Roman history from the chronological point at which Polybius' work terminated (146 BCE) and up to Strabo's own time.

However, Strabo's wording in the above passage does not support this assumption. For, he mentions two occasions on which he dealt with Parthian usages: the sixth book of the *Notes* and the second of the *Sequel to Polybius*. This implies the existence of two different works, one of which, the *Notes*, consisted of at least six books. Adding to this Strabo's statement that after the *Notes* he turned to geography, I tend to accept the basic lines of the old and now ignored interpretation of Ridgeway.[93] Thus, Strabo first wrote an historical work continuing Polybius and comprising forty-three books. Later, he wrote a second work, the *Notes* (*Hypomnemata historika*), in which he included also the deeds of Alexander.[94] This of course, could not have been part of the sequence to Polybius because it refers to a much earlier period. Moreover, a survey of at least 186 years in four books seems a rather presumptuous undertaking, that is, if we assume that Alexander's conquests were indeed Strabo's point of departure and if we accept the interpretation of Pédech according to which this survey was meant to emphasize the significance of these conquests to the history of the world.[95] Moreover, although Strabo titles his history of Alexander separately, his use of the verb *hypomnematizo* with reference to his survey of Alexander (2.1.9, C 70) seems to connect it specifically to the *Hypomnemata*. After these two historical works Strabo finally turned to his *Geography*.

It is difficult to tell at what chronological point Strabo's *History* ended. However, it is generally accepted that the survey concluded in the year 27 BCE with the fall of Antony and the organization of the Roman empire under Augustus.[96] Thus the work covered more than 120 years in forty-three books, each one encompassing roughly three years and therefore very detailed.

In view of the absence of a complete historiographical work, there are two ways, both rather sketchy, to evaluate Strabo's historiographical approach and methodology. First, the fragments which have survived can be discussed with the evident limitations due to their perhaps minor status in the original complete work. Second, an examination of some historiographical notions in the *Geography* may show Strabo's inclinations in terms of methodologies and approaches.[97]

Sixteen fragments of the historiographic works have survived in the form of allusions in the works of other authors.[98] These are a short reference in Tertullian, three in Plutarch's *Lives* and the other twelve in Josephus, mostly in the *Antiquities*, thus indicating the distribution of the work, which is not mentioned later than the second century CE.[99] The fragments from Josephus are not only superior in number, but also in quality, since five of them seem to be a direct quotation from Strabo.[100] Josephus also documents several of Strabo's sources for his *History*. These were Hypsicrates of Amisus (*FGrH* 91 F 17), Nicolaus of Damascus (F 12; F 13), Timagenes of Alexandria (F 11) and the Roman Asinius Pollio (F 16), all contemporaries of Strabo (chapter 5).

Although there is not enough material to form a thorough picture of the nature of Strabo's *History*, it is possible to understand very generally the chronological scope of the works and the issues under discussion. The earliest historical reference in the fragments is to Antiochus Epiphanes and his lack of money which caused him to plunder the temple in Jerusalem in 170 BCE (*FGrH* 91 F 10). Since this reference falls earlier than the chronological beginning of the *Sequel to Polybius*, it must have been derived from the *Historical Notes*. The latest event preserved in the fragments is the action of Antony against Antigonus in 37 BCE (F 18).

A close inspection of the fragments may offer some hints as to the general contents of the entire work. Strabo mentioned several Roman generals in describing events in Roman history. He narrated the exploits of Pompey (F 15) and Josephus ascribes to both Strabo and Nicolaus a reference to the expeditions of Pompey and Gabinius against the Jews (F 13). Strabo also indicated the gifts of gold sent from Egypt and from Judaea to Pompey, one of which he himself saw in Rome (F 14). Josephus quotes Strabo who said that Antony beheaded Antigonus (F 18). The comment on this fact shows the orientation and interest of Strabo, for he said, according to this quotation, that Antony was the first Roman to behead a king and that he did this because he thought that this was the only way to compel the Jews to accept Herod. It is clear that Strabo was interested in Roman behaviour with its political implications and he discussed this also by focusing on the personality of Antony himself. The interest in the personal traits of an historical character is again revealed in Plutarch's allusion to Strabo's contention that Sulla suffered from premonitory gout while in Athens (F 8). This seems a minor detail and may illustrate Strabo's interests and his particular sources of information. He was also aware of the omens preceding the death of Julius Caesar (F 19). Strabo again referred to the Romans and their actions and motivations in the comment cited by Plutarch, that the Romans were ashamed of their victory over Tigranes the king of Armenia because he was such a weak enemy (F 9). As far as we can tell from these fragments, and according to the historiographical notions in the *Geography*, Strabo was probably not interested in internal Roman affairs, but treated Roman history and its leading characters only when they were associated with the broader 'international' sphere.[101]

In speaking of Strabo's reference to the Jews and particularly the Jews in Cyrene, Josephus expounds the original context (F 7). Apparently Strabo wrote that when Sulla crossed over to Greece to make war on Mithridates, he sent Lucullus to put down a Jewish revolt in Cyrene. This event in the history of Roman politics connected with Mithridates and Cyrene caused Strabo to add a minor digression on the Jews. Thus, he said that they were spread everywhere in the *oikoumene*, that they had special territories and autonomy in Egypt and in Alexandria and that the Jewish people was originally from Egypt and therefore inhabited the adjacent regions. Referring once more to the Jews, Strabo apparently quoted other historians, for instance Timagenes of Alexandria, who said that the Hasmonean Aristobulus was good to his subjects, acquired additional territory and circumcised the conquered Ituraeans, thus converting them to Judaism (F 11).

Together with the Roman scene Strabo must have surveyed developments in Egypt. Josephus again adduces a direct quotation on the internal situation there. The kingdom, according to this fragment, was divided between Ptolemy Lathyrus and his supporters who were the majority, and his mother Cleopatra who was supported by the Jews in gratitude for her favourable conduct towards two of them (F 4). We can safely infer that Josephus was interested in one thing and Strabo in another, that is, in the political situation in Egypt. In another context Josephus quotes both Strabo and Nicolaus of Damascus on the manner in which Ptolemy Lathyrus treated the Jews. Both writers probably reported that he killed people and ordered his soldiers to eat them, in order to terrify the survivors (F 12).

Rome and Egypt, leading spheres of activity in the world politics of the early first century BCE, had contacts with another sphere, that of Asia Minor and King Mithridates of Pontus. Strabo related that Mithridates took some money which Cleopatra had deposited in Cos, including 800 talents belonging to the Jews (F 6). The context in Josephus, which was designed to show that the Jews had enough money to contribute to the temple in Jerusalem, should not be confused with the assumed context in Strabo, who was most probably interested in the more general political scene. Two other fragments contain another Strabonian historiographical reference to Mithridates, this time alluding to his invasion of Egypt with the help of Hyrcanus the high priest of the Jews and Antipater the procurator (F 16; F 17).

The general impression gained from the fragments is of an original universal history centred on the relationships between the most important Hellenistic forces of the last two centuries BCE, at the time of the gradual ascendance of Rome as an imperial power. Strabo seems to have been interested in world politics, so to speak, and not so much in internal affairs. He discussed the latter only inasmuch as they affected general developments. In this sense he must have inherited Polybius' universalistic approach to history, thus forming not only a chronological continuation of his famous predecessor, but also following his ideological and methodological footsteps, as we have seen in Strabo's universal approach to geography (above, p. 48). Interestingly enough, other universal *Histories* with similar tendencies were composed in the Augustan era by Diodorus of Sicily, Nicolaus of Damascus and Pompeius Trogus.[102]

I now turn to Strabo's ideas on historiography as they appear in the *Geography*. Pédech has presented a survey of Strabo's allusions to historical events and characters in the *Geography*, and Lasserre has attempted to identify historiographical parts of the *Geography* that do not rely on other authors, thus hoping to reconstruct Strabo's own *History*.[103] I, however, shall focus on Strabo's general notions concerning historiography.

Naturally Strabo is referring to historiographical matters in a geographical context, that is, he discusses mainly the relationship between geography and history. However, his notions also reflect his general ideas pertaining to the writing of history. Historical surveys should be an integral part of geography as long as they contribute to the practical needs of educated readers and especially of statesmen: 'the man who busies himself with the description of the earth (*ges periodos*) must needs speak, not only of the facts of the present, but also sometimes of the facts of the past, especially when they are notable' (6.1.2, C 253). Here too Strabo walks along traditional paths by insisting on the truth: 'the aim of history is truth . . . the aim of rhetorical composition is vividness . . . the aim of myth is to please and to excite amazement' (1.2.17, C 25), and also: 'history wishes for the truth' (11.5.3, C 504). He, therefore, strongly criticizes the historians of Alexander who distorted facts for the sake of flattery and betrayed the truth for propaganda purposes by 'moving' whole regions, such as the Caucasus, to the end of the world in order to create the impression that Alexander had reached the boundaries of the *oikoumene* (11.5.5, C 505–6 and chapter 4, p. 111).

Thus, Strabo discusses at some length the sources of his predecessors and their credibility, while himself trying to be critical and thorough. He sometimes presents several versions of the same event and tries to form an opinion when he can: 'As for myself, where it is possible to reach a decision, I set forth my opinion, but where it is not, I think that I should make known the opinions of others' (6.3.10, C 285).[104]

Since truth is his guideline, Strabo does not accept legends and myths into his historiography, unlike earlier historians whom he accuses of 'fondness for myths (*philomythia*)' (11.6.2, C 507). Accordingly, he rejects mythical genealogies (8.6.2, C 368–9) and various mythical and semi-legendary stories, for instance Polybius' notion that Tiberius Gracchus (cos. 177) destroyed 300 cities in Celtiberia (3.4.13, C 163). At the same time, perhaps because he is writing a *Geography* and not a *History*, he interweaves in his descriptions myths and legends which have no factual basis.[105] It is possible in some cases to find a didactic or pragmatic explanation for their inclusion in a specific context, and if not, it seems that Strabo's intention was to entertain his readers and to please them. He does indeed offer several excuses for the inclusion of myths in his supposedly serious geographical survey with its pragmatic goals. These pretexts emerge through the context in which the stories are presented or in some explanatory words. Usually the key to understanding the combination of myth and truth is rationality. For instance, Strabo tries to find factual roots in the story of Jason and the golden fleece (1.2.38–40, C 45–7) and he explains the name 'Myrmidons', meaning 'ants', by the tendency of the men thus called to dig, and not because they used to be real ants (8.6.16, C 375).

Strabo justifies the inclusion of myths in his work by a didactic-pragmatic motivation as well:

Man is eager to learn, and his fondness for tales is a prelude to this quality. It is fondness for tales, then, that induces children to give their attention to narratives and more and more to take part in them. The reason for this is that myth is a new language to them ... and what is new is pleasing, and so is what one did not know before; and it is just this that makes men eager to learn.

(1.2.8, C 19)

That is, the pleasure involved in the hearing of myths encourages learning and curiosity, and therefore it is justified to add appealing myths to geographical descriptions.

Since these problems occupy his thoughts, Strabo once more expresses the combination between pleasure and education and the conflict between entertainment and utility. Myths, he says, do not contribute to the pragmatic education of the reader unless they also have a moral message and a practical conclusion. In this way the deeds of the heroes can teach present-day men. A myth can also expand one's knowledge if it includes a description of the place where it occurred. And, finally, even men of affairs enjoy charming myths 'but they care for no great amount of them, since they are more interested in what is useful' (1.1.19, C 11).

The use of legends is natural and acceptable for poets but even historians use them, not out of ignorance but because they want to satisfy the reader's appetite for marvels and entertainment (1.2.35, C 43). Strabo himself uses this methodology by interweaving various stories into his descriptions in a way which calls to mind modern tourist-guides (chapter 6, p. 160). It seems to me that this is the way to understand the myth about the rivers Arnus and Ausar who 'promised' the people of Pisa 'not to deluge it and kept their pledge' (5.2.5, C 222–3). And, similarly, the myth about Typhon who lies under Italy and causes volcanic eruptions in the peninsula (5.4.9, C 248).

Let us turn now to specific historical allusions in the *Geography*. Pédech collected the historical references to Alexander and Engels has recently analysed their contents and their political relevance to Strabo's time.[106] Although naturally arranged according to the geographical scheme of the work without any chronological considerations, these references reveal Strabo's extensive knowledge of the campaigns and their consequences. He uses some of the primary sources including Nearchus, Onesicritus, Aristobulus and Cleitarchus (chapter 6, p. 184). This knowledge probably derived from his earlier historical studies, which were here collected and presented according to geographical considerations.

Strabo also alludes to some periods and events in Roman history, which figure in geographical contexts, usually pertaining to specific sites, throughout the entire work. Since this feature demonstrates the extent of the author's absorption of Roman culture, I shall discuss it more broadly in chapter 3. However, here we should note that Strabo is aware of earlier developments, from the foundation of Rome and the regal era to the political evolution of the Roman state after the second Punic war, although he seems to expose a chronological gap by ignoring Roman history of the first two and a half centuries of the republic.[107]

In conclusion, Strabo's words concerning his aims in his earlier historical work seem significant for the evaluation of his general approach:

> Just as in my *Historical Notes* only the incidents in the lives of distinguished men are recorded, while deeds that are petty and ignoble are omitted, so in this work also I must leave untouched what is petty and inconspicuous, and devote my attention to what is noble and great, and to what contains the practically useful, or memorable, or entertaining.
>
> (1.1.23, C 13)

That is, Strabo focused on major historical events, according to his understanding, particularly as they related to famous men, thus emphasizing the influence of outstanding persons.

HELLENICA VS. BARBARICA

Strabo wrote his works in Greek and exploited mainly Greek sources.[108] His views are clearly grounded in Hellenic traditions and Greek cultural values. Several contexts in the *Geography* reveal the author's concept of the distinction between Greeks and Barbarians, and these specific references make plain his attitude towards all nations other than the Greek. However, this sense of Hellenocentrism, so to speak, is more profoundly expressed in Strabo's description of the *oikoumene* as a whole and in his particular treatment of the various regions in it. Consequently, the concept of Hellenica vs. Barbarica is one of the keys to the *Geography*.[109]

Strabo's distinction between Barbarians and Hellenes is twofold. In referring to 'savage' tribes, mainly in the northern and western regions of Europe, such as Germany, Iberia and Britain, Strabo speaks of 'our mode of life', for instance in 7.3.7, C 301, taking the Greek and the Roman civilizations together. He differentiates between several traits he considers to manifest civilization and those which are typically savage (below). The Roman conquest is therefore a bearer of culture, law and peace to Barbaric peoples (chapter 4, p. 115). That is, his concept depicts 'us' against 'them', the Greeks and the Romans against the rest of the world. But, parallel to this picture, which is an outcome of the political developments of the time, Strabo makes a decided distinction between the Greeks and the Romans. The Greeks, in his opinion, are superior to the Romans, though admittedly not in the political sense. But they have chronological precedence, being more ancient, and cultural superiority in the world of scholarship and in the domain of visual art.

Strabo preserves the traditional Greek distinction between Barbarians and Greeks and rejects an attempt by Eratosthenes to modify this definition. There is a relatively long discussion of the matter in 1.4.9, C 66–7. Eratosthenes claimed that it would be better to divide humans according to their moral qualities. There are good people and bad people, just as there are bad Greeks and excellent Barbarians such as the Indians, the Romans and the Carthaginians. To support his proposal, Eratosthenes referred to the advice given to Alexander the Great to treat the Greeks as friends and the Barbarians as enemies. In Eratosthenes' interpretation Alexander did not accept this advice and welcomed all the good people, that is, those who are law-abiding, administer states and are well educated.[110] Strabo cites this whole story only to conclude that Alexander followed this advice because in fact there are people who are by nature law-abiding and have socio-political tendencies while others also by nature are the precise opposite. Thus, Strabo finds support for his own view that Greeks are naturally better than Barbarians.

In a typical Strabonian way, an Homeric verse is the basis for another discussion of the term 'Barbarians' and its meaning. The debate involves arguments by Thucydides and Apollodorus of Athens, the grammarian, both of whom Strabo rejects. It includes purely poetical considerations such as metre, and general grammatical conclusions pertaining to onomatopoeia. Strabo's general view of the term 'Barbarian' is, expectedly, based on his understanding of Homer:

> I suppose that the word 'barbarian' was at first uttered onomato-poeically in reference to people who enunciated words only with difficulty and raucously . . . accordingly . . . it appeared that the pronunciations of all alien races (*alloethne*) were likewise thick, I mean of those that were not Greek . . . and then we misused the word as a general ethnic term, thus making a logical distinction between the Greeks and all other races . . . and there appeared another faulty and Barbarian-like pronunciation in our language, whenever any person speaking Greek did not pronounce it correctly, but pronounced the words like Barbarians who are only beginning to learn Greek and are unable to speak it accurately as is also the case with us in speaking their languages.
>
> (14.2.28, C 661–3)[111]

Strabo's definition of 'Barbarians' is based on the general failure of a stranger to speak another language, just as the Greeks would have difficulty in pronouncing foreign languages. (But this does not make the Greeks into Barbarians . . .) However, it differs slightly from the definition based on the 'Barbarian' sound of the strangers' speech in any language, on onomatopoeic grounds, and narrows the notion to the sound of Greek as the others speak it. The underlying meaning of both definitions, however, is the same, and turns the words based on the root *barbar* into synonyms for non-Greek, as in Strabo's reference to southern Italy: 'today all parts of it ... have become completely Barbarised (*ekbebarbarosthai*)' (6.1.2, C 253). This unequivocally reflects the Greek point of view since the earliest inhabitants of these regions were Greek colonists of the Archaic period. It has particular significance in that it in fact relates to the process of the growing influence of Romans and thus presents the Romans as Barbarians, a feeling also transmitted by Strabo in other ways as shall be shown below.[112]

A phrase by Demetrius of Scepsis shows the grammarian's use of the ethnic distinction, but it seems to agree with Strabo's view as well. Demetrius argued that the inhabitants of Gargara became semi-Barbarians (*hemibarbaroi*) because the kings brought colonists from Miletopolis to join the original Aeolians who inhabited the city (13.1.58, C 611). Strabo also mentions Ephorus' differentiation between various tribes in Asia Minor, dividing them into three groups – Greeks, Barbarians and 'mixed' (*hoi migades*), that is, composed of both ethnic elements (14.5.23, C 678). The implication in both allusions is more of a racial distinction between Greeks and non-Greeks with less obvious moral or cultural emphasis. However, Strabo does not accept the definitions made by Ephorus: 'for even if they have become mixed, still the predominant element has made them either Greeks or Barbarians, and I know nothing of a third tribe of people that is mixed' (14.5.25, C 679).[113]

The superiority of the Greeks is implied even in relation to the Romans, let alone the uncivilized tribes of the farther northern and western regions of the *oikoumene*. The difference between Greeks and Barbarians is apparent through the contents and arrangement of the *Geography*. Aujac has pointed out that the parts of the work relating to Greek regions are much more elaborate and detailed than other sections.[114] While Strabo devotes three books to Greece proper (Books 8–10) and another four to Asia Minor (11–14), both obviously Greek regions, he surveys Italy in two books (5 and 6), and covers other territories in one book at the most. This, however, is not part of a deliberate wish to underestimate other nations or to cut short information on other regions, but simply reflects Strabo's naturally wider knowledge of his own culture.

Strabo's understanding of Barbarian behaviour is, then, determined by his own cultural orientation and his idea of the 'normal' way of life. The several cases in which he refers to the unusual customs of foreign people reveal his notions. For instance, he defines the habits of the inhabitants of the British Isle (Strabo does not include Ireland) as 'more simple and more Barbaric (*barbarotera*)' than those of the Celts, because 'although well supplied with milk, they make no cheese; and they have no experience in gardening

or other agricultural pursuits' (4.5.2, C 200). He quotes Homer with reference to the people who lived near the temple of Dodona. The poet described
them as 'men with unwashen feet that couch on the ground' (*Iliad* 16.235)[115]
and Strabo interprets this as 'Barbarians' (7.7.10, C 328). Strabo regards
some of the habits of the Iberians as Barbaric: 'bathing with urine which
they have aged in cisterns and washing their teeth with it' and 'sleeping
on the ground' (3.4.16, C 164). He also notes the Barbaric ornaments of
the Iberian women and their ferocity, for they preferred to kill themselves
and their children rather than be taken captive. They also showed much
courage and endurance by giving birth and continuing to work in the fields
(3.4.17, C 164–5). Or the wild nature of the inhabitants of Corsica who,
according to Strabo act like wild beasts (5.2.7, C 224). Strabo also refers
to what he holds to be customs of the Jews which seem to him particularly strange, that is, their abstinence from flesh, and their performance of
circumcisions and excisions (16.2.37, C 761). As for the Indians, Strabo
indeed admires their simple habits and their moral standards but fails to
grasp their custom 'of always eating alone and of not having one common
hour for all for dinner and breakfast . . . for eating in the other way is more
conducive to a social and civic life' (15.1.53, C 709). He also discerns a
difference between the objects of Barbarian trade and of civilized commerce.
The Barbarians sell slaves and hides in exchange for clothing, wine and
olive oil (4.6.2, C 202; 11.2.3, C 493), that is, they offer unprocessed products, and some of them 'know nothing about storing up food or about
peddling merchandise either, except the exchange of wares for wares' (7.3.7,
C 300). Finally, 'according to Eratosthenes, the expulsion of foreigners is
a custom common to all Barbarians' (17.1.19, C 802), and thus they are
socially isolated. Only religious worship is common to both Greeks and
Barbarians (10.3.9, C 467; 16.2.38, C 761–2).

Another expression of cultural difference, this time reversed, since the
Barbarians could not understand the Romans, is the case of the Vettonians
who failed to understand the Roman officers who walked around, 'thinking
they should either remain quietly seated or else be fighting' (3.4.16, C 164).

Generally speaking, Strabo's repeated allusions to the difference between
culture and savage life seem to indicate that culture means sophistication
and order whereas nomadic and wild life mean simplicity and ignorance.
As we have seen, sophistication is measured by the ability to make cheese,
to grow vegetables or to produce manufactured goods, and order is manifested not only in political and social organizations, but also in fixed eating
hours and a well-trained army: 'all Barbarian races and light-armed peoples
are weak when matched against a well-ordered and well-armed phalanx'
(7.3.17, C 306).

Some explanations are offered for these enormous differences between the
civilized and the Barbaric lifestyles. Quoting Plato, Strabo notes two civilizatory factors, the place of habitation and the distance from the sea (13.1.25,

C 592), and himself adds another factor, the proximity to more civilized people, whether the Syrians (16.2.11, C 753) or the Greeks themselves, for, as he contends, the Ethiopians lead a nomadic and resourceless life because of the climate and the lack of water, but also because of their 'remoteness from us' (17.1.3, C 787).

Strabo expresses some traditional Greek ideas to the effect that there are factors which determine the nature of nations and are unavoidable, such as geographical conditions, climate and position in the *oikoumene* and more specifically the latitude zone in which a nation or a tribe lives. But at the same time he adds to this deterministic concept the idea of evolution and possible change in the sense that some nations can learn and accept the civilized way of life which is manifested especially in political and social organizations. This phenomenon is feasible for nations invested with a special spirit and character and is particularly common, according to what Strabo viewed in his times, in Iberia, where peace and Roman influence have brought the formerly Barbaric and untamed tribes into a political order and civilized way of life (chapter 4, p. 116).[116]

Strabo's entire approach to the numerous nations and tribes which populate the *oikoumene*, in terms of describing their lifestyle and habits, that is his ethnography, can be understood only through his analysis of each people according to its position on a sort of conceptual spectrum lying between two extremities – Barbaric or civilized. Moreover, Thollard has shown in his convincing study that these notions are not only part of a conceptual approach rooted in moral and philosophical ideas, but that they form a systematic tool for describing the geographical space. Just as the order of the geographical description lies on linear grounds formed for instance by *periploi* and thus progresses according to the coastline (above, p. 40), so the ethnographical description lies on a sort of imaginary line between Barbarism and civilization and thus always begins with the more civilized peoples of a certain region and ends with the more Barbaric.[117]

Although the *Geography* is full of allusions and direct references to Roman political superiority in the world and to the benefits brought to Barbaric peoples by Roman conquest (chapter 4, p. 115), Strabo at the same time does not conceal his criticism of the Romans, stressing Greek cultural superiority (chapter 4, p. 119). Thus, he includes details in his descriptions of the Greek areas which do not appear in the survey of the rest of the *oikoumene*, referring to typically Greek cultural characteristics: scholarship and art. He consistently gives lists of scholars and famous men of letters according to their native towns scattered throughout the Greek regions. The *poleis* thus surveyed according to their famous sons are:

Southern Italy and Sicily: Elea (6.1.1, C 252); Croton (6.1.12, C 263).
The Greek mainland: Megara (9.1.8, C 393); Ascre in Boeotia (9.2.25, C 409); Plataea in Sicyon (9.2.31, C 412); Iulis in Ceos (10.5.6, C 486).

The Aegean islands: Paros (10.5.7, C 487); Syros (10.5.8, C 487); Amorgos (10.5.12, C 487).

Asia Minor and adjacent islands: Heracleia (12.3.1, C 541); Tieium (12.3.8, C 543); Sinope (12.3.11, C 546); Amisus (12.3.16, C 548); Bithynia (12.4.9, C 566); Laodicea (12.8.16, C 578); Proconnesus (13.1.16, C 589); Parium (13.1.19, C 589); Lampsacus (13.1.19, C 589); Scepsis (13.1.54–5, C 608–9); Assus (13.1.57, C 610); Adramyttium (13.1.66, C 614); Pitane (13.1.67, C 614); Mytilene (13.2.3, C 617); Eressus in Lesbos (13.2.4, C 618); Lesbos generally (13.2.4, C 618); Methymna (13.2.4, C 618); Temnus (13.3.5, C 621); Cyme (13.3.6, C 622); Pergamon (13.4.3, C 625); Sardis (13.4.9, C 628); Antiochia in Caria (13.4.15, C 630); Miletus (14.1.7, C 635); Priene (14.1.12, C 636); Samos (14.1.18, C 638); Ephesus (14.1.25, C 642); Colophon (14.1.28, C 643); Teos (14.1.30, C 644); Erythrae (14.1.34, C 645); Chios (14.1.35, C 645); Clazomenae (14.1.36, C 645); Magnesia (14.1.41, C 648); Tralleis (14.1.42, C 649); Nysa (14.1.48, C 650); Lindus (14.2.11, C 655); Rhodes (14.2.13, C 655); Cnidus (14.2.15, C 656); Halicarnassus (14.2.16, C 656); Cos (14.2.19, C 657–8); Caryanda (14.2.20, C 658); Bargylia (14.2.20, C 658); Iasos (14.2.21, C 658); Mylasa (14.2.24, C 659); Stratoniceia (14.2.25, C 660); Alabanda (14.2.26, C 661); Seleucia (14.5.4, C 670); Soli (14.5.8, C 671); Tarsus (14.5.14–15, C 674–5) Mallus (14.5.16, C 676); Salamis (14.6.3, C 682); Citium (14.6.3, C 682–3); Soli in Cyprus (14.6.3, C 683).

Phoenicia and Palestine: Seleucia in Babylonia (16.1.16, C 744); Apameia (16.2.10, C 753); Tyre and Sidon (16.2.24, C 757); Ascalon and Gadara (16.2.29, C 759).

Egypt: Cyrene (17.3.22, C 837–8).

The people listed are men of all ages who are part of Greek culture. Some of them lived before Strabo's time and others were his contemporaries (chapter 5). These lists demonstrate Strabo's personal acquaintance with the world of Greek scholarship and they merge well with the geographical context, creating a sort of 'map' of scholars according to sites. It is quite apparent that this map encompasses only regions where there were long-standing Greek settlements: Greece proper, south Italy and Sicily, Asia Minor, Syria, Palestine and Egypt.

It was of course well known that Ionia and southern Italy had been important cultural centres of the ancient world since the sixth century BCE, but the way in which Strabo creates his picture shows the importance of the issue in his eyes and exemplifies his acquaintance with these circles throughout the generations. This map of scholars also reveals exceptions. Several eastern cities famous for their learning, such as Athens and Alexandria, do not get similar treatment and do not have an attached list of scholars. It is possible that Strabo had before him a source which had already done this survey in the form of lists and therefore he omitted these cities.[118] However, it seems more probable that he had a method of his own. We know that he did not want to describe in detail all the attractions of Sparta, Argos and Athens because they were so famous and a thorough description would be too long and would repeat what so many others had said before him (8.6.18, C 376; 9.1.16, C 396; 9.1.19, C 397 and chapter 1, p. 28). It is quite likely that he did not want to give lists of scholars from Athens and Alexandria because everybody knew them and the list would be very long and would distract the reader from the main theme.

Another obvious feature of the lists is that there are no parallel lists of famous Roman scholars. The only exception is Ennius whom Strabo mentions as a native of Rudiae (6.3.5, C 282). The discrepancy is clear: one Roman against Greeks from sixty-six towns and cities. This is yet another way in which Strabo creates a separation or at least a specificity of the Greek world and its description, setting it off from the rest of the *oikoumene*.

This 'mapping' of the 'world of letters', so to speak, is supplemented by a similar map of works of art deriving from the Greek world.[119] The regions to which these monuments are ascribed correspond to the regions covered by the lists of scholars and thus complete the picture of cultural superiority and achievement. These references to famous works and to the artists when they are known are less numerous than the lists of scholars; however, they are conspicuous enough to emphasize the cultural superiority of the Greeks in this realm as well,[120] as shown in Table 1.

Thus the Greek world is depicted as richer than the rest of the world in artistic production. This of course is significant in itself but more so in comparison with the ignorance of the Romans and their habit of stealing works of art and carrying them off to Rome (chapter 4, p. 121). Culturally, then, Strabo thinks the Greeks are much superior to the Romans, and he expresses this view without concealing his contempt for the ignorance and simplicity of the Romans.[121] He alludes several times to the Greek appreciation of art in contrast to the Romans' philistine behaviour towards fine works and their sacrilegious handling of religious offerings. Respect and admiration for works of art is in itself typically Greek.[122] But this characteristic is brought out more sharply in contrast to the loutish conduct of the Romans as Strabo depicts it. The shock and rejection he expresses in describing this Roman characteristic is, of course, a natural reaction of a conquered people. But more than this, Strabo is deeply upset by the ignorance and roughness of the Romans.

In referring to geographical research and writing Strabo presents the Romans as mere imitators of the Greeks. They do not initiate contributions to information on newly acquired regions and the key to new knowledge is still in the hands of the Greeks (3.4.19, C 166). In early times the two peoples had different attitudes to the building of cities. The Greeks looked for beauty, sheltered position, harbours and fertile land, while the Romans

Table 1 Artists and works of art in Strabo's *Geography*

Work	Artist	Place of origin
Apollo	Calamis	Apollonia (7.6.1, C 319)
Capture of Troy	Cleanthes of Corinth	Alpheius (8.3.12, C 343)
Birth of Athene	Cleanthes of Corinth	
Artemis on a griffin	Aregon of Corinth	
Zeus of gold		Olympia (8.3.30, C 353–4)
Zeus	Phidias	
paintings	Panaenus	
statues	Polyclitus	Mycenae (8.6.10, C 372)
Dionysus	Aristides	Corinth (8.6.23, C 381–2)
Heracles tortured		
Nemesis	Diodotus or Agoracritus	Athens (9.1.17, C 396)
Eros	Praxiteles	Thespiae (9.2.25, C 410)
Labours of Heracles	Lysippus	Acarnania (10.2.21, C 459)
The globe	Billarus	Sinope (12.3.11, C 546)
Statue of Autolycus	Sthemis	
Colossal statue of Zeus		Galatia (12.5.2, C 567)
Asclepius		Epidaurus (12.5.3, C 567)
The Fallen Lion	Lysippus	Lampsacus (13.1.19, C 590)
A statue of Aias		Rhoetium (13.1.30, C 595)
Leto and Ortygia	Scopas	Ortygia (14.1.20, C 640)
A painting of Anaxenor		Magnesia (14.1.41, C 648)
A statue of Anaxenor		
The Colossus of Helius		Rhodes (14.2.5, C 652)
Ialysus	Protogenes	
Satyr	Protogenes	
Antigonus	Apelles	Cos (14.2.19, C 657)
Aphrodite	Apelles	

focused on the building of roads, aqueducts and sewers (5.3.8, C 235–6).[123] This time there is no specific evaluation of the two but an awareness of the difference in mentality – Greek aesthetic inclinations vs. the Roman tendency to undertake practical construction.

Strabo's attitude to the Romans seems best expressed by an expression and a concept formed by Eratosthenes. According to this, the Romans are in fact 'refined Barbarians (*asteioi barbaroi*)', just like the Indians, the Arians and the Carthaginians (1.4.9, C 66). For, according to Strabo's general concept, the Romans are indeed Barbarians since they are not Greek, but they are also refined because they live according to laws, order and civilized leadership. Strabo's attitude to Rome and the Romans is thus a combination of respect and admiration with a sense of Greek self-esteem and superiority. His view of the relationship between civilization and wilderness puts the Greeks at the top of the world pyramid of civilized society, but at the same time they share with the Romans a superiority to the rest of the nations in the world.

Historically, the Greeks are also superior to the Romans since their culture is earlier and older. In fact, Greek culture is the basis for the creation of Rome. This is why Strabo emphasizes the Greek foundations of the towns of Italy in Books 5 and 6 (chapter 6, p. 172). The Italian past as it appears in these books is connected to stories of the establishment of various towns. Their Greek beginnings are emphasized, so much so that Strabo, following the Roman historian Acilius, says that Rome itself was founded by Greek settlers and, like many other towns in Italy, had a Greek cultural basis (5.3.3, C 230).[124] The idea of the Greek origin of the Roman nation may reflect Strabo's 'national' pride as a Greek man of letters, for he believes that at the roots of Roman power lie Greek culture and values. The relation between Greek and Roman culture as Strabo sees it is completely opposite to the view of his teacher Aristodemus, who claimed that Homer, the greatest Greek poet, was originally Roman (chapter 1, p. 9). That is, Rome was the source of greatness and civilization. Strabo decidedly keeps the crown of cultural superiority 'at home'.

Politically, superiority was clearly Roman (chapter 4), but Strabo argues that the Roman conquest of the Greeks was different from the subjugation of the rest of the world. Through a reference to an excerpt from Ephorus, he declares that a conqueror should act according to the character of the conquered. Violent methods are not necessary with civilized nations such as the Greeks. In 9.2.2, C 401 Strabo quotes Ephorus' explanation for the fall of the Theban hegemony because 'they belittled the value of learning and of intercourse with mankind, and cared for military virtues alone'. He then adds his own opinion: 'Ephorus should have added that these things are particularly useful in dealing with Greeks, although force is stronger than reason in dealing with the Barbarians.' He goes on to demonstrate that the Romans in ancient times dealt differently with savage tribes but later adopted milder methods in their dealings with civilized nations and races 'and so established themselves as lords of all'. The inference is clear: the Greeks are more civilized.

Strabo shows again and again that after the conquest was completed the Greek world found itself in a privileged position in comparison to the rest of the conquered *oikoumene*, for the Romans allowed many *poleis* in the Greek territories to have their independence and freedom (*eleutheria*) out of respect towards Greek culture.[125] In surveying the gradual Roman expansion at the end of Book 6 Strabo mentions some cities which gained their freedom from the Romans either out of friendship or because of the honour in which they were held (6.4.2, C 288). These seem to have been mostly Greek cities respected by the Romans for their great past and their traditions. Strabo emphasizes time and again the deference of the Romans and the freedom given to the cities. For instance, a specific allusion to the Lacedaemonians who 'were held in particular honour and remained free (*eleutheroi*), contributing to Rome nothing else but friendly services' (8.5.5, C 365). And a more general summary at the very end of the *Geography*, applying probably to the Greek cities: 'there are also free (*eleutherai*) cities of which some came over to the Romans at the outset as friends, whereas others were set free by the Romans themselves as a mark of honour' (17.3.24, C 839).[126]

Lasserre thinks that this presentation of the political situation in the world while stressing the unique position of Greece is a special characteristic of Strabo's. It reflects Augustan ideology presenting Rome as a great world power but at the same time shows Strabo's attachment to the Greek ideal of freedom rooted in the tradition of the Classical *polis*. That is, Strabo appreciates the prosperity and peace brought by the Romans to various places, but insists that the freedom and the autonomy of the Greek regions must be preserved.[127] This point shows once again the duality in Strabo's character as a Greek in Roman surroundings.

3

STRABO AND THE WORLD
OF AUGUSTAN ROME

STRABO IN ROME

An educated Greek, descendant of a noble Pontic family which had inclined towards Rome at the time of the Mithridatic wars, and possibly a Roman citizen himself (chapter 1), Strabo spent a significant length of time in Rome. During his sojourn in the city he became part of a group of Greek intellectuals living and mingling socially in the city (chapter 5), and established relationships with several Romans. This direct contact with the city, its aristocratic inhabitants and its cosmopolitan atmosphere at the time of Augustus, considerably influenced Strabo's political views as they are revealed in the *Geography*. He devotes significant parts of his work to the Roman empire of his age, referring both to its political achievements and to its expanded geographical surface (chapter 4).

To reconstruct Strabo's journeys to and from Rome we need a combination of dated references together with some complementary guesswork. Thus, when Strabo says that he saw P. Servilius Isauricus (12.6.2, C 568) he does not specify the nature of this 'seeing', the time or the place where it occurred. But since we know that the ninety-year-old Isauricus died in 44 BCE in Rome, and we do not know that he journeyed outside Italy in his later years, we may assume that Strabo met him in the city and that this occurred at the latest when Strabo was about twenty years old and therefore at the time of his first visit.[1] In about 35 BCE[2] Strabo watched Selurus, the brigand from Aetna, being devoured by wild animals in the Forum (6.2.6, C 273). Hence, either he remained in the city from 44 BCE for some nine years or else this event alludes to another visit, possibly the second.

In the latter half of 29 BCE Strabo was again[3] on his way to Rome on the occasion of Augustus' triumph over Antony at Actium (10.5.3, C 485). After accompanying his friend Aelius Gallus, the governor of Egypt, on his mission in about 29–26 BCE[4] and living for several years mainly in Alexandria (chapter 1, p. 21), Strabo returned to Rome shortly after 20 BCE and continued there at least until 7 BCE, for he mentions the porticus of Livia dedicated in that year,[5] and possibly to the end of his life,

85

for he probably saw the triumphal procession of Germanicus on 26 May 17 CE,[6] approximately five years before he died, as his detailed description of the event implies (7.1.4, C 291–2). Thus, we have evidence of three, perhaps four, separate sojourns, but there is no specific information regarding their duration although Strabo's experiences in the city and his many Roman acquaintances indicate long stays rather than brief visits. It has also been suggested that Strabo composed his *Geography* in Rome where he finally died (chapter 1, pp. 3 and 15).

During his various excursions to Rome Strabo saw strange sights and experienced new encounters. He saw very tall British boys (4.5.2, C 200); he saw the painting of Dionysus by Aristides on the walls of the temple of Ceres (8.6.23, C 381); he saw the crippled man, called for his lack of arms 'the Hermes', given as a gift to Augustus (15.1.73, C 719);[7] and he saw Egyptian alligators (17.1.44, C 815). In the historiographical work quoted by Josephus Strabo wrote that he saw a golden statue given to Pompey by Aristobulus and placed in the temple of Jupiter (*FGrH* 91 F 14). He also testifies that from Rome one can see Tibur, Praeneste and Tusculum (5.3.11, C 238) and it is possible to buy a glass pitcher or a cup for one bronze coin in the city (16.2.25, C 758). These impressions evidently derive from direct experience.[8]

Strabo's visits account for his detailed description of Augustan Rome and some of its monuments (5.3.8, C 235–6). He admires the beauty of the city and the various buildings initiated by Pompey, Caesar, Augustus, and the latter's sons, friends, wife and sister. He mentions specifically the Campus Martius, its monuments and the view seen from it; all together 'present to the eye the appearance of a stage-painting . . . a spectacle that one can hardly draw away from' (5.3.8, C 236).[9] In a field near the Campus Martius there are porticoes, temples, theatres and memorials of the most illustrious men and women, and the Mausoleum, described in detail and clearly based on personal observation, possibly after Augustus' death:[10]

> The most noteworthy is what is called the Mausoleum, a great mound near the river on a lofty foundation of white marble, thickly covered with ever-green trees to the very summit. On top is a bronze image of Augustus Caesar, beneath the mound are the tombs of himself and his kinsmen and intimates. Behind the mound is a large sacred precinct with wonderful promenades. In the centre of the Campus is the wall, this too of white marble, round his crematorium. The wall is surrounded by a circular iron fence and the space within the wall is planted with poplars.
>
> (5.3.8, C 236)

It is noteworthy that the central piece in Strabo's description is the Mausoleum which expresses the high position of the *princeps* after his death.

Strabo is also the first literary source to apply the term Mausoleum to Augustus' tomb.[11]

During his sojourns in Rome, Strabo established social contacts with several Romans. His most significant relationship was with Aelius Gallus, whom Strabo calls his 'dear friend' (*philos kai hetairos*), saying that 'when Gallus was governor of Egypt, I accompanied him and ascended the Nile as far as Syene and the frontiers of Ethiopia' (2.5.12, C 118).[12] Strabo joined Gallus' entourage of 'friends and soldiers' in tours around Egypt which enabled the geographer to visit various famous sites in his own person (chapter 1, p. 20).

After completing his mission in Egypt, Gallus was sent by Augustus to lead a military campaign to Arabia. Strabo gives many details on the background of this mission and the particular circumstances encountered by the soldiers. First, Gallus was to establish friendly relations with the Arabs and to explore the country. The plan arose from rumours about the riches of the country and its spices and gems (16.4.22, C 780). Strabo was aware of every detail of the soldiers' adventures and difficulties: the extreme heat afflicted them with fatigue, hunger and thirst. The situation became even more serious when they all fell ill with scurvy, and were forced to depend on local guides, one of whom betrayed them and caused the army further losses.[13] Galenus, the second-century physician, says that Gallus imported from Arabia an antidote for snake and scorpion bites which saved many of his soldiers. On his return to Rome he gave Augustus the recipe of the ingredients of this concoction.[14]

Strabo's survey of the Arabian campaign specifies Gallus' strategy, his plans and his attempts to help his forces survive the many disasters that plagued them. The character of Gallus emerges favourably as that of a responsible and brave commander. Details about the campaign as well as information on the country and its geography were perhaps directly transmitted to Strabo by his friend.[15] This social relationship, manifested in the Greek scholar's accompanying his friend and then recording in writing the Roman commander's campaigns, seems to reflect a feature present also in other, similar, associations. As Rome became more involved in the eastern Mediterranean, from the second century BCE, friendships were formed between Greek intellectuals and Roman generals. A famous example is the close bond that developed between Polybius and Scipio Aemilianus whom the historian accompanied on his campaigns. This kind of tie became more common in the first century BCE as is shown by the cases of Theophanes of Mytilene and Pompey, Theopompus of Cnidus and Julius Caesar, and many others (chapter 5). The Roman generals usually enjoyed the scholarly society of their Greek companions, and could sometimes expect to have their military achievements recorded by their friends, whereas the Greeks gained personal favours, such as Roman citizenship and special attitudes and benefits for their native cities.[16]

Apart from Gallus, Strabo was acquainted with at least two other Romans. Cn. Calpurnius Piso, a friend of Augustus and Tiberius, who was consul in 7 BCE and governor of Libya between the years 5 BCE and 2 CE, told Strabo that Libya is similar to a leopard's skin because it has spots of inhabited settlements surrounded by dry desert (2.5.33, C 130).[17] It is difficult to infer the extent of their acquaintance from this comment, but at least we know that the two men spoke to each other. This Piso was the eldest son of the Piso who was Horace's friend, thus indicating that Strabo and Horace were associated with the same family.[18]

We have already seen that on his first visit to Rome Strabo probably met the old P. Servilius Isauricus who had been active in the southern parts of central Asia Minor, in the region of Isauria, pacifying the local brigands, and eventually destroying their strongholds along the coasts (12.6.2, C 568; 14.3.3, C 665).[19] Strabo recounts how Zenicetus, the leader of the brigands, set fire to himself inside his house when Isauricus captured the region around Olympus in Lycia (14.5.7, C 671). These details could of course have been common knowledge due to the importance of Isauricus' campaigns. Other than this, Strabo does not volunteer any details of the nature of his association with the old soldier. His words are open to the interpretation of one brief meeting, even a silent one, or of a more solid relationship.

Strabo mentions another thirty-eight contemporary Romans by name but he does not indicate any social contact with them, whether meeting or conversation. Most of these men were leading figures in Roman politics of the latter half of the first century BCE and the beginning of the first century CE[20] and it seems safe to assume that Strabo did not get to meet men of the highest class personally but merely heard about their actions. The one exception referring to information not connected to politics is the passing allusion to the marriage of Marcia, Cato's wife, to Hortensius, in the context of describing the custom of the Tapyri who dwell by the Caspian Sea to give their wives to other men after they have had several children from them (11.9.1, C 515).

Apart from social contacts, assimilation in the new cultural centre formed in Rome can be evaluated through the extent of a sojourner's knowledge of Latin and his ability to read literary documents. Strabo was clearly Greek not only in his perceptions but also in his language. As he was a descendant of a noble family affiliated to the Philhellenic Pontic monarchs (chapter 1, pp. 3 and 5), Greek must have been his mother tongue though he perhaps also knew the local Cappadocian, still current in Pontus at the time.[21] Strabo's contemporary, Dionysius of Halicarnassus, declares in his *Roman Antiquities* 1.7.2–3 that he learned the language of the Romans and read parts of their literature. Strabo does not say specifically that he knows Latin but he certainly does know some Latin words, or at least refers to translations of certain terms and names into and from this language which he calls *Latine phone*,

Table 2 Latin words in Strabo's *Geography*

Term	Context	Appliance	Reference
σφήν > κούνεος (*cuneus*)	'Pole' – name of a pole-shaped region in Iberia	transcription and translation	3.1.4, C 137
Ἰουλία Ἴοζα (*Iulia Ioza*)	place name in Iberia	transcription	3.1.8, C 140
Λοῦκεμ Δουβίαμ (*Lucem Dubiam*)	'Dubious Light' – place name in Iberia	transcription including case ending in Latin	3.1.9, C 140
Παξαυγούστα (*Pax Augusta*) Αὐγούστα Ἡμερίτα (*Augusta Emerita*) Καισαραυγούστα (*Caesaraugusta*)	Roman colonies in Gaul and Iberia	transcription	3.2.15, C 151 cf. 3.4.20, C 166 3.4.10, C 161
στόλατοι (*Stolati*)	'Wearers of the Stola' – Iberians who became Roman in their lifestyle	transcription	3.2.15, C 151
Διάνιον > Ἀρτεμίσιον (*Dianium*)	temple name in Iberia	transcription and translation	3.4.6, C 159
Ἰουγκάριον πεδίον (*Campus Iuncarius*)	plain named after the iuncus, 'rush'	transcription	3.4.9, C 160
Βεττέραι (*Veteres*)	soldiers' colony in Iberia	transcription	
Μάραθον πεδίον (*Campus Fenicularius*)	plain named after the fennel	translation	
Σπαρτάριον πεδίον > Σχοινοῦν πεδίον (*Campus Spartarius*)	plain named after the rush	transcription and translation	
θρίαμβος (*triumphus*) θριαμβεύω θριαμβικός	Roman triumphus (verb and adjective from same root)	corrupt transcription (derivation unknown).	3.4.13, C 163; 3.5.3, C 169; 5.2.2, C 220; 6.4.2, C 287; 10.5.3, C 485; 12.3.6, C 543.
Φόρον Ἰούλιον (*Forum Iulium*)	Augustus' naval base near Massilia	transcription	4.1.9, C 184
Κωνουέναι > συγκλύδαι (*Convenae*)	'assembled rabble' -men from around Lugdunum	transcription and translation	4.2.1, C 190 cf. 4.2.2, C 191

Table 2 Continued

Term	Context	Appliance	Reference
λαῖναι (*laenae*)	'lined cloaks' – Roman term for Gallic dress	transcription	4.4.3, C 196
Σαβάτων Οὔαδα (*Vada Sabatorum*)	where the Alps begin	transcription and adaptation into Greek case	4.6.1, C 201
λιγγούριον > ἤλεκτρον (*lingurium*)	'amber'	transcription and translation	4.6.2, C 202
Αὐγούστα (*Augusta*)	Roman town in the Alps	transcription	4.6.7, C 206
Νεοκωμῖται > Νοβουμκώμουμ (*Novum Comum*)	'New Village' – town near the Po, originally Greek	transcription and translation into Latin (not by Strabo)	5.1.6, C 213
Φόρον Κορνήλιον (*Forum Cornelium*)	towns in North Italy	transcription	5.1.11, C 216–7
Μακροί Κάμποι (*Macri Campi*)		transcription and adaptation into Greek	
Ἀκουαιστατιέλλαι (*Aquae Statiellae*)		transcription	
Ῥηγισούιλλα (*Regis Villa*)	site on the Tyrhennian coast	transcription	5.2.8, C 226
Οἰακουσυμφαλίσκον (*Aequum Faliscum*)	site in North Italy	corrupt transcription	5.2.9, C 226
Φόρον Φλαμίνιον (*Forum Flaminium*) Φόρον Σεμπρώνιον (*Forum Sempronium*)	towns in north Italy	transcription	5.2.10, C 227
Πύλλη Κολλίνη (*Porta Collina*)	gate in the wall of Rome	translation	5.3.1, C 228
Κυρίται (*Quirites*)	address to Roman citizens	transcription	
σίνος > κόλπος (*sinus*)	'gulf' – origin of name of Sinuessa	transcription and translation, Latin etymology	5.3.6, C 234
πῖκος > δρυκολάπτος (*picus*)	'Woodpecker' – origin of name of Picentini	transcription and translation, Latin etymology	5.4.2, C 240–1

Table 2 Continued

Term	Context	Appliance	Reference
Σεπτέμπεδα (*Septempeda*) Πνευεντία (*Pneuentia*) Ποτεντία (*Potentia*) Φίρμον Πικηνόν (*Firmum Picenum*) Καστρουνόουμ (*Castrum Novum*)	northern towns	transcription	5.4.2, C 240–1
Οὐουλτοῦρνος (*Vulturnus*)	coastal town in Italy	transcription	5.4.4, C 243
Γαλλιναρίαν ὕλην (*Silva Gallinaria*)	forest in north Italy	transcription and translation	
Ποτιόλοι (*Puteoli*)	Other name of Dicaearchia	transcription and explanations for the name based on Latin etymology	5.4.6, C 245
caput (κεφαλή) > Capua	'head' – Capua as capital city	Latin etymology	5.4.10, C 249
βασίλειον > Ῥήγιον (*Rhegium*)	'kingly' – etymology for the town's name	transcription and translation	6.1.6, C 258
Γερμανοί > γνήσιοι (*germani*)	'blood kins' origin of nation's name	transcription and translation	7.1.2, C 290

Latine glotte (3.4.9, C 160), *Latine dialekton* (6.1.6, C 258), *he Romaion dialekton* (7.1.2, C 290) or simply *Latine* (3.1.4, C 137). Table 2 presents all his allusions to Latin terms. The use of Latin varies between mere transcription, mainly of names, and translation of meaning. Most references are to toponyms, as is appropriate to a geographical treatise. The references never extend to expressions or sentences but are restricted to single words.[22]

The list includes many names of new colonies and Roman settlements, some relating specifically to Augustus, all situated in the regions of Iberia, Gaul and Italy, and therefore, with one exception, found in Books 3–6 of the *Geography*. This up-to-date information on new Latin toponyms is certainly taken from his sources for these regions, some of which were probably in Latin. One might have been the *Commentaries* of Agrippa recording recent conquests at the time of Augustus (chapter 4, p. 127), where Strabo may have found the toponyms and transcribed them into Greek. These terms transcribed or translated from Latin cannot in themselves attest an active knowledge of Latin. However, Strabo probably had at least enough passive knowledge to be able to read and transcribe, and to consult Roman sources, some of which will be discussed shortly. There is no reason to exclude the possibility that after so many years in Rome, Strabo did not share the experience of Dionysius of Halicarnassus.

It goes without saying that Strabo's recourse to Latin is far more extensive than his use of other languages, in which he gives only a handful of terms (table 3).

Table 3   Foreign words in Strabo's *Geography*

Language	Word	Meaning	Reference
Gallic	μάδαρις > παλτοῦ τι εἶδος	spear	4.4.3, C 196
Samnite (Oscan)	ἵρπος > λύκος (*hirpus*)	'wolf' in Samnite dialect – origin of the name of the Hirpini	5.4.12, C 250
Mesapic	βρεντέσιον	ram's head	6.3.6, C 282
Thracian	βρία > πόλις	young donkey	7.6.1, C 319
Molossian	πελίαι πελίοι	old men and women	7 fr. 1a; 2
Medic	τίγρις > τὸ τόξευμα	arrow	11.14.8, C 529

Note that the terms always explain a toponym or aetiologize a myth. There are not enough of them to suggest a real knowledge of the language concerned and it is likely that Strabo found them in written sources or in oral information acquired from local inhabitants.

From words sentences are built and with them literature. Could Strabo do more than transcribe Latin words and names and could he actually read Latin literature? He does refer to several Roman authors and their works, sometimes quoting or paraphrasing some pieces of information taken from them. These Roman sources are presented below in chronological order from the earliest to the latest. Naturally, they appear in the *Geography* according to the context, quoted as sources.

Strabo labels Q. Fabius Pictor an historian (*syngrapheus*) and cites his notion that the Romans first became rich after their conquest of the Sabines (5.3.1, C 228). Pictor, a Roman senator, wrote a history of Rome in Greek and was a source of Polybius, Dionysius of Halicarnassus and Diodorus of Sicily.[23] He surveyed Roman history from the beginnings to 216 BCE, presenting an analogy between the Greek and the Roman cultures, a theme which must have appealed to Greek authors. Strabo could therefore either have read him directly in the Greek original or found his ideas in an intermediary source, possibly Polybius. This case, therefore, does not in itself indicate an ability to read and understand Latin.

D. Iunius Silanus, the historian, is mentioned by Strabo as Artemidorus' source of information on a spring in Gades that reacted inversely to the flux and reflux of the sea (3.5.7, C 172). Strabo says there about Artemidorus that 'he does not seem to me to have stated anything worth recording, since both he himself and Silanus are, you might say, laymen with respect to these matters'. Here Strabo knows the Roman source through a Greek one, that is, Artemidorus, and therefore did not necessarily read Silanus himself.[24]

In Book 5, discussing the assumed Greek origins of Rome, Strabo alludes to 'a Roman historian' who indicated that the sacrifice to Heracles in Rome is performed according to the traditional Greek ceremony (5.3.3, C 230). The manuscripts of the *Geography* present the name of this historian as *Kylios* or *Kekylios*. The editors Kramer and Meineke emended the text to read *Koilios*, assuming that this was the annalist L. Coelius Antipater who, at the end of the second century BCE, composed a history of the second Punic war.[25] Schwegler, however, preferred to emend the text to *Akylios* thus identifying the historian as C. Acilius. Coelius, he pointed out, focused on the second Punic war whereas the quotation in Strabo refers to the foundation of Rome, a period beyond the scope of Coelius' work but within Acilius', for the latter surveyed Roman history from the beginnings to 184 BCE.[26] Moreover, Acilius wrote in Greek and so it is more probable that Strabo read him and not Coelius. It may be added that Dionysius of Halicarnassus, who lived and wrote in Rome at the same time as Strabo, also exploited Acilius' work in his *Roman Antiquities* (3.67.5), a fact which makes the identification with Acilius still more probable, for he must have been popular with Greek scholars at the time, perhaps because of the language but perhaps also because of his Philhellenic opinions, accentuating the Greek origins of Rome. Thus, once again Strabo refers to a Roman author who wrote in Greek.

Cicero is mentioned twice in the *Geography* but only once as a source of information. In 10.2.13, C 455 Strabo alludes to him as an orator who was consul with Antony, and in 17.1.13, C 798 he quotes 'some speech' of Cicero, not extant today, as his source for the fact that 12,500 talents were paid as taxes to Ptolemy XII Auletes. Perhaps Strabo got this piece of information from someone who had actually read the speech without himself reading it in the original, for he does not tell us its exact title.

Strabo knew and exploited Julius Caesar's commentaries (*hypomnemata*) of the *Bellum Gallicum* (4.1.1, C 177). Apparently most of the description of Gaul and Britain in Book 4 is based on Caesar. Klotz suggested that Strabo in fact used the report of Timagenes of Alexandria, who gathered new information on Gaul and described it on the basis of the surveys of Artemidorus, Posidonius and Caesar. He therefore treated Strabo's words in Book 4 as if they were 'pure' Timagenes and compared them with Caesar's

Bellum Gallicum. Even the criticism of Asinius Pollio's estimate of the length of the Rhine in 4.3.3, C 193 is considered by Klotz to be in Timagenes.[27] According to this suggestion Strabo could have absorbed the contents of the *Bellum Gallicum* and the notion of Asinius Pollio without having to read a single Latin word, but there seems no real reason to exclude the possibility that he read Caesar directly and supplemented him with other sources.[28]

Q. Dellius, 'the friend of Antony, who wrote an account of Antony's expedition against the Parthians, on which he accompanied Antony and was himself a commander' (11.13.3, C 523), is cited as a source for the position of a Medic royal citadel and its distance from the river Araxes. The text reads *Adelfios*, an unknown author, but the attributes quoted support Casaubon's emendation to *Dellios*.[29] This time too there is no reason to dismiss Strabo's direct reliance on the author.

Strabo quotes Asinius Pollio for the length of the Rhine – 6,000 stadia – but remarks that 'it is not' (4.3.3, C 193). Asinius Pollio was the consul of 40 BCE who established the first public library in Rome, financed by booty from the Illyrian war.[30] After a triumph was celebrated in his honour he retired from politics to write history. His *Histories* were later translated into Greek by his own freedman, named after him Asinius Pollio of Tralleis. Therefore Strabo could read Pollio directly, or, what seems possible, preferred to read him in the Greek translation. He could also have derived the information from Timagenes of Alexandria who found refuge in Pollio's home after his expulsion from Augustus' court. On the basis of Strabo's use of other Latin sources, it is easier to assume that he read the Greek translation without having to think of an intermediary source.

In 17.3.8, C 829 Strabo refers to 'one of the Roman historians' who did not refrain from telling marvellous tales about Mauretania, such as the uncovering and then burial of the skeleton of Antaeus by Sertorius and the way in which elephants fight fire and men. The best manuscript (Vatican no.1329) reads 'Tanusius'.[31] This historian, Tanusius Geminus, who after Caesar's death wrote on Sertorius' campaign and on Caesar's times, is perhaps also the source for Book 3 on Iberia. This suggestion is based on Strabo's relatively abundant use of Latin words and names in the third book (above); on his use of Roman miles; and on his particularly elaborated descriptions of Sertorius' actions in Spain.[32]

Out of eight Latin authors mentioned by Strabo, two wrote in Greek, one was translated into Greek, and three others were perhaps used through an intermediary source. It is therefore reasonable to assume that whenever he had a chance Strabo preferred a Roman source written in Greek or translated into it. At the same time it is unlikely that he could not read Latin at all after spending so many years in Rome.[33] Hence it may be suggested that he also exploited two other Roman sources which he does not mention specifically. Both are genuinely Augustan in the sense that they are simultaneously products of the atmosphere in Rome at the time of Augustus, expressing its new horizons and achievements, and enhancers of this same spirit by transmitting it to the public. These are the *Commentaries* of Agrippa (chapter 4, p. 127) and the *Res Gestae Divi Augusti* (below, p. 97).[34] Strabo probably saw the *Commentaries* in the form of some sort of monumental lists initiated by M. Vipsanius Agrippa in order to explicate the Roman conquest of the *oikoumene*, as his allusions to a chorographic work and his use of Roman miles imply. Likewise, his description of Rome as a world empire together with the presentation of Augustus himself seem to echo details and ideas from the *Res Gestae*, Augustus' record of his own achievements publicly displayed on a monumental inscription in Rome and at least three others in Asia Minor where it was also translated into Greek. There is reason to assume that Strabo saw the inscription in Rome. His version differs from the Greek one displayed in Asia, but remains close to the Latin original. Further, he was present in Rome after Augustus' death when the monument was already publicly visible.

Whether Strabo read his Roman sources in Latin or in Greek, he was evidently familiar with some chapters in Roman history. Even if the direct and exact authority for this information is not always detectable, it is evident that he was aware of some traditions on the beginnings of Rome. He alludes to the events leading Aeneas and the refugees from Troy to land in Latium, referring to certain details of the journey, such as the burning of the ships by the women (6.1.12, C 262). He knows the story of the birth of the twins Romulus and Remus and the foundation legend, including the story of the abduction of the Sabine women (5.3.2, C 229–30). The names of characters from the early Roman epoch are relatively numerous and indicate the use of a source well acquainted with Roman traditions. Thus Strabo refers to Teucer, Antenor, Anchises, Aeneas, Ascanius, Latinus, Numitor, Faustulus, Rhea Silvia, besides Romulus and Remus.[35] He also knows something of the history of the regal era, for he alludes to six early kings of Rome: Titus Tatius, Numa Pompilius, Ancus Marcius, Tarquinius Priscus, Servius Tullius and Tarquinius Superbus,[36] and refers to the cruelty of the last king and the revolution and change to the republican constitution (6.4.2, C 288). Impressive as all this is, it should be borne in mind that detailed references to early Roman history were already appearing in Greek sources from Hesiod[37] to Polybius and clearly in some of the works of the Roman authors mentioned above which were written in Greek. It is therefore not surprising that Strabo incorporates them into his *Geography* without necessarily having read them directly in a Latin source.

Strabo's knowledge of Roman history from the Punic wars onwards may also derive from Greek sources, mostly Polybius. Among the events he mentions are the siege of Saguntum and the outbreak of the second Punic war (3.4.6, C 159), Hannibal's passage through the Alps, clearly taken from Polybius (4.6.12, C 209), the battle of Cannae (6.3.11, C 285) and

Hannibal's strategy at Lake Trasimene (5.2.9, C 226–7).[38] It should be kept in mind that these pieces of historiographical information occur in geographical contexts and that Strabo alludes to these events only by way of mentioning their venues.

Although Strabo provides some quite extensive lists of Greek scholars born in various eastern cities, the only Roman poet he mentions is Ennius, listed as a famous native of Rudiae (6.3.5, C 282 and chapter 2, p. 81). This fact emphasizes an important difference between the two cultures, the Greek having a much more ancient history of poetry and scholarship, and it seems also to reflect Strabo's attitude towards the two, admiring his own and perhaps somewhat underestimating the Roman. This attitude is also indicated in his reference to Roman geographers who merely translate and copy what the Greeks have to say (3.4.19, C 166).

Evidently Strabo must have absorbed some Roman cultural traits. He established social relationships with Romans and he introduced some facts from Roman history and even some Latin words into his work. It is very likely that he could do more than simply transcribe a few words and was probably able to read whole texts such as the *Res Gestae Divi Augusti*. But at the same time he seems to keep to his Greek identity and background. His use of Greek ideas and literary conventions and his sense of Hellenic superiority, particularly over the Romans, is typical of the Greek intellectuals who saw their culture as essentially different from and superior to all other human societies. This ideological separation of cultures was also maintained during the political ascendance of Rome towards the end of the first century BCE. Greek intellectuals and Roman aristocrats meeting in Rome would employ Greek, for to all appearances the scholars did not bother to learn foreign languages.[39] But whereas Strabo is clearly Greek in his culture, in one aspect he seems to comply with the Roman point of view, and that is the political. He absorbed contemporary Roman politics, was deeply influenced by them and interwove them in his work, particularly because they had geographical consequences and significance (chapter 4).

THE IMAGE OF AUGUSTUS IN STRABO'S WORK

In the Latin literature of the Augustan period, Rome was usually depicted as a great empire bringing peace and prosperity to the *oikoumene*, and ruled by a great and benevolent leader, Augustus.[40] Similar characteristics appear also in the writings of some Greek scholars who lived at the time and were in contact with Roman society. Thus, Nicolaus of Damascus and Timagenes of Alexandria, Strabo's contemporaries who probably belonged to the same intellectual and social milieu in Rome (chapter 5), each composed a biography of Augustus. The very choice of theme indicates the laudatory inclination of these works and their place against the background of Augustan Rome. Strabo no doubt absorbed much of this atmosphere during his long sojourn in Rome and through his relations with Romans such as Aelius Gallus, the governor of Egypt. He did not write a biography of Augustus, and his earlier historiographical survey ended in 27 BCE (chapter 2, p. 70), but the numerous allusions to the emperor scattered throughout the *Geography* clearly display his positive attitude. In fact Strabo is the earliest author to use the Greek 'Sebastos' as an equivalent to the Latin 'Augustus'.[41] He does not devote any one concentrated passage to the emperor but various allusions add up to a full picture of a man with great personal qualities and political accomplishments. The emperor is thus depicted as a conqueror who restored cities and bestowed tranquillity on extensive regions, a personality whose fame reaches the boundaries of the earth from which envoys are sent to him with gifts of honour, a man who initiated building projects and benevolent legislation in Rome and outside the city, a faithful worshipper of the gods who also respects human beings.

At the age of seventy-six, shortly before his death, Augustus completed a summary of the actions he had undertaken for the benefit of the Roman state, and surveyed his political career. This text, known as the *Res Gestae Divi Augusti*, was posted after Augustus' death on 19 August 14 CE at the Mausoleum in Rome and also at least in Asian Galatia where three different copies of the document, in Latin and in Greek, have been found.[42] Strabo's references to Augustus seem to echo some details from this document, suggesting that he perhaps saw it and adapted its contents into his geographical treatise. The geographer could have seen the Latin original at the Mausoleum after Augustus' death, as his detailed description of the site and its surroundings may imply (5.3.8, C 236 quoted above, p. 86).

Strabo presents Augustus in an extremely favourable light and his admiration of the political achievements of the Romans, which had also some geographical significance, focuses on the character of the emperor. Thus, he attributes several military successes particularly to Augustus, who personally subdued the Cantabrians (3.3.8, C 156; 6.4.2, C 287); finally subjected the Salassi, sold them as booty and carried them to a Roman colony (4.6.7, C 205); wore down the warlike Iapodes on the Illyrian border (4.6.10, C 207; 7.5.4, C 314); acquired Cisalpine and Transalpine Gaul and Liguria in one general war (6.4.2, C 287); sent an expedition against the German Getae (7.3.11, C 304); set five Dalmatian cities on fire (7.5.5, C 315); while his generals sacked a fortress on the Euphrates after a long siege and destroyed its walls (11.14.6, C 529). All these incidents and the variety of regions where they occurred create the impressive image of Augustus as a great conqueror.

Augustus' power over foreign nations was not manifested only through conquest and subjugation, but also by patronage over kingdoms whose rulers he himself appointed. Thus he installed Herod as king of Judaea (16.2.46, C 765) and nominated Juba king of Mauretania (17.3.7, C 828). Similarly, the priest in charge of the Museum in Alexandria, formerly appointed by the Ptolemies, was 'now' appointed by Augustus (17.1.8, C 794). The continuation of the Ptolemaic authority and, in the case of Herod who was formerly appointed by Antony, the inheritance of Antony's dominance in the east, emphasize Augustus' supreme power.

Augustus' image and the special aura of his time clearly derive from achievements based on wars and conquests. But Strabo, like other Augustan authors, emphasizes the beneficial outcome of this situation and tries to reconcile the aggressive connotation of conquests and wars with the specially lenient character of Augustus himself. He therefore presents the character of the emperor as benevolent and merciful by describing actions promoting the general state of tranquillity and order in the empire, such as the suppression of the brigands in the Alps (4.6.6, C 204), and the abrogation of the earlier extension of the *temenos* in Ephesus because it provided refuge for criminals, fostered crime and harmed the inhabitants (14.1.23, C 641).

Strabo stresses Augustus' moderate and wise policy, even though there were clear military and political considerations behind it:

> he supposed that he could conduct the war in hand more success-fully if he should hold off from those outside the Albis, who were living in peace, and should not incite them to make common cause with the others in their enmity against him.
>
> (7.1.4, C 291)

And, emphasizing Augustus' practical aspirations for Aelius Gallus' campaign in Arabia rather than an aggressive desire for conquest, he contends: 'he expected either to deal with wealthy friends or to master wealthy enemies' (16.4.22, C 780).

Thus, although a great conqueror with magnificent military achievements, Augustus is not depicted as a merciless, ruthless and power-motivated man but rather as cautious and restrained. This moderate policy is brought out by Augustus himself in his *Res Gestae*, denying any aggressive tendencies: 'when victorious I spared all citizens who sued for pardon. The foreign nations which could with safety be pardoned, I preferred to save rather than to destroy' (*RG* 3);[43] 'The Alps . . . I brought to a state of peace, without waging on any tribe an unjust war' (*RG* 26).

As part of the image of Augustus as eager not to destroy but to construct, Strabo recounts Augustus' acts of foundation, colonization and restoration in the conquered areas. His soldiers colonized Baetis in Iberia (3.2.1, C 141); he sent 3,000 Romans to found Augusta Praetoria in Gaul (4.6.7, C 206); he sent soldiers to Rhegium to compensate for its demographic decline and restore the ruins caused by earthquakes (6.1.6, C 259); he restored and strengthened Syracuse in order to bring back her lost fame (6.2.4, C 270); he restored the cities on the island of Ortygia, Catana and Centuripa, the latter due to its role in Sextus Pompeius' defeat (6.2.4, C 272); he founded and settled Nicopolis in memory of his naval victory over Antony and Cleopatra at Actium (7.7.5–6, C 324–5); and he restored many Asian cities seriously damaged by earthquakes such as Tralleis and Laodicea (12.8.18, C 579).

Augustus not only restored and developed the newly acquired territories of the empire, but also adorned the city of Rome. Strabo describes in detail the beauty of Augustan Rome (5.3.7–8, C 234–6) and specifically ascribes to Augustus the construction of roads 'through masses of rock and enormous beetling cliffs' (4.6.6, C 204).

In Rome, Strabo testifies, there was an extensive process of new construction going on because of fires and collapsing buildings. Constant property sales also caused the destruction of old houses and the erection of new ones according to the buyer's taste.[44] Augustus tried to minimize the occurrences of the two primary causes of loss, jerry-building and fire:

> Augustus Caesar concerned himself about such impairments of the city. For protection against fires, he organised a militia composed of freedmen, whose duty it was to render assistance, and as action against collapses, he reduced the heights of the new buildings and forbade that any structure on the public streets should rise as high as seventy feet.
>
> (5.3.7, C 235)[45]

Strabo depicts Augustus not only in relation to his political and constructive achievements, but also as an educated man surrounded by Greek scholars. Apollodorus of Pergamon was Augustus' teacher of rhetoric, and thus became the emperor's friend (13.4.3, C 625); Xenarchus of Seleucia, who was also Strabo's teacher, enjoyed Augustus' friendship and also that of Arius whom we know to have been another of Augustus' Greek teachers (14.5.4, C 670 and chapter 5); and Athenodorus of Tarsus, a friend of Strabo, was also Augustus' honoured teacher (14.5.14, C 674). The character of Augustus as an emperor surrounded by Greek intellectuals, two of whom interestingly enough had personal contact with Strabo, was a trait of some importance in our author's eyes.[46]

Augustus' philhellenic inclinations are also apparent in his attitude towards the city of Amisus in Pontus, which he set free (12.3.14, C 547). His treatment of spoils of war, and especially of Greek works of art, also has to do with his moral character and his approach to Greek culture. This theme especially worried Strabo, who dwells several times on the outrageous theft by Roman commanders of works of art and dedications from Greek temples in the east (chapter 4, p. 121). Strabo's outspoken reproaches accentuate all the more his attitude to Augustus, who seems to be pardoned and excused for similar deeds. Augustus is said to have spared the treasures of the eastern temples and, unlike other Romans, did not plunder them, appreciating their religious and artistic value. He did in fact bring to Rome from the island of Cos a painting of Aphrodite by Apelles, but it was in a good cause, 'Augustus thus having dedicated to his father the female founder of his family' (14.2.19, C 657). Moreover, the people of Cos got a reduction in taxes as compensation for the painting. In this way Augustus is presented as an honest man who did not steal the work of art outright. Another positive quality shown here is Augustus' respect towards his adoptive father, Julius Caesar, descendant of Aeneas, son of Aphrodite.

In another case Strabo presents Augustus as a pious man who, unlike Antony, and as a man who appreciates Greek art, would not offend the gods. Thus he refers to a statue of Aias from Rhoetium that

> was taken up by Antony and carried off to Egypt, but Augustus Caesar gave it back again to the Rhoetians, just as he gave back other statues to their owners. For Antony took away the finest dedications from the most famous temples, to gratify the Egyptian woman, but Augustus gave them back to the gods.
>
> (13.1.30, C 595)

On another occasion Augustus made amends for Antony's depredations by sending back sculptures taken from Samos. He left one of them in Rome but erected a small temple for it:

> of these [sc. statues], three of colossal size, the work of Myron, stood upon one base. Antony took these statues away, but Augustus Caesar restored two of them, those of Athene and Heracles, to the same base, although he transferred the Zeus to the Capitolium, having erected there a small chapel for that statue.
>
> (14.1.14, C 637)

The contradiction between the characters of Antony and Augustus is thus another way of praising the emperor.

Augustus' character and morals are further flattered in a story that shows his compassion and understanding. After his victory over Adiatorix of Galatia, the emperor 'resolved to put him to death together with the eldest of his sons' according to the law of war, that is, not because he was cruel.[47] But a younger son, with his parents at his side, persuaded the eldest to stay alive and let him die instead, 'for he being more advanced in age, would be a more suitable guardian for his mother and for the remaining brother'. And so the young brother died with his father, and the eldest

> was saved and obtained the honour of the priesthood. For learning about this, as it seems, after the men had already been put to death,

Caesar was grieved, and he regarded the survivors as worthy of his favour and care, giving them the honour in question.

(12.3.35, C 558–9)

In the concluding parts of Book 6 of the *Geography*, which is devoted to Italy, Strabo expands his description with an appendix on the advantages of Italy as the centre of an empire and on the historical causes for Rome's territorial expansion and political success (6.4.1–2, C 285–8). In what may be entitled *Res Gestae Populi Romani*, he surveys Rome's development from a small town ruled by kings, through a republic combining monarchic and aristocratic institutions, into a world empire governed by Augustus and his successors, Germanicus and Tiberius. The last lines of this short historical survey reflect a special image of Augustus:

> It were a difficult thing to administer so great a dominion other-
> wise than by turning it over to one man, as to a father . . . never
> have the Romans and their allies thrived in such peace and plenty
> as that which was afforded them by Augustus Caesar, from the
> time he assumed the absolute authority, and is now being afforded
> them by his son and successor, Tiberius, who is making Augustus
> the model of his administration and decrees . . .
>
> (6.4.2, C 288)

Strabo here emphasizes the compatibility of the form of government, that is monarchy, and the geopolitical situation of the Roman empire.[48] But this particular monarch, Augustus, is presented as the father of the Roman nation, a metaphor calling to mind the official title *Pater patriae* given to Augustus by the Senate on 5 February 2 BCE, and mentioned by Augustus himself in his *Res Gestae* (35). Although Strabo does not use the exact trans-lated form – *Pater patridos* – he is evidently expressing the same idea.[49]

Admiration for the emperor was expressed also through monuments erected to honour him. Strabo mentions such monumental projects outside Italy, paying homage throughout the wider empire. Thus, he alludes to an elaborate monument erected by sixty Gallic tribes in Lugdunum at the junction of the rivers, composed of an altar, an inscription bearing the names of the sixty tribes, images of each tribe and another large image, possibly of Augustus (4.3.2, C 192). And indirectly we hear of statues of Augustus set up in southern Egypt at the Ethiopian border which were pulled down by the Ethiopians (17.1.54, C 820).

Foreign nations living at the remote frontiers of the *oikoumene* also showed their respect for Augustus by sending personal emissaries. Leaders and rulers of distant communities appointed gift-bearing embassies to greet him. Strabo mentions an Indian tribute: 'From India, from one place and from one king, Pandion, and another Porus, came to Caesar Augustus presents and gifts of honour' (15.1.4, C 686). He also quotes the full testimony of Nicolaus of Damascus who met the embassy on its way in Asia Minor and saw the enclosed letter and the gifts:

> He says that . . . the letter was written in Greek on a skin, and that it plainly showed that Porus was the writer, and that, although he was ruler of six hundred kings, still he was anxious to be a friend to Caesar, and was ready, not only to allow him a passage through his country, wherever he wished to go, but also to co-operate with him in anything that was honourable . . . that the gifts carried to Caesar were presented by eight naked servants, who were clad only in loin cloths besprinkled with sweet smelling odours, and that the gifts consisted of the Hermes, a man who was born without arms . . . and large vipers, and a serpent ten cubits in length, and a river tortoise three cubits in length, and a partridge larger than a vulture
>
> (15.1.73, C 719–20)

There were connections with other nations, in all cases particularly remote or Barbaric peoples. Referring to Britain Strabo says:

> At present, however, some of the chieftains there, after procuring the friendship of Caesar Augustus by sending embassies and by paying court to him, have not only dedicated offerings in the Capitolium, but have also managed to make the whole of the island virtually Roman property.
>
> (4.5.3, C 200)

To this we may add the personal contact between Augustus and Maroboduus before the latter became the leader of the German tribes (7.1.3, C 290), and the gesture made by the Cimbri who 'sent as a present to Augustus the most sacred kettle in their country, with a plea for his friendship and for an amnesty of their earlier offences' (7.2.1, C 293).[50] And, finally, ambassadors of the Ethiopian queen Candace came to Augustus when he was in Samos, although they had not heard of Augustus until then, apparently to pledge friendship after the governor Petronius checked their attack on the Roman garrison in Ethiopia (17.1.54, C 821).

The nations mentioned by Strabo as paying special tributes to Augustus all signify typically remote races who, according to Greek tradition, dwelt at the edges of the world (chapter 2, p. 44). The Indians, representing the east, the Ethiopians – the south, the Germans – the north, and even the Britons, are not just polite and impressed envoys, but symbolize the entire *oikoumene* acknowledging Augustus' greatness. In his *Res Gestae* Augustus himself emphasizes this unprecedented diplomatic achievement, saying that 'a large number of other nations experienced the good faith of the Roman people during my principate who never before had had any interchange of embassies or of friendship with the Roman people' (*RG* 32), and especially mentions the Indian embassy 'a thing never seen before in the camp of any general of the Romans' (*RG* 31).

One of the most striking signs of subjugation to Augustus' rule is the case of the royal Parthian hostages committed to him in exchange for his friendship: 'Phraates has entrusted to Augustus Caesar his children and also his children's children, thus obsequiously making sure of Caesar's friendship by giving hostages' (6.4.2, C 288).

Strabo indicates the exact circumstances in which Phraates gave his sons as hostages, gives their names, and adds the fact that two of their wives and four of their sons were given with them, concluding that 'all his surviving children are cared for in royal style, at public expense, in Rome, and the remaining kings have also continued to send ambassadors and to go into conferences' (16.1.28, C 749).

The surrender of the Parthians to Augustus is particularly significant for the attainment of his exclusive position as the ruler of the world, for at some point they were considered the most threatening rival of Rome (chapter 4, p. 113). The Parthian submission is mentioned also by Augustus himself as an outstanding event (*RG* 32).

Strabo barely refers to Augustus' actions in the domain of internal Roman politics prior to the foundation of the principate and avoids referring to his earlier years, his titles, *cursus honorum*, adopted sons and his gradual political ascendance. He merely implies the internal clashes between Augustus and Sextus Pompeius and Augustus and Antony.

The allusions to the war between Sextus Pompeius and Augustus are indirect, that is, they are not introduced for themselves but rather as points of reference for chronological or geographical matters, such as 'after ejecting Pompeius from Sicily' (6.1.6, C 259) or referring to Messina as a central point in the war between Sextus Pompeius and Augustus (6.2.3, C 268). Strabo brings in these occasions only when his focus is the actions of Augustus himself; for instance, he alludes to Sextus Pompeius' abuse of Syracuse in order to emphasize his main point, Augustus' restoration of the city (6.2.4, C 270), or he mentions the restoration of other cities in Sicily, one of them being favoured because it contributed to the overthrow of Sextus Pompeius (6.2.4, C 272).

Augustus' earlier career and internal Roman doings did not find their way into Strabo's geographical work for he did not propose to write a biography or a history. His aim was not the glorification of Rome and Augustus as such, and his theme was not Roman history or Roman power. All he intended to do was to describe the *oikoumene*, the extent of which was naturally dependent on recent Roman conquests. Rome and Augustus eventually emerge from the *Geography* in a very favourable light, but this outcome may be considered as a sort of by-product.

Besides the direct references to Augustus, his character is also enhanced by allusions to three other personages who emphasize his unique features by contradiction or similarity. These are Alexander the Great, Antony and Tiberius, each reflecting a different epoch in history, all referred to by Strabo in analogy to Augustus.

There is an implied resemblance between the period of Alexander the Great and his character and Augustus' age and his image. This semblance is rather hinted at and not fully developed, but it seems to add some dimension to the already magnificent portrait of the emperor. Strabo compares the geographical and political achievements of Alexander and those of Rome at the time of Augustus. Nations formerly subdued by Alexander are 'now' under the rule of Rome (1.2.1, C 14; 12.7.3, C 571). In both periods the extension of empire to the boundaries of the *oikoumene* resulted in political superiority as well as an increase in geographical knowledge. Strabo is aware of the attempts of Alexander's historians to flatter the king by emphasizing the extent of his conquests through geographical distortions, but points out that, unlike them, he himself is trying to be accurate and reliable (chapter 4, p. 111).

Both rulers had a similar personal experience: 'From India . . . came to Caesar Augustus . . . the Indian sophist who burnt himself up at Athens, as Calanus had done, who made a similar spectacular display of himself before Alexander' (15.1.4, C 686). This spectacle is not a mere ethnic peculiarity but accentuates the submission of India, first to Alexander and then to Augustus.

There is not enough information to form a full comparison between the two rulers, but the hints we have in the *Geography* seem to echo the idea current in Rome of a conscious confrontation of the Romans and their leaders with the character of Alexander. Pompey saw Alexander as his example and even his cognomen *Magnus* and his physical appearance are connected with this inclination. There are also various testimonies to Julius Caesar's association with Alexander and Augustus himself emphasized his resemblance to the great king. This *Imitatio Alexandri* was manifest in the Romans' aspiration to expand the empire to the boundaries of the *oikoumene*, their ambition focused on Britain and the northern sea, as Alexander's was on the conquest of India.[51] It is interesting to note that this competition with Alexander's image was used also by Timagenes of Alexandria who was hostile towards Rome and Augustus. He used the analogy to denigrate the Romans, claiming that had they encountered Alexander in battle, they would have been defeated.[52] Again, Alexander is the standard for measuring Roman achievements.

While the character of Alexander represents an image to be imitated, Antony is presented in the *Geography* as the antithesis to Augustus. Strabo mentions Antony in almost every book of the work, sometimes specifically comparing his frivolity and uncouthness to Augustus' piety, modesty and moderation. The contrast between their respective manners of ruling is apparent. Referring to Egypt, Strabo depicts the beneficial turn from the joint reign of Antony and Cleopatra to Roman rule under Augustus: 'After this Augustus Caesar pursued them, destroyed both, and put an end to Egypt's being ruled with drunken violence' (17.1.11, C 796).

As we have seen (p. 99), Strabo speaks of the ruthless plunder of works of art by Antony, while stressing in the same context the opposite actions of the pious Augustus who returned the stolen pieces to their lawful owners.

Antony gave Cleopatra not only confiscated temple dedications but also territories belonging to the Roman people. He gave her Hamaxia in Cilicia because of the good wood it had for building ships (14.5.3, C 669); referring to Cyprus which was formerly a province as it is 'now', Strabo says that Antony gave it to Cleopatra and to her sister Arsinoe, and 'when he was overthrown all his organisation was overthrown with him' (14.6.6, C 685). Here one may feel Antony's betrayal of the property rights of the Roman people and a sort of 'happy ending' because the island is 'now' in Roman hands and all Antony's plans have collapsed. Only once did Augustus take some land for himself but note how this act is mentioned:

> The people of Naples took possession of this island too, and although they lost Pithecussae in war, they got it back again, Augustus Caesar giving it to them, though he appropriated Capri to himself personally and erected buildings on it.
>
> (5.4.9, C 248)

The emphasis is on Augustus' giving property to the people of Naples and not taking.

Another topic relating to Antony and appearing in various contexts and with different emphases is his defeat at Actium in 31 BCE. Strabo refers several times to the victory at Actium but not to its internal Roman political significance, being more interested in its effect on the situation in the world and in its significance as a turning point marking the dominance of Roman power. However, he does go into some local detail. Cleopatra was present at the battle (7.7.6, C 325; 17.1.11, C 797); Bogus king of Mauretania belonged to Antony's faction (*stasis*) and was executed at Actium by Agrippa (8.4.3, C 359); after the defeat Antony felt abandoned and betrayed and withdrew to his palace in Alexandria (17.1.9, C 794);[53] and finally he was forced to commit suicide and Cleopatra surrendered to Augustus but later killed herself by a snake bite or a poisonous ointment (17.1.10, C 795). He also mentions two cities named Nicopolis, that is Victory City, one in Epirus founded by Augustus to commemorate the Actian victory (7.7.6, C 325), the other in Egypt near Alexandria, where supporters of Antony were defeated (17.1.10, C 795).

Tiberius is drawn against the giant image of his adoptive father, Augustus. Strabo deliberately accentuates the similarities between the two and the fact that Tiberius was consciously continuing Augustus' policies and attitudes. In this way not only does Tiberius' character gain another dimension, but the glory of Augustus is further enhanced. Tiberius is mentioned several times in a favourable and complimentary way but there is no deeper elaboration of his character as there is of Augustus' image. Strabo presents Tiberius as Augustus' heir who took his predecessor as an example and imitated his policy (6.4.2, C 288), as Tiberius himself claimed.[54] Most of the information on Tiberius concerns his conquests and other military undertakings: he stationed three legions in Iberia (3.3.8, C 156); he subjugated some tribes on the Adriatic coast (4.6.9, C 206); he was engaged in a naval battle with the Vindelici (7.1.5, C 292); he turned Cappadocia into a Roman province (12.1.4, C 534); and he was sent to Armenia by Augustus (17.1.54, C 821).

Strabo also mentions Tiberius' close friendship with Marcus Pompeius, Theophanes of Mytilene's son (13.2.3, C 618 and chapter 5, p. 136).

In one context Tiberius is drawn as very compassionate, almost like a god. Strabo reports his restoration of cities that suffered losses and damage by earthquake (12.8.18, C 578–9; 13.4.8, C 627) and mentions the providence (*pronoia*) of Tiberius, a word usually reserved for the supreme powers of nature (chapter 2, p. 63). But even this benevolent act is presented by way of comparison with Augustus: 'The emperor restored them by contributing money, just as his father in earlier times, when the inhabitants of Tralleis suffered their misfortune . . . restored their city, as he also restored the city of the Laodiceans' (12.8.18, C 570).

Augustus is thus clearly a very dominant character in Strabo's work as far as any personage can be accentuated in a geographical context. Only Alexander could ever be compared to him. This image puts Strabo once again in the same category as other Augustan authors, both Latin and Greek. Although he probably wrote his *Geography* at the time of Tiberius, the work and particularly the allusions to the politics and conquests of the *oikoumene* are clearly Augustan, in the sense that they express notions similar to other contemporary literary expressions which depicted the time as an age of peace and prosperity and attributed these Roman achievements to a single man – Augustus.

4

GEOGRAPHY, POLITICS
AND EMPIRE

THE EMPIRE AND THE BOUNDARIES OF
THE *OIKOUMENE*

The geographical survey encompassing the entire known world of Strabo's time is much more than a simple account of regions and peoples. In it Strabo also reveals his opinions on various matters, scholarly and moral, and in particular he exposes his political views. These were clearly affected by recent developments in his own time, the age of Augustus, during which, at the end of almost a century of wars and conquests, the Roman empire reached an unprecedented size and achieved peace at most of its frontiers. Strabo's contacts with Romans and his sojourn in Rome enabled him to absorb the atmosphere at the centre of the empire. He shows how the vast Roman conquests and with them the expansion of the empire to the ends of the inhabited earth contributed to the widening of geographical knowledge while they established the position of Rome as a world power. Imperial might induced changes in the political map of the world and in the cultural character of remote Barbaric tribes who adopted the Roman way of life. Internal feuds were concluded and external security was enhanced. In some cases, the Roman presence alone carried with it a new age of peace and prosperity.[1] At the same time Strabo's Asiatic origin and Greek orientation also affected his attitude towards Roman political ascendance. These factors are evident particularly in his criticism of what he considers to be the immoral consequences of the Roman conquests. Thus, Strabo approaches this whole issue of Roman power from several angles – geographical, moral and political – and the overall representation reveals his general attitude and his political thoughts.

Twice in the *Geography* Strabo specifically and directly discusses Roman growth and the state of the Roman position in the world. At the end of Book 6, which is devoted to Italy, he presents the natural advantages of the Italian peninsula that contribute to its function as the ideal centre of an empire, announcing his intention to indicate the most important things which caused the Romans 'at present to be exalted to so great a height' (6.4.1, C 285). As one could expect from a geographer, he first enumerates geographical and physical causes pertaining to the natural characteristics of Italy, which was 'a base of operation for the universal hegemony'. These are, briefly, natural fortifications, Italy being a peninsula surrounded by seas and mountains; the small number of harbours, which adds to its security but, these being large, favour commerce and the navy; climatic variety producing a wide range of fauna and flora (see also 5.3.1, C 228); the topographical alternation of mountains and plains which offers the advantages of both; the many rivers, lakes and healthy springs; the existence of various mines; abundant food supply for men and beasts; and, finally:

> Since it lies intermediate between the largest races on the one hand, and Greece and the best parts of Asia[2] on the other, it not only is naturally well-suited to hegemony, because it surpasses the countries that surround it both in valour (*arete*) of its people and in size, but also can easily avail itself of their services, because it is close to them.
>
> (6.4.1, C 286)

That is, the natural position of Italy in the middle of the *oikoumene*, together with its topographic, climatic, hydrologic and agronomic conditions, contributes to its power.[3]

This type of causation in which changes in the extent of human habitation are explained by natural factors is rooted in the theory of climate and natural conditions as determinants of human character. Strabo here combines this Greek theory with an actual political situation and tries to apply theory to practice, whether following Posidonius or perhaps another author. It is likely that in observing the political phenomenon of ascending Roman power, contemporary philosophers made the connection between practice and theory as it suited their theoretical models. Polybius had done something of the kind by applying the theory of the ideal mixed constitution to the constitution of the Romans. Cicero also applied the Aristotelian theory about ruling and ruled nations corresponding to the law of nature in order to justify Roman power.[4]

Moving from the country, Italy, Strabo goes on to describe the historical and political causes for Roman expansion. He briefly surveys Roman history from the regal era up to his own period (6.4.2, C 286–8), giving an up-to-date picture of the political situation at the time of writing, with reference to the geographical scope of the empire, the nature of the relations between Rome and various kingdoms and tribes around the world, and the currently active war fronts. In this short account at the end of Book 6, Strabo lists in one breath, so to speak, a great many nations around the world, creating the image of an empire reaching the four cardinal points whether by its actual presence or by respectful recognition. He is careful to differentiate between the varying status of the nations, some being provinces of the empire, others autonomous client kingdoms and still others independent entities paying homage to Augustus. But the general outcome is an impressive image of Roman power.

At the end of Book 17, in his closing remarks to the entire *Geography*, Strabo again gives a summary of the Roman provinces:

> Since the Romans occupy the best and the best known portions of the *oikoumene*, having surpassed all former rulers of whom we have record, it is worth while, even though briefly, to add the following account of them . . . of the continents, being three in number, they hold almost the whole of Europe . . . of Libya the whole of the coast on our sea is subject to them; and the rest of the country is uninhabited or else inhabited only in a wretched or nomadic fashion . . . of Asia also, the whole of the coast on our sea is subject to them . . . some further portion is constantly being taken from these peoples and added to the possessions of the Romans.
>
> (17.3.24, C 839)

He goes on to specify the status of the subject peoples and the administration of various Roman provinces throughout the *oikoumene* (17.3.25, C 840). In this respect, the limits of the empire are the limits of the *oikoumene*. Those parts which are outside the empire are deserted or inhabited by nomads and pirates (below, p. 110).

In addition to these long and detailed digressions which deal wholly with the political, geographical and cultural prowess of Rome, Strabo refers to Roman policy on many other occasions in brief and sometimes random allusions. The recurrent idea is the identification of the boundaries of the empire with those of the *oikoumene*.

'We call *oikoumene* the world which we inhabit and know' (1.4.6, C 65). This world is vast but has clear limits, since it is a large island surrounded by the Ocean (chapter 2, p. 43). It contains various countries and nations and tribes, all different from each other in their histories and their customs. The limits of the *oikoumene* known to men are determined by the surrounding Ocean, by deserts and uninhabited regions or by unexplored areas. Strabo is well aware of the limits of information and the obscurity of data on certain places near the boundaries of the *oikoumene*.

In a parallel way, the Roman conquests are also wide. Their scope emphasizes the greatness of Roman achievement. Through his geographical descriptions Strabo stresses the size of the empire and the great importance of this condition. He does not always express in so many words his enthusiasm about the distances covered by the Roman army; however, his survey implies the fact that the Romans rule over many regions, remote countries and unknown nations. This is done in two ways, one demonstrating the

Roman influence over various nations through allusion to numerous sites in the *oikoumene*, and the other making a strict identification between the scope of conquest and the limits of information, that is, the boundaries of the *oikoumene*. Roman conquest has enlarged the knowledge of remote regions, and beyond the conquered areas nothing is known.

Strabo's idea of the *oikoumene* is traditional and rooted in early Greek experience (chapter 2). At the same time, owing to his practical purposes in the *Geography* and with his intended readers in mind, he focuses on the *oikoumene*: 'The geographer undertakes to describe the known parts of the inhabited world, but he leaves out of consideration the unknown parts of it just as he does what is outside of it' (2.5.5, C 112).[5] However, he is aware that the boundaries of countries and the political organization of tribes change constantly (9.5.8, C 433). The boundaries of the *oikoumene*, or, at least, the boundaries of knowledge about them, were therefore expanded by the Roman conquests:

> The spread of the empires of the Romans and of the Parthians has presented to geographers of today a considerable addition to our empirical knowledge of geography, just as did the campaign of Alexander to geographers of earlier times . . . I therefore may have something more to say than my predecessors.
>
> (1.2.1, C 14)

and again: 'The supremacy of the Romans and that of the Parthians has disclosed considerably more knowledge than that which had previously come down to us by tradition' (11.6.4, C 508).[6]

More specifically, in referring to the regions beyond the Albis and the northern parts of Europe, Strabo shows that acquaintance with territories originates in conquest, and unconquered places are relatively unknown. He associates this correlation with the Romans in particular. Augustus' decision to proceed with conquest or to renounce it determined the flow of information about new places and peoples: 'These tribes [sc. the Germans] have become known through their wars with the Romans . . . and they would have been better known if Augustus had allowed his generals to cross the Albis' (7.1.4, C 291); and

> Those parts of the country beyond the Albis that are near the Ocean are wholly unknown to us. For of the men of earlier times I know of no one who has made this voyage along the coast to the eastern parts . . . and the Romans have not yet advanced into the parts that are beyond the Albis . . . what is beyond Germany and what beyond the countries which are next after Germany . . . it is not easy to say; nor yet whether they extend as far as the Ocean along its entire length, or whether any part is uninhabitable by reason

of the cold or other cause, or whether even a different race of people
. . . is situated between the sea and the eastern Germans. And this
same ignorance prevails also in regard to the rest of the peoples
that come next in order towards the north.

(7.2.4, C 294)[7]

Strabo is quite clear on the issue. If conquests determine acquaintance with
new regions, the boundaries of the empire and the limits of the *oikoumene*
correspond to each other. The aspiration to identify the two worlds – the
inhabited and the conquered – has to do with the Homeric concept of
the *oikoumene* surrounded by the Ocean. Whereas Alexander wanted to
reach the Ocean in the east, the Romans wished to arrive at its western coast
and thus to rival Alexander's successes and complete what he had begun.[8]

Strabo elaborates further on the Roman achievement through his use of
the geographical background. Throughout the *Geography*, in the course
of the systematic description of the *oikoumene*, he emphasizes the Roman
presence in widespread parts of the world. The Romans are in Iberia (1.1.4,
C 2); in Sardinia and Corsica (5.2.7, C 224); reaching the German tribes
and particularly the Cimbri (7.2.2, C 293–4); in Greece (8.7.3, C 385); in
Crete (10.4.9, C 477; 10.4.22, C 484) and in Egypt, where three legions
are posted (17.1.5, C 791; 17.1.30, C 807). He also includes regions and
nations not officially subjected to Roman rule and which do not form one
of the provinces of the empire, each having its own status from client
kingdom to wholly independent political entity. A disastrous military
campaign was attempted in Arabia by Aelius Gallus, Strabo's friend (2.5.12,
C 188); the Britons enjoy autonomy but have to pay taxes to the Romans
(4.5.3, C 200); and in Coele Syria, the Nabataeans, the Sabaeans and the
Syrians each have their own status in relation to the Romans (16.4.21,
C 779). The regions in this category fill out the mosaic that depicts the
Roman empire stretching to the boundaries of the *oikoumene*.

Kingdoms and regions not defined as Roman provinces nor directly super-
vised by the Romans, nevertheless acknowledge Roman power and the glory
of its ruler, Augustus (chapter 3, p. 101). The Parthians on their own initiative sent hostages to Rome as a token of friendship (6.4.2, C 288). The
Indians sent embassies with gifts (15.1.4, C 686; 15.1.73, C 719–20). Even
the Ethiopians, ruled by their mannish one-eyed queen, Candace, learned
about Augustus through envoys (17.1.54, C 820–1). It is significant that
these nations, particularly the Indians and the Ethiopians, are those who
traditionally dwell at the boundaries of the world (chapter 2, p. 44). Their
recognition of Roman rule completes the picture of Rome as a world power
whose fame has reached even the farthest peoples.[9]

Strabo is aware of earlier attempts to distort geographical detail for propaganda purposes. The historians of Alexander 'moved' the boundaries of the
oikoumene in order to promote his fame:

The stories that have been spread far and wide with a view to glorifying Alexander are not accepted by all; and their fabricators were men who cared for flattery rather than truth. For instance, they transferred the Caucasus into the region of the Indian mountains ... which is more than thirty thousand stadia distant from India ... for these were the farthermost mountains towards the east that were known to writers of that time ... it was a more glorious thing for Alexander to subdue Asia as far as the Indian mountains than merely ... to the Caucasus, yet the glory of the mountain, and its name ... led writers to suppose that they would be doing the king a favour if they transferred the name Caucasus to India.

(11.5.5, C 505–6)

and

It is not easy to believe most of those who have written the history of Alexander; for they toy with facts, both because of the glory of Alexander and because his expedition reached the ends of Asia, far away from us; and statements about things that are far away are hard to refute.

(11.6.4, C 508)

and again:

Many false notions were also added to the account of this sea [i.e. Caspian] because of Alexander's love of glory ... it was resolved to manipulate the account of Alexander's expedition so that in fame at least he might be credited with having conquered those parts of Asia too.

(11.7.4, C 509)[10]

The effect of Strabo's own geographical descriptions is similar to the message of Alexander's historians, for Rome, ruled by Augustus, appears as a powerful empire which has reached unknown regions of the *oikoumene* and whose fame has spread almost to the whole of humankind. This corresponds exactly to the propaganda presenting Alexander as a conqueror who reached new and unprecedented horizons.[11] All this of course is not pure invention in Strabo. Alexander was in fact the first to reach new regions, especially in the east, which were known to the Greek world only by hearsay. Similarly, the Roman forces encountered nations and tribes who until then were remote from Mediterranean culture.

The propaganda theme in Strabo's *Geography* is more subtle. The presentation of the new geographical and ethnographical information provided by recent conquests had a primarily didactic purpose but at the same time it served political goals. This aspect reflects the atmosphere in Strabo's time and corresponds to similar inclinations among contemporary authors, Roman and Greek alike.[12]

Although Rome is presented as the leading political and cultural power in the world, Strabo is aware of the existence of other powers at the outskirts of the empire which are not entirely subjected to the Romans. These are particularly the eastern kingdoms of India, Media and Parthia.[13] He emphasizes especially the power and strength of the Parthian empire which rules over some parts of the *oikoumene* beyond the Roman realm and mentions many regions which are subordinated to the rule of the Parthian kings.[14] This is the same technique that he uses to promote the fame of the Roman empire, as we saw, and he presents the view in some detail:

> Later they [sc. the Parthians] grew so strong, always taking the neighbouring territory, through successes in warfare, that finally they established themselves as lords of the whole country inside the Euphrates . . . and at the present time they rule over so much land and so many tribes that in the size of their empire they have become, in a way, rivals of the Romans. The cause of this is their mode of life and also their customs, which contain much that is Barbarian and Scythian in character, though more that is conducive to hegemony and success in war.
>
> (11.9.2, C 515)

A direct result of the political and military achievements of the Parthians is their contribution to the increase of geographical knowledge. In the passages quoted above (p. 110) Strabo indeed ascribes the addition to geographical knowledge to the Romans, but also to the Parthians. Another expression of their political power as compared to Rome is the friendship of the Medes towards the emperor in Rome at the same time as towards the Parthians (11.13.2, C 523).

In his treatment of the correlation between familiarity with topography and military success, Strabo cites a Roman defeat by the Parthians caused by the Romans' ignorance of the local layout (1.1.17, C 10). This example, although used to illustrate the matter under discussion, is evidence that the Parthians were an able and important enemy of Rome.[15]

At the same time he sets them within the general picture of nations who accept the power of Rome. Here the superiority of the Romans is undoubted:

> As for the Parthians, although they have a common border with the Romans and also are very powerful, they have nevertheless yielded so far to the pre-eminence of the Romans and of the rulers of our time that they have sent to Rome the trophies which they once set up as a memorial of their victory over the Romans, and,

what is more, Phraates has entrusted to Augustus Caesar his children
and also his children's children, thus obsequiously making sure of
Caesar's friendship by giving hostages; and the Parthians of today
have often gone to Rome in quest of a man to be their king, and
are now about ready to put their entire authority into the hands
of the Romans.

(6.4.2, C 288 and chapter 3, p. 103)

Pompeius Trogus, a contemporary of Strabo, who wrote a universal history
in forty-four books, drew a similar yet somewhat more extreme picture,
according to the summary of his work made by Justinus in the third century
CE.[16] Referring to the Parthians, Trogus wrote: 'now the rule (*imperium*) of
the east is theirs, as if there was a division of the world (*divisio orbis*) with
the Romans' (Justin 41.1.1).[17] Thus, the Parthians are a great power which
succeeded in confronting the Romans and reached the boundaries of the
world: 'only they from all nations were not only equal [to the Romans] but
also victors' (41.1.7) and: 'the power (*imperium*) of the Parthians extended
from the mountain Caucasus to the river Euphrates after many people were
reduced under their authority' (41.6.8). All these are common expressions
that also use some geographical indicators to describe an unprecedented
power of great political and spatial significance.

In this view, which in a way spoils the image of the Romans as sole
rulers of the *oikoumene*, Livy detected signs of opposition to Rome. He said
that the presentation of the Parthians as protagonists equal to the Romans
is typical of the 'silliest of the Greeks (*levissimi ex Graecis*) who exalt the
reputation even of the Parthians against the Romans' and 'are fond of
alleging that the Roman people would have been unable to withstand the
majesty of Alexander's name', and so they deprecate the power and glory
of the Romans.[18] Therefore the source for the concept of Parthian power as
it is presented by Trogus is thought to be Timagenes of Alexandria, who
had good reason for hostility towards Augustus and Rome and whose work
contained anti-Roman expressions (chapter 5, p. 135).[19]

Strabo either formed this notion about the powerful Parthians in response
to what he saw in the political situation in his time, or got it from another
source, possibly Timagenes himself. Apparently Strabo had heard of this
critical attitude which undermined the image of Rome as sole world power,
and chose to insert it in the *Geography*. It is also possible that both Timagenes
and Strabo absorbed the concept independently since it was probably current
in Rome side by side with the official version. Perhaps it existed only in Greek
circles, for we find references to it only in Greek sources such as Timagenes,
Strabo and Trogus, as is implied in Livy's words about the 'silly Greeks'.

The main point in the present discussion is that Strabo combines this
concept with the official image which identifies the borders of the Roman
empire with the boundaries of the *oikoumene*. His view as a whole is still

Romanocentric in the sense that he shows Parthian subordination, particularly to Augustus (chapter 3, p. 103).[20] What then is the explanation for the coexistence of two concepts which create a somewhat contradictory image of Rome, once as the sole power and again as a great power which has a significant rival – the Parthians? Syme detects in this discrepancy an indication of different parts of the *Geography* composed at different times. The change in concept would thus reflect a real change in the world political situation. While in the assumed earlier version of the work Parthia was inferior to the Romans, in the later edition it had regained power and became the rival of Rome.[21] Syme's supposition seems forced, first because it presupposes the existence of two versions of the *Geography* and second because it leaves untouched the primary difficulty that the final (theorized) edition of the work is lacking if Strabo had indeed left unedited traces of two contradictory political concepts from the earlier versions. Even if we observe some inconsistency in Strabo this does not seem to call for a theory of two versions of the work. I suggest another possibility, which I find again in what I consider the key to Strabo's approach to various problems, that is, his Greek background combined with his sojourn in Rome. It is more likely that he consciously presented these two concepts, one reflecting the official Roman image, the other touching on a marginal idea with anti-Roman undertones which was possibly extant in Greek circles. Strabo adopts mainly the official concept of Rome as sole world power and Augustus as its leader. But at the same time he reveals the parallel line of thought which probably went around in Rome, and stressed the presence of other powers on the periphery of the empire, powers which had strength and military abilities of their own. His bottom line, however, is that Rome surpasses all the rest, if not always in political power, certainly in its fame, which is recognized also by its rivals.

STRABO'S IDEA OF JUSTIFIED CONQUEST

Strabo evidently admired Rome for its power and political achievements and was fully aware of the new political and geographical age. But at the same time he resented the conquests and saw some bad consequences arising from the Roman military advance. The *Geography* reveals this double attitude. Strabo presents the Roman conquests as bearing peace and progress but at the same time he does not refrain from demonstrating their negative aspects and the unfavourable characteristics of the Roman conquerors.

As Strabo tells us, the condition of the regions of the *oikoumene* conquered by the Romans changed not only politically but also culturally. The Romans brought a different lifestyle with them and introduced Barbaric nations and tribes to their imperial administration and their language. Strabo's notions in these contexts are clearly affected by his ideas of Barbaric customs vs.

civilized norms of life (chapter 2, p. 75). He generally sees the Roman influence as beneficial, since Roman conduct was cultivated and refined in comparison with the life of the Barbarians, and it liberated the subdued peoples from their primitive customs:

> The Romans took over many nations that were naturally savage owing to the regions they inhabited . . . and thus not only brought into communication with each other peoples who had been isolated, but also taught the more savage how to live under forms of government (*politikos zen*).
>
> (2.5.26, C 127)

This idea of presenting higher standards of cultured life to wild nations, and thus improving their situation, is mentioned many times, particularly with reference to the tribes in Iberia and Gaul:

> The Turdetanians . . . have completely changed over to the Roman mode of life, not even remembering their own language any more . . . they are not far from being all Romans.
>
> (3.2.15, C 151)

> On account of the overmastery of the Romans, the Barbarians who are situated beyond the Massiliotes became more and more subdued as time went on, and instead of carrying on war have already turned to civic life and farming.
>
> (4.1.5, C 180)

> [The Cavari] are no longer Barbarians, but are, for the most part, transformed to the type of the Romans, both in their speech and in their modes of living, and some of them in their civic life as well.
>
> (4.1.12, C 186)

The Romans who carry their culture to conquered peoples perform a civilizing mission by implanting progressive characteristics in the place of former savage usages. Accordingly, poverty, anarchy, lack of commercial activity, wild and violent customs, give way to sociability, law and order, discipline, frugality, trade, art, literacy and urban life.[22]

Strabo perceives two principal expressions of savage life: incessant fighting and lack of social and political awareness due to the distance from other human beings. The contact with the Romans affects both: it ends the fighting by enforcing peace, and it brings Roman culture, causing people to organize themselves socially and politically until they become '*politikoi*':[23]

The quality of intractability and wildness in these people [of northern Iberia] has not resulted solely from their engaging in warfare, but also from their remoteness; for the journey to their country, whether by sea or by land, is long, and since they are difficult to communicate with, they have lost the instinct of sociability (*to koinonikon*) and humanity (*philanthropon*). They are less so now because of the peace and of the sojourns of the Romans among them. But wherever such sojourns are rarer the people are harder to deal with and more brutish (*theriodesteroi*) ... but now, as I have said, they have wholly ceased carrying on war, for Augustus Caesar subdued the Cantabrians and their neighbours ... Further, Tiberius, his successor, has set over these regions an army of three legions ... and it so happens that he already has rendered some of the people not only peaceable but civilised (*politikoi*) as well.

(3.3.8, C 156)

In some places the conquest put an end to security problems and brought with it order, peace and prosperity. This was a new situation for people who had no social or political organization and whose sole occupation was war. This idea is expressed many times in the *Geography*, in referring to various regions of the *oikoumene*, and is usually applied to a comparison between the bad situation in the past and the relief caused directly by the Roman presence:

Added to that, too, is the present peace, because all piracy has been broken up, and hence the sailors feel wholly at ease.

(3.2.5, C 144)

Most of the people had ceased to gain their livelihood from the earth, and were spending their time in brigandage and in continuous warfare both with each other and with their neighbours ... until they were stopped by the Romans, who humbled them.

(3.3.5, C 154)

[In Celtica] ... the men are fighters rather than farmers. But at the present time they are compelled to till the soil, now that they have laid down their arms.

(4.1.2, C 178)

In the past there was hostility between the Aedui and the Sequani; 'now, however, everything is subject to the Romans' (4.3.2, C 192). And in Arabia the threat of robbery 'has been broken up through the good government established by the Romans and through the security established by the Roman soldiers that are kept in Syria' (16.2.20, C 756). Thus, 'now that all peoples have been brought into subjection to a single power, everything is free from toll and open to all' (9.4.15, C 429). The confrontation of the past with the present is a constant theme which appears in other places as well, for instance 4.1.5, C 180–1; 10.4.9, C 477; and 14.5.6, C 671.

In accordance with this view, Strabo implies that friendship with the Romans is an asset that brings benefits to its seekers and that those who support them prosper and those who betray them are lost, for instance: 'As for Libya, so much of it as did not belong to the Carthaginians was turned over to kings who were subject to the Romans, and, if they ever revolted, they were deposed' (6.4.2, C 288); and 'Tenea prospered more than the other settlements, and finally even had a government of its own, and, revolting from the Corinthians, joined the Romans, and endured after the destruction of Corinth' (8.6.22, C 380); and again: 'Having shown a friendly disposition towards the Romans in the conduct of their government, the people of Prusa obtained freedom' (12.4.3, C 564).

Strabo is clearly affected by the view current in Augustan Rome that the time was an age of economic prosperity, of open boundaries, of peace and tranquillity, of order and licence to engage in agriculture and scholarship. It is notable that he presents the conquered regions of the west differently from those of the east. In referring to the eastern parts he mentions administrative improvements brought by the Romans, for instance in Egypt (17.1.13, C 798), and the defeat of pirates and robbers (14.5.6, C 671; 16.2.20, C 756), whereas his allusions to the western regions specify the cultural aspects of the conquest which brought some civilizatory changes (see quoted passages mainly from Books 3 and 4). He thus implies that the east had its own ancient culture before the Romans arrived, but the west was Barbaric, wild and uncivilized.

Strabo points out that the Romans indeed conquered vast areas and reached the boundaries of the *oikoumene*, but in some remote and deserted regions they chose to go no further. These unconquered regions produced no profit for them, either political, since they were mostly uninhabited, or economic, for they were bare and poor:

> for governmental purposes there would be no advantage in knowing such countries and their inhabitants, and particularly if the people live in islands which are of such a nature that they can neither injure nor benefit us in any way because of their isolation. For although they could have held even Britain, the Romans scorned to do so, because they saw that there was nothing at all to fear from the Britons, for they are not strong enough to cross over and attack us, and that no corresponding advantage was to be gained by taking and holding their country . . . and the unprofitableness of an occupation would be still greater in the case of the other islands about Britain.
>
> (2.5.8, C 115–16)

the Nomads, on account of their lack of intercourse with others, are of no use for anything and only require watching.

(6.4.2, C 288)[24]

Another revealing passage shows Augustus' considerations behind his decision to send an expedition led by Aelius Gallus to explore the tribes in Arabia and Ethiopia. Impelled by his wish to win the Arabians over to himself or to subjugate them, and influenced by their famous wealth, 'he expected either to deal with wealthy friends or to master wealthy enemies' (16.4.22, C 780).

Finally, in the concluding remarks of the work Strabo says that the Romans occupy the best parts of the *oikoumene* and he describes exactly what is inside the Roman world and what is outside, the latter being mostly uninhabited regions or else populated by Nomads and pirates (17.3.24, C 840 quoted above, p. 109). The idea behind all this is that conquest is not always to be welcomed and other considerations of utility and risk should be taken into account.

The concept of the Romans as carriers of peace and order, and especially the imposition of one rule uniting the entire world under itself, is based on Posidonian ideas with Stoic roots (chapter 2, p. 64). There are some indirect quotations from Posidonius, thus transmitting their factual content as well as their ideological meaning. Posidonius himself, as a disciple of Panaetius and as the head of the Stoic school in Rhodes who was also involved in Roman circles, had a clear view of the benefits of Roman rule. At the same time he contended that whereas it is right for the strong to rule over the weak, the former should not oppress the latter but rather should take care of them. Accordingly, Posidonius too, and after him Strabo, described the negative sides of the Roman conquest.

Strabo's enthusiasm about the power and size of the Roman empire and the enlightenment and peace brought by the Romans to the most distant parts of the *oikoumene* is not without reservations. The geographer presents also some negative and unfavourable sides of the Roman conquest. These include the corruption of provincial officials and the luxurious and extravagant habits of the Romans.

Like many other ancient authors, Strabo compliments simplicity and modesty and scorns luxury, greed and hypocrisy:

> Our mode of life has spread its change for the worse to almost all peoples, introducing among them luxury (*tryphe*) and sensual pleasure, and to satisfy these vices, base artifices that lead to innumerable acts of greed . . . much wickedness of this sort has fallen on the Barbarian peoples also, on the Nomads as well as the rest . . . the things that seem to conduce to gentleness of manner, corrupt morals and introduce cunning instead of straightforwardness.

(7.3.7, C 301)

Strabo finds negative features in his own culture.[25] These spoil innocent and simple people who were not 'contaminated' prior to their contact with the Greeks and the Romans. This notion probably derives from Strabo's Stoic inclinations and is further revealed in his reproach of riches and luxury: Sybaris, in southern Italy, was destroyed by luxury and *hybris* (6.1.13, C 263); the people of Tarentum suffered politically and socially because of overindulgence caused by prosperity (6.3.4, C 280); and luxurious living corrupted the Ptolemies in Egypt and caused failures in leadership and administration (17.1.11, C 796).

On one occasion Strabo presents the reverse idea, showing the Romans as moderators of licence and carriers of culture. The Campani tended towards lavishness and excessive extravagance because their region was very fertile. So much so that Hannibal said that they had turned his soldiers into women. But when the Romans took the region they brought back wisdom and moderation (5.4.13, C 250–1). This picture, which presents the Romans as a civilized and modest people, may be explained by the difference in period. In earlier times the Romans were moderate and cultured but in his own age Strabo witnessed moral decline among them. He argues that the destruction of Carthage and Corinth marked a turning point in Roman history. After these events morals declined because of the riches acquired by conquest (14.5.2, C 668).[26]

Strabo has decided views about the reasons for moral decline. In discussing spring waters in Caria which are thought to cause weakness and over-indulgence he says: 'It seems that the effeminacy of man is laid to the charge of the air or of the water; yet it is not these, but rather riches and wanton living, that are the cause of effeminacy' (14.2.16, C 656). He ascribes the change in morals to transformations in the mode of life. Although here he is not referring to the Romans, it may be possible to infer his ideas about the Roman decline which began with changes in values and certainly not with changes of climate.

Strabo depicts exceptional extravagance in a way which may be understood as more than a factual report. Referring to timber in Pisa which had been used for ship building, he says: 'at the present time most of it is being used up on the buildings at Rome, and also at the villas, now that people are devising palaces of Persian magnificence (*basileia Persika*)' (5.2.5, C 223). 'Persian magnificence' probably expresses criticism of Romans who indulge in extravagant styles.[27] This particular note is especially acerbic since the same wood served in the past to build ships for war and defence. Similarly, Strabo emphasizes the lavish and expensive (*polyteleis*) houses in Antium which were built as a resort for the Roman leaders (5.3.5, C 232) and mentions the luxurious construction in Tarracina (5.3.6, C 233). In Tusculum there are 'magnificently devised royal palaces' (5.3.12, C 239) and in Baiae 'palace on palace has been built' (5.4.7, C 246). The criticism is focused on central Italy, although there is no doubt that extravagant houses existed also in other places.

Strabo's numerous allusions to various marble quarries in the empire[28] may also represent an attempt to illustrate Roman extravagance in exploiting the rich material to satisfy the demand for lavish construction in the capital. He mentions several causes for the destruction of buildings in Rome: sudden collapse, fire and deliberate destruction. The latter is due to the incessant buying and selling of houses. People destroy old houses in order to build and buy new ones according to their taste (5.3.7, C 235). This is another indirect critical note. The fact that Strabo reverts several times in the *Geography* to his criticism of the Roman way of life probably indicates that his awareness of this subject was based on his philosophical inclinations and was not to be set aside for political considerations.[29]

Strabo criticizes the Romans also for their sacrilegious attitude towards Greek art, being particularly distressed by the behaviour of Roman generals who pillaged works of art and brought them to Rome (chapter 2, p. 81). Sculptures or pictures were wrenched from their original settings, mostly Greek sites. In some cases Strabo's opinion of these acts is evident. He mentions the grief of Polybius who described the destruction of Corinth and the shameless behaviour of the soldiers towards works of art and temple dedications. Polybius even saw Romans dropping pictures on the ground or using them as a table for a game of dice. Expressing similar feelings, Strabo calls Lucius Mummius, the consul of 146 BCE who destroyed and plundered the treasures of Corinth, 'arrogant[30] rather than fond of art' (8.6.23, C 381). Lucullus took the statues which Mummius brought to Rome in order to adorn the temple of Good Fortune that he built, promising to give them back after the dedication. He failed to do so, but told Mummius he could take them whenever he wanted; however, 'Mummius took it lightly for he cared nothing about them' (8.6.23, C 381). Strabo goes on to describe the plundering of Corinthian graves by Roman colonists who wanted to expose pieces of art in order to sell them in Rome. On another occasion Strabo mentions the statue of Aias taken by Antony from Rhoetium in order to delight Cleopatra, but Augustus gave it back (13.1.30, C 595). Thus the extent of Antony's crime is revealed, for he offended the gods by using sacred dedications for improper purposes, in contrast to the piety of Augustus who returned the statues (chapter 3, p. 99).[31]

The references to these acts of robbery reveal two characteristics that trouble Strabo. First, such doings reveal the disrespect of the Romans towards works of art, for they are too ignorant and rude to appreciate their value. Second, most of these works were dedications in temples and thus the men who stole them from their religious context offended the gods. Strabo's sensitivity probably derives from his Greek background. This is another instance where he expresses the discrepancy between the Greek and the Roman cultures (chapter 2, p. 79). It is also the background for his citing the words of Timagenes who thought that the plundering of temples by the Romans was a terrible thing which deserved suitable punishment;

Q. Caepio the Roman consul of 106 BCE who coveted sacred treasures from Tolossa 'ended his life in misfortunes for he was cast out by his native land as a temple-robber, and he left behind as his heirs female children only, who . . . became prostitutes . . . and therefore perished in disgrace' (4.1.13, C 188).[32] Again, contempt towards art and offending the gods are combined.

Other Roman targets for Strabo's criticism are corrupt officials and the failures of Roman leadership. Thus, he reports that the greed of the tax-contractors sent to the gold mines in the Alps caused turbulence among the native Salassi (4.6.7, C 205) and in this way the corruption of the Roman officials damaged the imperial system.[33]

In the description of the Achaean coastline Strabo refers to piracy at sea and to the abductions for ransom which constantly bother the inhabitants. He goes on to say that 'in those places which are ruled by local chieftains the rulers go to the aid of those who are wronged . . . but the territory that is subject to the Romans affords but little aid, because of the negligence (*oligoria*) of the governors who are sent there' (11.2.12, C 496), thus exposing a flaw in the Roman imperial system. He alludes also to earlier faults of leadership which caused further damage to the Roman name: 'On account of the bad managers which the city had at the time, the Romans do not seem to have remembered the favour of the Caeretani with sufficient gratitude' (5.2.3, C 220), thus referring to the Romans not acting properly towards the people of Caere who helped them during the Gallic invasion in the fourth century BCE. On one occasion Strabo indeed comes up with an explanation for the Romans' neglect: 'it is hard to condemn the Romans of negligence, since, being engaged with matters that were nearer and more urgent, they were unable to watch those that were farther away' (14.5.2, C 669). Still, the critical notions which accompany Strabo's main admiration of Rome can hardly be ignored.

ROMAN GEOGRAPHY, THE FORUM AUGUSTI, AND AGRIPPA'S PROJECT

Ever since the conquests of Julius Caesar Roman interest in geographical matters was on the increase. Caesar's invasion of Britain in 55–54 BCE engendered feelings of excitement about the new geographical and political horizons thus revealed. Riding on this tendency and aware of its impact on the people, Caesar incorporated in his *Bellum Gallicum* short geographical and ethnographical digressions describing the nature of the British Isle and the character of its inhabitants.[34] This added another dimension to the glory of the Romans, together with personal publicity for Caesar himself.

The new horizons and the awakening awareness of space and *oikoumene* probably account for the indications of a lively demand for geographical information in first-century BCE Rome.[35] Cicero planned to write a geographical treatise but was held back by the likelihood of criticism from Tyrannion the grammarian who was Strabo's teacher. This revelation, appearing in Cicero's letters to Atticus, implies that Tyrannion also had geographical tendencies, perhaps even a real plan to write a *Geography* himself (chapter 1, p. 9). This preoccupation of the two – Cicero and Tyrannion – though insufficiently defined, suggests that the idea of a *Geography* was considered in practical terms, and it has implications for a possible influence of Tyrannion the teacher on Strabo's enterprise.

Cicero was not alone in his geographical pretensions. Cornelius Nepos composed a geographical work which is quoted by Pomponius Mela and Pliny; the fragments show a survey of locations, distances and toponymy.[36] Varro Atacinus wrote a poem entitled *Chorographia* which described various parts of the world such as India and Egypt and referred to boundaries and general layout.[37] Crinagoras, a Greek poet of Strabo's period (chapter 5, p. 14), expressed in an epigram the practical potential of a geographical work as a useful tool for any tourist. Addressing Menippus of Pergamon who wrote a *periplous* he wrote: 'I am looking for a circumnavigator-guide . . . Menippus, give me a little help, my friend, writing me a scholarly Tour, my expert in all geography.'[38] Thus he reversed the purpose of the *periplous* (chapter 2, p. 40), not only to describe practical experience but also to contribute to it.

The upsurge of interest in geography also affected works of prose and poetry which were not primarily geographical. Catullus in his eleventh poem described the boundaries of the world and included recent Roman conquests in the Alps and in Britain. The poem refers to Catullus' friends, Furius and Aurelius, who are asked by the poet to deliver a message to his mistress. The first fourteen lines praise their loyalty to Catullus, for they will be willing to travel dangerously with him to the most remote places in the world: 'whether he makes his way even to distant India . . . or to Hyrcania and soft Arabia, or to the Sacae and archer Parthians, or those plains which sevenfold Nile dyes with his flood, or whether he will tramp across the high Alps, to visit the memorials of great Caesar, the Gaulish Rhine, the formidable Britons, remotest of men'.[39] Although this poem has no political significance, other than the implied glory of Julius Caesar, the poet borrows geographical vocabulary, so to speak, in order to transmit a poetic idea of extreme distances.

The *Carmen Saeculare* of Horace, written with the encouragement of Augustus himself, deliberately sets out to exalt him and accordingly alludes to recent remote conquests by naming various distant nations: 'Already the Parthian fears the hosts mighty on land and sea, and fears the Alban axes. Already the Indians and Scythians, but recently disdainful, are asking for our answer.'[40] The ethnographical names used are more or less similar to the geographical ones and correspond to the indicators of the boundaries of the *oikoumene*, for instance India and the Indians, and other nations and sites representing geographical extremities (chapter 2, p. 44).

Virgil expressed the idea of extensive conquests over many nations and regions in his description of a triumph for Augustus modelled on the shield of Aeneas. The variety of nations and the detailed description of their weapons add to the glory of the event. Note also the specific ethnonyms and toponyms which relate to remote peoples and boundary points:

> The conquered peoples move in long array in fashion and dress and arms as in tongues. Here Mulciber had portrayed the Nomad race and ungirt Africans, here the Leleges and Carians and quivered Gelonians. Euphrates moved now with humbler waves, and the Morini were there, furthest of mankind and the Rhine of double horn, the untamed Dahae, and Araxes chafing at his bridge.[41]

Finally, Livy's son is quoted by Pliny among his sources for the fifth and sixth books of the *Natural History*. Since these parts of the work deal with geographical matters it is possible that Livy's son also had some geographical composition in mind.[42]

The Greek-writing scholars who gathered in Rome and formed an intellectual circle that had social contacts with the Roman elite (chapter 5) also produced works associating geographical terms with the glory of the political strength of Rome. Like the Roman poets, they all referred particularly to remote geographical points or sites at the boundaries of the *oikoumene* in order to emphasize and exemplify the scale and dimension of recent achievements. Thus, Antipater of Thessalonike praised the victory of the young Gaius Caesar, Augustus' grandson, over the Parthians, and said that he carried Roman glory eastward 'to the Ocean'.[43] Crinagoras, the Greek poet from Mytilene, used geographical terminology in his epigrams for purposes of glorification. He applauded Germanicus for his victory over the Celts by calling as witnesses the Pyrenees and the Alps 'that face the Rhenus'.[44] He praised the conquests of Tiberius in Armenia and Germany and stressed that as a result Roman power lies between the rivers Araxes and Rhine – both indicators of the boundaries of the Cosmos, and the points at which the sun rises and sets, respectively.[45] This is an excellent example of the use of geographical terminology to indicate extensive space. In another epigram Crinagoras presented various sites and parts of nature which tell of the emperor's fame: 'the depths of Hyrcania's forest or outermost Soloeis and the fringe of the Libyan Hesperides' and finally 'the waters of the Pyrenees'.[46]

Even Augustus himself chose to combine political achievement with geographical data. In his *Res Gestae*, meant to present his personal contributions to the welfare and progress of Rome (chapter 3, p. 97), the emperor documented the regions and kingdoms subjected to Rome in his time. By enumerating in detail names of nations and of countries and other toponyms of rivers and towns, Augustus tried to create an impressive picture of new horizons also in the mind of the common beholder who was not well-informed enough to know exactly where each site was located.

Thus, it is quite evident that the interest of the Romans in geography grew towards the end of the republic and developed significantly under Augustus. This development went hand in hand with the new conquests and the expansion of the empire. And so, like a circular line in which cause and effect constantly switch roles, conquests stimulated geography and geography encouraged more conquests. Recent conquests confronted Rome with new regions and unknown nations, giving rise to a need for documentation of the new facts in order to laud and publicize these unprecedented political and military achievements. At the same time, the drive for new victories drew on geographical information which contributed to the assumption that the world was small enough to be subjected. An ideology of world conquest was born.[47]

It should be emphasized that the geographical interest of the Romans was not scientific either in goal or expression. In addition to its propaganda aspect, Roman geography was mainly practical in the sense that it was meant to give its readers useful information. This included itineraries, distances and descriptions which could help the traveller or tourist or military commander to find his way easily in a foreign land.[48] In this sense Strabo complies with Roman needs and tendencies by providing a practical geography in a descriptive and non-scientific genre. Compared to the scientific and accurate approach of Claudius Ptolemy who wrote in the second century CE, Strabo's *Geography* is more of a tourist-guide with political orientation. There is nothing discreditable about this. It is simply what Strabo meant to achieve (chapter 6, p. 154).

The enhanced Roman interest in geography with its political and practical tendencies was the stimulating factor behind certain literary and other productions in the Augustan Age. Strabo's project was one of these since it expressed the global politics conducted by Rome. Other examples are found in some visual monuments, constructed mainly in Rome, and the *Commentaries* of Agrippa which described the boundaries of the new empire. Some of the monuments erected in Augustan Rome used a geographical 'vocabulary' in a visual form and context. These elements began to appear towards the end of the Roman republic and in this way correspond to the similar developments in Roman literature indicated above.[49]

In 55 BCE a theatre with 10,000 seats was erected in the Campus Martius in commemoration of Pompey's third *triumphus* in 61 BCE. Part of the decoration was a series of personifications of conquered peoples. Suetonius refers to these '*simulacra gentium*' and Pliny gives Varro's testimony that the theatre was decorated with fourteen sculptures of different nations designed by Coponius.[50] These sculptures were probably accompanied by inscriptions with the names of the tribes. Plutarch remarks in his detailed description of the triumphal procession of Pompey (*Pomp.* 45.1–5) that: 'Inscriptions borne in advance of the procession indicated the nations over which he triumphed.' He gives a list of these nations, thus illustrating the achievement in detail. The captives led in the procession also reflected the success of the campaign since there were kings and hostages from various nations who, as one can imagine, were probably dressed in national costume, making the extent of the conquest almost visible.

> Others before him had celebrated three triumphs; but he celebrated his first over Libya, his second over Europe, and his last over Asia, so that he seemed in a way to have included the whole world in his three triumphs.[51]

The glory of Pompey the conqueror was thus enhanced by the captives, the inscriptions with the names of the nations, the booty and also by the sculptured titled portraits of the subdued nations.

This use of ethnic and geographic elements for propaganda purposes was extended and elaborated in the age of Augustus. At this time the emperor planned and constructed the Forum Augusti in the centre of Rome. The architectonic and sculptured composition of the Forum included also the *Porticus ad nationes* in which portraits (*simulacra*) of all the tribes conquered by Augustus were placed. Next to these or in addition to them were inscriptions with names of conquered nations.[52] That is, the conquered people were shown in two ways, epigraphically and visually, transmitting to the visitor a sense of the number and variety of the conquered, and through this, of the magnitude of the achievement led by Augustus. This effect is the same as the one Virgil created in the *Aeneid* quoted above, also referring to Augustus. Finally, at Augustus' funeral 'all the nations he had acquired, each represented by a likeness which bore some local characteristics' were carried.[53]

The sources indicate a similar exploitation of geographical and ethnographical details in a visual context outside Rome as well. One such monument was the Sebasteion in Aphrodisias which was dedicated to Augustus and contained a series of sculptures combined with bas-reliefs and inscriptions.[54] The full-length sculptures were of women in ethnic dress, and on their bases were portrait reliefs with typical ethnic physiognomy. Below these reliefs were inscriptions with the name of the specific nation or tribe thus represented. The peculiarity of this monument is the multiplicity of nations and the fact that all of them are mentioned in the *Geography* of Strabo and in the *Res Gestae* of Augustus.

Strabo himself describes a temple for Augustus near Lugdunum in Gaul, erected on the initiative of all the Gauls together: 'in it is a noteworthy altar, bearing an inscription of the names of the tribes, sixty in number; and also images (*eikones*) from these tribes, one from each tribe' (4.3.2, C 192).[55]

The effect of the multiplicity of names of conquered nations seems to have been exploited also in inscriptions meant to announce the emperor's victories. By enumerating tribal names in the form of lists, the inscription demonstrated the extent of the achievement. To this type belong the inscription on a triumphal monument in the Alps enumerating forty-five names of tribes subdued by Augustus[56] and an inscription from a triumphal arch in Segusio dedicated to Augustus and including the names of fourteen tribes who set up the monument.[57] Some milestones in Spain also used geographical terminology to aggrandize the extent of the conquests by indicating that Augustus had gone 'ad Oceanum', implying the uttermost boundary of the *oikoumene*.[58]

Such monumental expressions of the new geographical and political situation were exposed publicly in Rome and throughout the empire. These were mainly triumphal arches depicting relief images of foreign races and nations offering their submission to a Roman general;[59] trophies indicating specific victories also by depicting Barbaric captives;[60] and coins using symbols of the *oikoumene* and personifications of conquered peoples.[61]

Among the special projects created in Augustan Rome and using geography for political purposes was the one initiated by Agrippa. The exact nature of this project is unknown, but several literary references throw some light on its creation and political context. Pliny provides the clearest testimony to the nature of this undertaking:

> Agrippa was a very painstaking man and also a very careful geographer; who therefore could believe that when intending to set before the eyes of Rome a survey of the world he made a mistake and with him the late lamented Augustus? for he [Augustus] completed the portico that had been begun by his [Agrippa's] sister[62] in accordance with the design (*destinatio*) and memoranda (*commentarii*) of Marcus Agrippa.[63]

Pliny's testimony puts forward several facts about Agrippa's plan:

a   Agrippa somehow depicted the world so that Rome could see it.
b   This 'world' was intended to stand in a portico.
c   Agrippa attached a written work (*commentarii*) to this project.
d   Augustus completed this project which was begun by Agrippa's sister.

Until recently Agrippa's project has been widely accepted to have consisted of both written commentaries and a map describing the *oikoumene*. This conjecture was based mainly on Pliny's statement that Agrippa intended 'to set before the eyes of Rome a survey of the world', which was understood as a visual means of showing the *oikoumene* publicly and therefore as a sort of large-scale map. However, the exact nature of this supposed map has never been defined, though some suggestions as to its size and shape have been put forward.[64]

Brodersen has recently proposed a rather convincing and surprisingly simple solution to this much-discussed and evasive Augustan monument.[65] He showed that most probably there was no map at all, and the project first initiated by Agrippa involved only the *Commentarii*, which presented in a monumental inscription posted at the portico lists of regions, cities and distances, as well as mountains, rivers, islands, and even names of tribes and nations, thus presenting 'before the eyes of Rome' the entire *oikoumene*. This was similar in form and in purpose to Augustus' own *Res Gestae* and to the monumental inscription near Lugdunum, both publicly transmitting lists of a geographical and ethnographical nature meant to express political achievement.

Pliny himself mentions Agrippa more than thirty times as his source for distances and geographical measures.[66] He probably saw the public list which supplied him with information about regions outside the Roman empire as well.

Some Strabonian allusions imply the geographer's possible acquaintance with this public representation of the world. He alludes to a chorographic list or tablet (*chorographikos pinax*[67]), which includes various details such as 'continents, nations, favourable positions of cities' as well as 'the multitude of islands scattered both in the open seas and along the whole seaboard' (2.5.17, C 120). This remark conveys the impression that Strabo saw this tablet himself.

Further, Strabo refers to a '*chorographia*' that includes distances in Roman miles (*miliasmo*) and divisions according to regions (6.2.1, C 266). He also alludes to a certain chorographer in five different contexts: length and width of Sardinia and Corsica (5.2.7, C 224); the distance of the shortest passage from Libya to Sardinia (5.2.8, C 225); the circumference of the bay of Tarentum by sailing (6.1.11, C 261); the distances between the Liparean islands and between them and Sicily (6.2.11, C 277); the distance between Brundisium to Garganum and from there to Ancona (6.3.10, C 285). All distances are given in Roman miles (*milia*), and all the references to the chorographer occur in the description of the Italian regions.

On five other occasions Strabo uses Roman miles without referring specifically to the chorographer: the distance between the temple of Heracles to Gades (3.5.3, C 169); distances between various sites in north Italy and south Gaul (4.1.3, C 178–9); the distance between Ticinum and Oceleum in north Italy (5.1.11, C 217); the length of the Via Appia from Rome to Brundisium (6.3.7, C 283); the length of the road from Apollonia to Macedonia which is marked with milestones (7.7.4, C 322–3). Here, too, four out of five deal with Italian regions, mostly northern, and the fifth with the Ocean (i.e. the Atlantic) beyond the Pillars of Heracles.

In two cases the source for Strabo's information is Polybius. In 6.3.10, C 285 Strabo cites Polybius as saying that the distances in the region of

Iapygia are indicated in miles (*memiliasthai*). In 7.7.4, C 322–3 he quotes Polybius' calculation of the Roman mile in Greek measures, and also gives, in Polybius' name, distances in miles.[68] The source for the other instances where Strabo uses miles is unknown. However, there are several possibilities if we accept the assumption that the original source was Roman. It could again be Polybius as an intermediate between Strabo and a Roman source, and Strabo simply did not mention Polybius in these cases. The source may be the chorographer who used Roman miles and who was quoted in other references. Finally, it could be another Roman source that Strabo does not name specifically. Naturally, it is easier and more probable to assume that the source is one that Strabo exploits on other occasions citing Roman miles. Therefore, the possibility that the source is Polybius or the chorographer is preferable to the notion of a third source not mentioned specifically even once.

The chorographer is important in Strabo's eyes, for he gives him a title: 'the chorographer (*ho chorographos*)'. From other references in a different context we learn that Strabo's use of the article with a noun adds a meaning of importance, fame and greatness. For instance, he remarks that in the past people thought that the Black Sea was the largest sea in the world and called it 'the Pontos', that is 'the sea', just as people call Homer 'the poet' (1.2.10, C 21). We may therefore conclude that the chorographer was indeed the greatest and best-known of chorographers and perhaps the only one.

It is thus clear that Strabo saw a certain chorographic tablet and that he alludes to a chorographic work written by a chorographer. The only doubt is the exact identification of the chorographer with Agrippa, and the chorographic work with Agrippa's *Commentaries*. I incline to accept the suggestion that Strabo indeed saw Agrippa's tablet laid out in Rome.[69] First, the chorography in Strabo is clearly Roman since it applies Roman distances. Second, the proposed time when Strabo composed his *Geography*[70] and his probable sojourn in Rome coincide with the completion and public presentation of the tablet. What seems to run counter to this assumption is the fact that Strabo does not allude specifically to Agrippa's project and does not ascribe it to its initiator; however, as we have seen, Agrippa himself did not live to complete the monumental plan which was executed by his sister and by Augustus himself.

5

GREEK SCHOLARS IN AUGUSTAN ROME

Roman imperial expansion into remote parts of the *oikoumene* and the peace that prevailed under Augustus enabled Greek scholars as well as other inhabitants of the empire to travel widely and to visit various intellectual and commercial centres, mainly Alexandria, Athens and Rome itself. In the last decades of the republic a circle of scholars emerged who taught Roman aristocrats philosophy, rhetoric and grammar, bringing the influence of Greek culture and values to bear on the higher echelons of society. This social and intellectual phenomenon flourished under the auspices of Augustus and within the cosmopolitan atmosphere of Rome at the time, but it went back to the second century, when the Romans became well acquainted with Greek culture through the wars in the east and the sojourn of Roman generals and governors in eastern regions. Thus there were several waves of Greek scholars arriving in Rome, some of them as prisoners of war, e.g. after the capture of Tarentum in 209 BCE, after the third Macedonian war in 168, and after the suppression of the Achaean revolt in 146. Other waves followed the persecution and expulsion of Alexandrian scholars by Ptolemy VIII Euergetes in 145, the annexation of Pergamon in 133, and the victories of Sulla and Pompey in the east in the first century BCE.[1]

Strabo, himself a Greek scholar who spent many years in Rome, was well aware of the unique and colourful human mixture created in the city and of the opportunities to meet people from all over the empire. Referring to the scholarly reputation of Tarsus, he reflects on the social and intellectual atmosphere in Augustan Rome: 'it is Rome that is best able to tell us the number of learned men (*philologoi*) from this city, for it is full of Tarsians and Alexandrians' (14.5.15, C 675).

In the *Geography* Strabo alludes to many of his contemporaries, scholars from various fields of knowledge, most of whom visited Rome at some stage of their lives. He knew them at least by name and may have met some of them personally. With additional information on these scholars, their social relations with both Greeks and Romans and their scholarly interests, a composite picture emerges of the literary circles gathered in Rome. The Greeks who lived in the capital for some while usually knew certain of their fellows and at the same time established relations with well-known Romans. This resulted in a large network, so to speak, of associations on a social and intellectual basis, reflecting the cosmopolitan character of Augustan Rome and enhanced by the peaceful conditions of those years. Within this larger milieu there were probably smaller circles that crystallized according to scholarly field, according to place of origin in the east, or around the same Roman patron, while some groups overlapped, so that a Greek scholar or a Roman general could have contacts in more than one society.

The number of Greek intellectuals who spent some time in Augustan Rome far exceeds those mentioned by Strabo. There were obviously some whom he did not meet, or at least decided for some reason not to include in his work. Nevertheless, the group of learned men whom Strabo does cite is quite impressive in size and background, for it is comprised of more than forty Greek scholars from various fields of knowledge, mainly philosophy, grammar, rhetoric and historiography. Strabo does not refer to these intellectuals as a group in a specific context; their names are scattered throughout the *Geography*, many of them introduced as famous natives of various eastern cities (chapter 2, p. 79).

In this chapter the scholars are presented according to their intellectual interests, thus showing the variety and complexity of this social phenomenon. I shall give precedence to the historians, first because Strabo himself started his career in this discipline, so that knowing his peers would to some extent have influenced his attitudes as a Greek historian dealing with current affairs. Second, because relatively large portions of their writings have survived, making them more significant simply because we know more about them. Three especially stand out, Dionysius of Halicarnassus, Nicolaus of Damascus, and Timagenes of Alexandria. All three, like Strabo, were born in eastern cities, were educated in Greek traditions, came to Rome at some stage in their lives and established social relationships with the Roman aristocracy. All of them refer in their writings to Rome and the expansion of the empire though each does this in his own way.

The historian Dionysius, a native of Halicarnassus (14.2.16, C 656), says in the introductory remarks to his *Roman Antiquities* that he arrived in Rome in the middle of the 187th Olympiad (30/29 BCE), that is, shortly before Strabo's second visit to the city.[2] He remained there for twenty-two years during which time he conversed with notable Romans, some of whom became his friends, acquired students and patrons and read some Roman works (*AR* 1.7.2–3). This social and cultural experience influenced him so much that he decided to record in Greek the history of Rome, a work filled with his unreserved admiration for Rome and its rule. Dionysius was motivated by his sense of gratitude towards the city which gave him an education and other benefits, but he stresses that he writes according to the standards of justice and truth and does not employ flattery (*AR* 1.6.5). He declares that a good historian wishing to transmit excellent works to posterity should focus on excellent topics that will benefit the reader and be very useful to him (*AR* 1.1.2). Hence he himself chose to describe the power and prosperity of Rome, realizing that Roman superiority was an unprecedented phenomenon in terms of duration and extension (*AR* 1.2.1). He also wishes to counteract the prejudices of certain Greeks who think that the Romans are of Barbaric and nameless origin and that fortune has smiled on them by mistake and not as of their due (*AR* 1.4.1–5.3).

Dionysius' admiration of the Romans is apparent in his introductory remarks describing the vast regions on land and sea ruled by Rome:

> Rome rules every country that is not inaccessible or uninhabited, and she is mistress of every sea . . . except that part of it which is not navigable; she is the first and only state recorded in all time that ever made the risings and settings of the sun the boundaries of her domination. Nor has her supremacy been of short duration, but more lasting than that of any other city or kingdom.
>
> (*AR* 1.3.3)[3]

In his own time, he says, Rome governs the world and no nation denies her right to legitimate rule or challenges her power (*AR* 1.3.5). Dionysius also thinks that more excellent and noble men have lived in Rome than ever in any Barbaric or Greek city (*AR* 1.5.3).

Dionysius' intended audience was the Greek reader in whose language no comprehensive work had been composed on Roman antiquities and who was mistaken in his opinion about the modest beginnings of the empire (*AR* 1.4.1; 1.5.4). The first founders of Rome, he maintains, were of Greek descent, thus trying to appeal particularly to his Greek audience.[4] His attitude towards Rome and the Romans seems more extreme than Strabo's for he presents Roman qualities as superior to Greek and describes the Romans as gentle conquerors for they did not destroy conquered cities and they did not enslave citizens and kill the males, but founded colonies and bestowed Roman citizenship on other people, unlike the Greeks who were very strict about citizenship and did not bestow it easily (*AR* 2.16.1–19.5). Nevertheless he mentions the moral decline in later Roman generations, indicating the turning point as the time of the Gracchi.[5]

Dionysius was an important critic of rhetoric and presented his opinions in a series of shorter works. In these treatises he also expressed his view of Rome as a carrier of progress, prosperity and justice.[6] Surveying the philosophical basis of oratory, he points out the decline in the quality of speeches, which have become shallow and extravagant. At the same time he perceives a return to the ancient style, encouraged by the world domination of Rome and by its excellent leaders and contends that proficiency in rhetoric is not merely a technical skill but contributes also to practical purposes in developing and implementing political rights.

Dionysius' point of view and his reference to Roman achievements in the Augustan period is set against his universalistic outlook. He does not emphasize Augustus' character and does not compliment him personally, but rather discusses the combination of Greek moral principles with Roman political experience, together forming the basis of the empire. He is more interested in the social and cultural meaning of the new situation and less in the personality and the ideology of the *princeps*, Augustus. Here his approach differs slightly from the attitude of Nicolaus of Damascus and Timagenes of Alexandria, both of whom composed biographies of Augustus (below). He does, however, emphasize the return to moral and religious values, the military and cultural accomplishments and the unity of this world empire, thus complying with Augustan propaganda and the general tendencies of the Latin literature of the time.[7]

In his rhetorical writings Dionysius addressed some of his friends, patrons and pupils, thus revealing part of his social milieu, even if we cannot identify all his interlocutors. He called the philosopher and historian Caecilius of Calacte his dear friend, and dedicated his work on Thucydides to Q. Aelius Tubero, possibly the consul of 11 BCE who was an historian and jurist. Metilius Rufus and his father, 'my most esteemed friend', Romans otherwise unknown, are also among intimates who figure in his shorter works.[8] Dionysius had contacts with Greeks such as Cn. Pompeius Geminus, and Ammaeus, to both of whom he addressed a letter, and he also hints at scholarly relations with a certain Demetrius and Zeno.[9]

Another Greek scholar of major importance spent some time in Rome, absorbing its influence on his writings and his social relations. Nicolaus of Damascus was the loyal adviser and friend of King Herod of Judaea.[10] As his position required, he visited Rome several times and appeared twice before Augustus on diplomatic missions to promote Herod's interests, first in 8 BCE and then in 4 BCE, accompanying Archelaus, the king's son.[11] At this time Strabo was again in the city after the years he had spent in Egypt with Gallus. Nicolaus' visits brought him closer to Roman culture and to the emperor, with whom he eventually established a friendly relationship. He used to send the emperor Syrian dates that Augustus called 'Nicolaean dates' to mark his fondness of the fruit and of his friend from Damascus.[12]

Nicolaus was a very prolific writer and composed several works of varied nature.[13] His major production was a universal history, perhaps the longest ever written in Greek, in 144 books, from the earliest times to the death of Herod. The fragments show that it probably began with some mythological details. Among its topics were the history of Assyria, Babylonia and Media (*FGrH* 90 F 1–6); Greece to the Trojan War (F 7–14); the history of Syria and Judaea (F 17–20); and early Roman history (F 69–70). Rome, therefore, had a place in this work but as part of the general picture in a universal context. Josephus, who used it as a source, said that Nicolaus included only details intended to flatter and to benefit the king, sometimes covering up his misdeeds. In this sense he did not write a history for the general public but one to make propaganda for Herod.[14]

Another work by Nicolaus, important in the Augustan context, was his *Life of Augustus* based on the emperor's autobiography and surveying his actions until 25 BCE (*FGrH* 90 F 125–30). Nicolaus' attitude towards Roman affairs is especially apparent in this biography. The very nature of such a work was to focus on the character of the emperor and thus to highlight his importance. Further, Nicolaus did not include mere factual biographical details but also disclosed his admiration of his subject matter. He dwelt on Augustus' good qualities, already revealed in his youth: he was strong in body yet gentle in soul, he respected the law and was pious towards the gods (*FGrH* 90 F 127, 4–10), he was moderate and talented (F 128, 28–30), wise and philanthropic (F 125, 1). Nicolaus presents the moral and legal justification for Augustus' reign: he inherited Julius Caesar's position and therefore the rule is his 'by nature and by law' (F 130, 53). He describes Augustus' rule over the world as an unprecedented phenomenon: people on islands, in continents, in cities and of nations around the world honour him with sacrifices and temples and glorify his generosity. At first they did not even know his name but they soon became his subjects, first surrendering to his power and then acknowledging him of their own free will because Augustus brought security to the world and 'made the boundaries of the Roman kingdom longer than ever' (F 125, 1).

Apart from the contents of the biography, there are indications of Nicolaus' appreciation of Rome and its accomplishments in a detail supplied by Josephus. He says that Nicolaus joined Herod when he sailed to Ionia in order to convince Agrippa to come to Judaea. On this occasion the Ionian Jews addressed Agrippa in the presence of Herod and protested against their usage by the Greeks who restricted their freedom to conduct themselves according to their religious laws and treated them harshly in matters of taxes and military service. Nicolaus presented the Jews' claims to Agrippa and at the end of his speech Agrippa granted the Jews their privileges. Nicolaus' speech, as Josephus cites it, reveals his respect and admiration for Roman rule:

> Is there any people or city or national community for which the protection of your empire and the power of the Romans have not come to be the greatest of blessings? Would anyone want to revoke the favours coming from here? No one, not even a madman.
>
> (*AJ* 16.38–9)[15]

Strabo quotes Nicolaus' testimony of his encounter in Antiochia, near Daphna, with an Indian embassy on its way to Augustus in Rome (15.1. 72–3, C 719 quoted partially in chapter 3, p. 134). The detailed description of the ambassadors, their appearance, their offerings and their actions, as well as Strabo's use of the verb 'he said (*ephe*)', may imply a direct relation-ship between himself and Nicolaus, who perhaps told the geographer the whole story in person.[16]

A third Greek Augustan author was Timagenes, who was brought to Rome from Alexandria as a captive of Gabinius in 55 BCE, that is, more than a decade before Strabo arrived there for the first time.[17] Timagenes was freed by Faustus Sulla, and gradually made his way in Roman society, eventually establishing a school of rhetoric. Seneca the elder gives a short and compre-hensive description of Timagenes' character, psychology and career:

> a man of acid tongue, and over-free with it, because . . . he hadn't been free himself over a long period. From a captive he had become a cook, from a cook a chair-carrier, from being a chair-carrier he had struggled into the friendship of the emperor. But he despised both his present and his past fortunes to such an extent that, when the emperor, angry with him on many counts, barred him from his house, he burned the histories he had written recounting the emperor's deeds, as though barring him, in his turn, from access to his genius. He was a fluent and witty man, who came out with many outrageous but attractive things.
>
> (*Con.* 10.5.22)[18]

Timagenes did indeed manage to find his way into the highest circles of society but his relationship with Augustus was evidently tense, his sharp tongue causing the emperor to be offended by the gossip he spread about his family and to prevent Timagenes from re-entering his house. Timagenes' hot temper made him destroy the biography he had written of Augustus, and he went to live with the statesman and historian Asinius Pollio.[19]

The incident marring the relationship between Augustus and Timagenes, and the other pieces of information show that the Alexandrian was hot-tem-pered and did not hesitate to express his hostility towards Rome and Augustus. Two fragments of his historical work reveal criticism of Roman greed. He presents Pompey as motivated in his military actions by consider-ations of profit, an accusation rejected by Plutarch who quotes Timagenes (*FGrH* 88 F 9). Strabo himself quotes a notion of Timagenes concerning Q. Servilius Caepio, consul 106 BCE, who coveted Greek sacred treasures and eventually endured family disgrace (4.1.13, C 188 and chapter 4, p. 121). Timagenes' hostile attitude towards the Romans emerges again in the elder Seneca's claim that Timagenes, 'who had a grudge against Rome and her prosperity', said that he was sorry Rome was damaged by fire because he knew that instead of the destroyed buildings, others, better and more beautiful, would be constructed.[20] Livy's allusion to the 'silliest of the Greeks who exalt the reputation even of the Parthians against the Romans'[21] is taken by some scholars as alluding to Timagenes. As Seneca suggested, perhaps the circumstances in which Timagenes came to Rome as a prisoner of war were the cause of his bitterness towards the Romans, although Polybius, who arrived there in similar circumstances and Tyrannion, Strabo's teacher, both reacted differently.

The few fragments of Timagenes' writings, as far as they reveal anything at all, show that he too wrote a universal history from the earliest times to Julius Caesar, including references to ethnographic, geographic and cultural matters.[22] The fact that he composed a biography of Augustus, which must have been laudatory, indicates one of the features of the literary activity of the age, influenced by the actions of one central and significant character. Timagenes' occupation with Roman subjects, and particularly with the character of Augustus, even if he himself expressed a critical opinion, again shows the importance of these matters in the writings of the Greek scholars in Rome in the Augustan age.[23]

Dionysius, Nicolaus and Timagenes were all 'politically obsessed',[24] by their awareness, each in his own way, of Roman power and of the character of Augustus. Together with Strabo, all four demonstrate Greek pride, writing in Greek for a Greek audience, and expressing ideas and messages with a Greek orientation.[25] Like Strabo, Dionysius emphasized the pragmatic aspect of his writing and the benefit he hoped to bestow on his readers. This approach was probably influenced by Polybius' procedure, but the Roman context in which they all composed their works naturally affected their practical orientation.

Other Greek historians, contemporaries of Strabo, are also mentioned in the *Geography*. Theophanes of Mytilene, 'the most illustrious of all the Greeks' (13.2.3, C 618), was a leading statesman in Mytilene.[26] His good and virtuous qualities made him a friend of Pompey whom he accompanied in the Third Mithridatic War and in other campaigns (11.5.1, C 503; 13.2.3, C 617). In return, Pompey granted Theophanes Roman citizenship and in a ceremony held before the army Theophanes was named after his patron Gnaeus Pompeius Theophanes. Arriving in Mytilene, Theophanes' city, Pompey gave the inhabitants their freedom as a tribute to his Greek friend. The close relationship with Pompey influenced Theophanes' historiographical writings and he recorded Pompey's campaigns, comparing him to Alexander the Great. Cicero also knew Theophanes but did not approve of his adoption of Balbus of Gades. After his death in 36 BCE Theophanes was honoured in Greece as a god for his actions and virtues. Strabo says that his son, Marcus Pompeius, was appointed by Augustus as procurator of Asia and is 'now' considered one of the prime friends of Tiberius (13.2.3, C 618).

The social position and scholarly interests of Theopompus of Cnidus were very similar to those of Theophanes.[27] Theopompus was a friend of Julius Caesar and had great influence with him (14.2.15, C 656). He too received Roman citizenship and appears in several inscriptions from Cnidus and Rhodes as Gaius Julius Theopompus. When in Asia, Caesar spared the people of Cnidus, Theopompus' homeland, and gave them their freedom in order to delight his friend and protégé. Theopompus visited Cicero in Tusculum in 45 BCE and gave him news of Rome, and it is Cicero who tells us of Theopompus' later destiny: he was expelled by Trebonius and found refuge in Alexandria. Theopompus' scholarly interests focused on collections of myths and legends. Artemidorus, Theopompus' son (14.2.15, C 656), an orator and teacher of Greek philosophy, still maintained close relations with Caesar.[28] Some sources contend that Artemidorus tried to warn Caesar before his assassination through a written note exposing the plot, others say that he rushed at the wounded and dying Caesar.

The same pattern of relationship between a Greek historian and a famous Roman may be ascribed to Hypsicrates of Amisus. He too was probably a friend of Caesar, who gave Amisus its freedom.[29] Hypsicrates is quoted twice by Strabo, as his source for the story of the fortification of the Chersonessus against the Scythians by Asander (7.4.6, C 311), and for the habits of the Amazons (11.5.1, C 504), and he was probably also a source for Strabo's earlier historical work.[30] Hypsicrates, who lived to be ninety-two, wrote also on Homer and Hesiod and dealt with the cultural bond between Greece and Rome through etymologies of Greek and Latin words, tracing the Greek roots for Latin, as did Tyrannion the grammarian, Strabo's teacher. Hypsicrates' works are thus another example of Greek scholarly discussions influenced by Roman issues.

Strabo mentions several Greek orators who were his contemporaries. Although some of these came to Rome before Augustus' principate, they reflect the same social and intellectual phenomemon. Among them was Aristodemus of Nysa, Strabo's teacher (chapter 1, p. 8). Aristodemus was an eminent scholar and the head of schools of rhetoric in both Nysa and Rhodes, but he too spent some time in Rome teaching the sons of Pompey (14.1.48, C 650). In his writings, focusing on Homeric studies, he expressed the close relationship between Greeks and Romans by tracing the roots of Homer, the greatest Greek poet, to Rome.

Potamon and Lesbocles, both from Mytilene (13.2.3, C 617), were two other orators known to Strabo.[31] Potamon came to Rome as a member of the Mytilenic embassies together with the poet Crinagoras (below) in order to renew the amity between their city and the Roman empire. He appeared twice before Julius Caesar, in 47 and in 45 BCE, and once before Augustus, in 26 BCE. Potamon remained in Rome and became famous for his oratory and for his self restraint, for, according to Seneca the elder, after his son's funeral he immediately continued to lecture in his school, unlike his fellow-citizen Lesbocles who also lost his son but closed his school and never delivered a speech again.[32] The story about the two orators is rather intimate, and of course carries a moral, but it shows that the elder Seneca knew them personally and that they were celebrated in Rome. Potamon wrote a history of Alexander, a work *On the Perfect Orator*, and poems in honour of Brutus and Caesar, thus both absorbing and expressing the Roman atmosphere.[33]

Strabo knew the two most celebrated Greek orators, each of whom represented a different approach to rhetoric. These were Apollodorus of Pergamon and Theodorus of Gadara (13.4.3, C 625; 16.2.29, C 759).[34] Apollodorus, both in his written work on rhetoric and in teaching at his school, advocated firm argument and restrictive rules whereas Theodorus' principles were flexible composition and free organization of speech. Quintilian, who mentions them frequently, emphasized the difference between the two, which was more than mere personal preference: 'These rhetoricians taught different systems, and two schools have arisen known as the Apollodoreans and the Theodoreans, these names being modelled on the fashion of certain schools of philosophy' (*Inst.* 3.1.18).[35] Thus, as with the philosophical schools, their respective theories were manifested also in their definition of oratory and its purpose, Apollodorus focusing on the persuasion of judges, Theodorus including in his definition notions of art, invention and ornament.[36]

Apollodorus taught both Greeks and Romans, some of whom were central figures in Rome. Dionysius Atticus of Pergamon, a sophist, historian and speech writer, was one of the students who published Apollodorus' ideas. Caecilius of Calacte later became a famous orator in his own right and was also a friend of Dionysius of Halicarnassus, thus playing a double role, so to speak, in the Augustan social structure. Another example of the composite pattern of interrelations is C. Valgius Rufus, who was the Roman advocate of Apollodorus' theories and was also rather closely associated with Horace, being part of the poetic circle promoted by Maecenas, Augustus' friend and counsellor.[37] The most famous and distinguished of all Apollodorus' students was Augustus himself, who studied with the Greek scholar before he became *princeps*, both men developing a deep friendship.[38] Apollodorus also addressed written work to C. Matius, one of Augustus' intimates, and probably wrote a letter to the poet Domitius Marsus, two Romans active in Augustan Rome.[39]

Theodorus, younger than Apollodorus but still his scholarly opponent, taught the young Tiberius in Rome around 30 BCE.[40] Another student of his was the Greek orator Hermagoras, who lived in Rome at the time of Tiberius.[41] In Rome Theodorus surpassed Potamon and Antipatros in his orations; this comparison appears in the Suda and perhaps implies a connection between the three. He later founded a school of rhetoric in Rhodes. Theodorus composed the historiographical works *On Coele-Syria* and *On History*, which might have been of some interest to Strabo as sources for his earlier *History* as well as for his *Geography*, though he does not specify them as such.

Strabo mentions several other contemporary Greek orators, famous in their profession, who did not live in Rome but had Roman connections on an administrative basis as advocates of the interests of their homelands. They are not part of the social and intellectual milieu described in these pages but at the same time they seem to round out the picture of Strabo's intellectual world at the time.

Aeschines of Miletus (14.1.7, C 635), a contemporary of Cicero, had a rapid and lively style of oration.[42] Strabo says that he spoke freely and carelessly in the presence of Pompey and was therefore deported and died in exile shortly before 46 BCE. Euthydemus from Mylasa in Caria was very wealthy and respected throughout Asia Minor (14.2.24, C 659). He held an influential position in his city and on meeting Cicero in Ephesus promised to send a Mylasan embassy to arrange financial matters.[43] Euthydemus' rival in Mylasa was Hybreas, 'the greatest orator of my time' (13.4.15, C 630).[44] Strabo implies two possible sources of information on Hybreas, both oral. These are Hybreas' own stories in his school and the tales told by Hybreas' fellow citizens. This may indicate a personal acquaintance with Hybreas himself or at least with his social surroundings. Hybreas' father left him a mule and a driver. After studying with Diotrephes the sophist in Antiochia, he returned to Mylasa and was an *agoranomos*. Not earning enough he turned to politics, where he was successful, and acted in what he saw, perhaps mistakenly, as the best interests of his city. He encouraged the inhabitants to revolt against Labienus, thus causing the Romans to turn against Mylasa. Hybreas himself fled to Rhodes and Labienus plundered his magnificent house, but later he came back and restored his house and his city's fortunes. Hybreas became a famous orator in Rome, using his talents to protect Mylasa from the burden of Roman taxes (13.4.15, C 630; 14.2.24, C 659–60). Another orator, Zenon of Laodicea, was the father of Polemon king of Pontus and husband of Queen Pythodoris (12.8.16, C 578), and like Hybreas he too caused his city to revolt against Roman occupation (14.2.24, C 660).

Several philosophers from different schools are known to have come to Rome at the time and to have established relationships with fellow Greeks and with Roman notables. Some of them became teachers and intimates of renowned Romans. Such was Athenodorus Cordylion of Tarsus, a Stoic, who was the first head of the library of Pergamon, visited Cato the younger in 67 and stayed with him as his house philosopher (14.5.14, C 674).[45] Another Stoic, Antipater of Tyre (16.2.24, C 757), a disciple of Stratocles of Rhodes, studied with Panaetius and Antidotus.[46] In Rome he, too, befriended Cato who was influenced by the Stoa. Along the same pattern, Nestor of Tarsus, an academic philosopher, was the teacher of Marcellus, Octavia's son and Augustus' nephew and his intended heir up to his sudden death (14.5.14, C 674).[47] He inherited Athenodorus' position as the head of the local government in Tarsus and was respected also by the Roman administrators.

The Greek teachers of Augustus himself stand out among other philosophers in Rome. Among them are Strabo's own teacher, the peripatetic Xenarchus of Seleucia, and the Stoic Arius of Alexandria (14.5.4, C 670).[48] Arius wrote a letter of consolation addressed to Livia on the death of her son

Drusus in 9 BCE, suggesting that he had a special relationship with Augustus' family. Another teacher of Augustus was Strabo's friend Athenodorus of Tarsus (chapter 1, p. 10), who also knew Cicero and dedicated one of his works on Tarsus to Octavia, Augustus' sister.

Athenaeus the Peripatetic of Seleucia, a fellow citizen of Xenarchus, was politically active in Seleucia and later became a friend of L. Licinius Murena.[49] When Murena was accused of *ambitus*, Athenaeus fled with him, was caught but was released after being proved innocent. Athenaeus established social relationships with prominent Romans, but later returned to his homeland. There he was welcomed by his fellow citizens but was killed when his house collapsed in the night (14.5.4, C 670).

One of the most influential philosophers in Rome who was also well known among politicians was the Epicurean poet Philodemus of Gadara (16.2.29, C 759).[50] He became a friend of the Pisones and especially of L. Calpurnius Piso Caesoninus (consul 58), who was his patron and whom he may have accompanied to Greece on Piso's visit as proconsul of Macedonia during 57–55 BCE. This type of relationship resembles patterns developing between other Greek scholars and Roman generals such as Theopompus and Caesar, Theophanes and Pompey, and Strabo and Gallus. Philodemus was very prolific and wrote on various themes from philosophy to poetry, while his Epicurean texts and erotic epigrams were praised by Cicero and influenced the great Augustan poets Propertius, Horace and Ovid. He also composed a history of philosophers and works on the theory of art. One of his essays dealt with the theme of the good king according to Homer. In his various writings he addressed the poets Varius Rufus, Virgil, Plotius Tucca and Horace, who formed circles of their own.

Eudorus the Eclectic and Ariston the Peripatetic, both from Alexandria, each wrote an *On the Nile*, and the two works were, says Strabo, identical in content and style but different in composition (17.1.5, C 790).[51] Eudorus also produced an astronomical work, perhaps a commentary on Aratus, and a geographical one, all subjects relevant to Strabo's interests. In this case Strabo's allusion to the two does not reveal any acquaintance other than purely academic.

Finally, Strabo relates that Andronicus of Rhodes the Peripatetic (14.1.41, C 648) was engaged in Aristotelian studies and arranged the works of Aristotle and Theophrastus with the assistance of Tyrannion. The scholarly collaboration may also indicate that Strabo may have been acquainted with Andronicus through his teacher.[52]

Strabo refers to several Greek grammarians who were active at his time. Some of them, like their fellow scholars, visited Rome and some had social contacts with Romans. In most cases he alludes to them in Homeric contexts, since many discussed these themes in their studies. Naturally the closest to Strabo was his teacher Tyrannion the grammarian from Amisus (chapter 1, p. 9). Tyrannion came to Rome as a prisoner of war and became rich and famous. He handled the books from Apellicon of Teos' library, perhaps with Andronicus of Rhodes, helped Cicero with the latter's library, and taught his nephew Quintus.

Other contemporary grammarians are also mentioned by Strabo. Aristonicus of Alexandria, among other studies on Homer and Hesiod, wrote a work on the wanderings of Menelaus (1.2.31, C 38) and spent some time in Rome.[53] Asclepiades of Myrleia in Bithynia, 'a man who taught grammar in Turdetania and has published an account of the tribes of that region' (3.4.3, C 157) and is one of Strabo's sources of information (3.4.19, C 166), also composed some commentaries on Homer, Theocritus and Aratus, monographs on the cup of Nestor and on the Pleiades, influenced by Crates of Mallus, and local histories of Bithynia and Turdetania. He too sojourned in Rome as a teacher and visited Spain.[54] Aristocles of Rhodes (14.2.13, C 655) wrote *On Poetics*, dealt with the theory of music and composed an historical-philological commentary on Plato. Although there is no evidence for his presence in Rome, Dionysius of Halicarnassus knew him as an orator, implying his fame among other Greek Augustan writers.[55]

Strabo mentions two Greek poets with characteristics similar to those of other members of the circle here discussed. Crinagoras of Mytilene (13.2.3, C 617) joined Potamon in the embassies sent from their city to Rome.[56] The poet spent a long time in Rome and was a member of the social and cultural circle gathered around Octavia, Augustus' sister. He dedicated some of his epigrams to an unidentified Lucius, to M. Claudius Marcellus and to the younger Antonia, Antony's daughter and Augustus' niece. He also used geographical terminology for purposes of glorification, and emphasized the practical potential of geographical surveys as tourist guides (chapter 4, pp. 123 and 124). One of his epigrams on Augustus clearly manifests the tendency of the Greeks to amalgamate in various ways their cultural background with their contemporary politics, in this case in order to express the overwhelming glory of Augustus:

Man's mimic, the parrot, left its wicker-work cage and went to the woods on flowery wings, and ever practising for its greetings the glorious name of Caesar, forgot it not even among the hills. So all the birds, quickly taught, came running in rivalry, who should be first to say 'Greetings' to the god. Orpheus made beasts obey him on the hills; to you, Caesar, now every bird tunes up unbidden.[57]

Diodorus of Sardis, Strabo's friend, was another Greek poet and historian who spent some time in Rome (chapter 1, p. 11). In his epigrams Diodorus complimented and glorified Tiberius and his brother Drusus, thus repeating the pattern of Greek absorption and reflection of Roman atmosphere. Diodorus compared Tiberius to Achilles' son, crowning him as 'leader among the sons of Aeneas' and concluding that 'the other was vigorous with the

141

spear, this one both in war and in wisdom'. In another epigram he prays for Drusus' health, youth and spirit, all qualities of 'the children of the blessed Immortals'.[58]

In addition to the Greek literary scholars, Strabo also knew some of his contemporaries who were engaged in medicine. He speaks of Asclepiades of Bithynia, who spent some time in Rome, was a friend of Crassus and was also known to Cicero (12.4.9, C 566). And he is also familiar with Zeuxis of Tarentum who founded the Herophilic school in Carura in Laodicea and his heir Alexander Philaletes of Laodicea (12.8.20, C 580); Heracleides of Tarentum, who was educated as a Herophilian but later became the most important and famous empiricist doctor in antiquity, and his fellow-student Apollonius Mys (14.1.34, C 645); and Apollonius of Citium (14.6.3, C 683).[59]

Although varying in age and academic interests, all these scholars were Greeks who preserved their traditions and scholarly position, but at the same time many of them came to Rome, either as suppliants or as teachers and friends to the Romans. It was mainly the philosophers and orators who were teachers, whereas the historians formed a different kind of relationship by accompanying their patrons and documenting their campaigns and actions. In all cases the Greek was the scholarly authority for the Roman practical man.

Strabo's own Roman associations (chapter 3, p. 87) could also have afforded him opportunities to meet other Romans and Greeks. The Piso who communicated his impressions of Libya to Strabo was probably the eldest son of Horace's friend Piso to whom the poet addressed his *Ars Poetica*. Thus Strabo and Horace may have been associated with the same family. This does not necessarily suggest that the two men met each other. In fact it has been recently noted that the Roman poets at this time were hardly associated with Greeks, and out of tens of acquaintances mentioned in their poems only a handful are Greek, in some cases none.[60] Thus, the poets probably kept to their own exclusive circle, except for instance with regard to Philodemus of Gadara. This may explain why Strabo does not mention any of the Roman poets other than Ennius. He probably simply did not meet them.

The relationship, sometimes rather close, between Greek intellectuals and Romans from the upper classes, is a feature which creates a repeated pattern in this social milieu. Thus we saw that Dionysius of Halicarnassus knew Q. Aelius Tubero, Metilius Rufus and his father, and Caecilius of Calacte. The latter was also a student of Apollodorus of Pergamon who taught C. Valgius Rufus and addressed Matius and Domitius Marsus in his writings. Apollodorus also taught Augustus himself, around whom a large cluster of scholars gathered, several of whom Strabo mentions. The intellectuals who surrounded the emperor, some as friends, others as teachers or envoys, were Nicolaus of Damascus, Xenarchus of Seleucia, Arius who also had a personal acquaintance with Livia, Athenodorus of Tarsus who knew Cicero and

Octavia, and Timagenes of Alexandria who was close to Asinius Pollio. Most of the Greek intellectuals evidently knew more than one Roman aristocrat. Smaller circles clustered around other central Roman figures such as Pompey, who was surrounded by Aristodemus of Nysa and Theophanes of Mytilene, who also knew Cicero and Balbus of Gades. Julius Caesar associated with Theopompus of Cnidus who knew Cicero, his son Artemidorus and possibly Hypsicrates of Amisus. Another Greek scholar who was close to Cicero was Tyrannion of Amisus, who also taught Cicero's nephew Quintus. Athenodorus Cordylion of Tarsus and Antipater of Tyre were both close to Cato the younger. Octavia, Augustus' sister, had her own society including Athenodorus of Tarsus and the poet Crinagoras who also knew M. Claudius Marcellus and the younger Antonia, Augustus' niece. Nestor of Tarsus was close to Marcellus, Octavia's son, Potamon and Lesbocles of Mytilene to Seneca the elder, and Athenaeus of Seleucia to L. Licinius Murena. Tiberius, Augustus' heir, also associated with some Greek scholars, such as Marcus Pompeius, the son of Theophanes of Mytilene, and Theodorus of Gadara. Philodemus of Gadara had his own Roman patron, L. Calpurnius Piso Caesoninus, and was mainly associated with poets such as Varius Rufus, Virgil, Plotius Tucca and Horace. And, last but not least Strabo himself, who talks of his contacts with Aelius Gallus, Servilius Isauricus and Cn. Calpurnius Piso, and his familiarity at least in name with Aelius Catus (cos. 4 CE) (7.3.10, C 303) and Asinius Pollio (chapter 3, p. 87).

Let us not forget that the complexity of this society as it is presented here is derived entirely and exclusively from Strabo's *Geography*. This suggests some conclusions for we may safely deduce that these circles were still broader and encompassed many other Greeks and Romans. Strabo knew all the Greek scholars in this description, some of them rather well. This may imply that he also had the chance to meet some of their Roman friends, and if not in person, he probably heard about them at first hand.

What adds colour and depth to this picture of the scholarly milieu is the contact between various members of the group. Dionysius knew Aristocles of Rhodes. Theodorus knew Apollodorus and Potamon, who in turn knew Lesbocles. Both Potamon and Lesbocles associated with Crinagoras. Tyrannion of Amisus knew Andronicus of Rhodes and Strabo knew them all.

Many of these scholars refer to Roman matters in their writings, frequently on a favourable note, trying to find a connection between Greek and Roman cultures. For example Dionysius of Halicarnassus in his *Roman Antiquities*; Nicolaus of Damascus, particularly in his biography of Augustus; Timagenes in his biography of Augustus before he burned it; Theophanes of Mytilene in his biography of Pompey; Hypsicrates in his etymological research on the relation between Greek and Latin; Aristodemus of Nysa in his claim that Homer had Roman roots; Tyrannion of Amisus in his grammatical etymologies; Potamon of Mytilene in his poems in honour of Brutus and

Caesar; Crinagoras in his laudatory epigrams on Augustus and his era; Diodorus of Sardis in his epigrams on Tiberius and Drusus; and, finally, Strabo in his *Geography*.

Strabo's biography, his Greek education, his sojourn in Rome and his friendship with Aelius Gallus thus repeat a pattern emerging in Rome and reaching its peak at the time of Augustus. His works, their contents and particularly his admiration of Roman rule may therefore be considered not only as a product of his personality, but as part of a social milieu producing similar literary expressions. This similarity places Strabo in a very specific social and cultural context of Greek intellectuals and particularly historians, who used Greek traditions and expressions to demonstrate Roman political dominance as they witnessed it by living in Rome and talking to Roman aristocrats.

6

THE *GEOGRAPHY* – A 'COLOSSAL WORK'

THE TEXT: ITS DATE AND INFLUENCE

Strabo's later work, written after his first historiographical undertaking, is the *Geography*, so named after the contents and on the basis of the title in some ancient sources. Strabo himself refers to his composition by several appellations, each alluding to its nature and scope. He speaks of his 'description of the earth (*geographia*)', 'description of the land (*chorographia*)', 'an outline (*periegesis*)' (3.4.5, C 158), 'circuit of the earth (*periodos ges*)' (6.1.2, C 253) and 'circuit of the land (*periodeia tes choras*)' (9.5.14, C 435).[1] Later sources refer to the work by various yet cognate names. The second-century lexicographer Valerius Harpocration of Alexandria has *Geographoumena*; Athenaeus and the Byzantine historian Jordanes *Geographika* and the Suda has *Geographia*.[2] The main medieval manuscripts of the text are headed *Geographika*.

The *Geography* as we have it today is based mainly on the tradition of several manuscripts from the tenth to the mid-fifteenth century as well as on Byzantine epitomes. The earliest versions of some parts of the work were found on Egyptian papyri dated to the second and third century CE, containing short excerpts of Books 2, 7 and 9. Some corrupt traces of sections of Book 1 and Books 8 to 17 were found on a palimpsest holding the Pentateuchs in Latin dated to the end of the fifth century.[3] The text comprises seventeen full books, except for a fragmentary part at the end of Book 7. This is the entire *Geography*, as its contents and construction show and as both the Suda and Stephanus of Byzantion confirm by their reference to seventeen books.[4] The division into books was probably made by Strabo and, as will be discussed below (p. 165), is not random but has stylistic and thematic foundations. The text is lengthy in comparison with other whole or fragmentary ancient texts, and holds approximately 377,000 words. The 1620 Paris edition of Isaac Casaubon presented the text in 840 pages. This numeration has become standard to some extent and it is usual to indicate Casaubon's pagination by the letter C.

There are several milestones in the history of the publication of the *Geography*.[5] The first printed edition (the *editio princeps*) was done by Aldus in Venice in 1516 and was the basis for the editions of Casaubon and later, in 1815, of Corais. Critical editions based on readings of some of the manuscripts were published by Kramer in 1844–52, followed shortly by Meineke in 1852–3. For a century these were the leading editions and, although they had some methodological shortcomings, form the basis for the text and the English translation by Horace L. Jones published in 1917–32 in the Loeb Classical Library. Niese's plan to work on a new edition of Strabo was interrupted by his sudden death. In the last three decades of our century several attempts were made to prepare a critical edition with a fresh and thorough reading of the manuscripts, but none have been completed. Aly published the Strabonian palimpsest and his posthumous critical edition appeared in 1968, containing Books 1 and 2. Sbordone published Books 1–6 in two volumes (1963–70) and almost simultaneously, in 1966, the Budé edition began issuing the text, which was edited by Lasserre, Baladié and Aujac, but not in the numerical order of Strabo's books; the first volume contained Books 3 and 4 of the *Geography*. The volume presenting Book 9 was published in 1996, leaving Books 13–17 still to appear.

New hope for the resuscitation of the *Geography* has emerged with the initiative of the Groningen team directed by Stefan Radt, who in 1982 began working on a critical edition accompanied by a German translation. This is expected to appear at the beginning of the millennium, and is planned to comprise separate volumes of text, translation and commentary.[6]

Establishing when Strabo composed his *Geography* is a matter of some controversy.[7] This is more than a chronological question; it is also essential for a better understanding of Strabo's life and scholarly accomplishments. Our assessment of his work will naturally be different if we imagine an experienced octogenarian writing his *magnum opus* in less than two years, rather than a person engaged in research and writing throughout most of his lifetime.

There are two principal approaches to this question. One considers the work as we have it as the product of two editions or versions composed at different periods. According to this view, Strabo later updated the early version, taking some geopolitical changes into account. Protagonists of the other approach argue that he composed the *Geography* in one writing session, so to speak, creating one extensive and continuous composition. These two views have given rise to several suggestions for the date of composition.

The first real attempt to find dating clues in the text of the *Geography* occurs in a short discussion by Fabricius (1717).[8] In Book 4 Strabo mentions the Alpine tribes, the Carni and the Norici: 'Tiberius and his brother Drusus stopped all of them from their riotous incursions in one summer, so it is already thirty-three years that they have been in a state of tranquillity and have been paying their tributes regularly' (4.6.9, C 206).

Since these tribes surrendered to Tiberius in the summer of 15 BCE,[9] this passage, written thirty-three years later, dates to the summer of 19 CE.

From this it may be inferred that at least part of the work was composed about that time. Although Fabricius does not offer a thorough investigation into the matter, he here indicates a key passage which indeed seems to pinpoint a moment at which Strabo was engaged in writing.

Niese took Fabricius' brief remark further, deriving definite conclusions from it.[10] He suggested that Strabo wrote the whole work in the years 18–19 CE, when he was about eighty years of age, which would mean that the labour of composition was continuous and completed in a very short time. Niese's argument is based on dating chronological references in the *Geography*. Strabo occasionally uses the words 'now' (*nyn*) and 'recently' (*neosti*). Assuming that these words reflect the actual time of writing, they may serve as pointers to the date of composition (and see chapter 1, p. 1).

A major weakness in Niese's method is his disregard of the fact that the *Geography* abounds in passages that contain the terms 'now' and 'recently', yet refer, when such may be ascertained from the context, to a wide range of dates. Were we to accept Niese's guiding principle that these words indicate the time at which a specific piece was composed, we would be obliged to conclude that the various parts of the work were produced over a long period and not necessarily in the order in which they are currently arranged.

However, this is highly improbable. The work is pervaded by internal cross-references which create the impression of a composition written in a relatively short space of time and according to the present order of the books. Each of the fifteen descriptive books (excluding the first two introductory ones) opens with a short summary of what has been treated up to that point and what will be dealt with in the pages to follow. Sometimes Strabo incorporates similarly brief summaries between subjects. This pattern helps the reader by dividing the long work into smaller units and it gives the impression of a structured plan of writing and editing. Besides these, the *Geography* incorporates numerous cross-references, all of which seem to reflect a well-planned and fully detailed scheme present in the author's mind (below, p. 166).

Following the line of thought that considers the *Geography* as written in one version only and not later revised, Aly suggested an alternative view for the duration of the composition.[11] He proposed a longer period than Niese had inferred, beginning in the second decade BCE. It should be pointed out, however, that Aly did not engage in a thorough investigation and merely voiced his personal impression that Strabo was active as a scholar for about fifty years of his life. Since he invested about half this time in his historiographical work, he would have begun the *Geography* only later, in the second decade BCE. ·

At first sight this conjecture seems to conform with the various passages dealing with different periods of time from the peak of Augustus' reign and up to Tiberius, but it has no apparent basis. The assumption has an advantage in that it helps to explain the references to a wide range of dates in Strabo, without one having to scrutinize his sources or consider the possibility of later revision. However, this is clearly too easy and evasive a solution to the complex issue. Moreover, it runs counter to the obvious indications of careful and detailed editing throughout that make the work into a unified whole and support the conclusion that the work of composition took a relatively short period of time. The claim that it covered about forty years seems highly unlikely.

Another approach advocates the existence of two versions of the *Geography*: an earlier draft and a later improved text which incorporated some additions made by Strabo himself to update his work. Supporters of this line of thought, however, differ as to the time when the supposed drafts were written.

Pais suggested that most of the work was completed by the year 7 BCE, and that Strabo added some recent information and retouched parts of it in 18 CE.[12] This would mean that he had been writing the *Geography* for some years up to the age of sixty, and revised it and added new data when he was eighty years old.

Pais, in effect, fiercely contests Niese's conclusions. He thinks it highly improbable that Strabo produced this entire massive undertaking at the age of eighty and in the short space of time that Niese proposed. A vast work of this nature would certainly have required longer to compose, and would have demanded acute physical and mental faculties very rare at such advanced years. Pais also points out that if indeed, as Niese says, the whole composition was carried out at the late date, it is difficult to explain the absence and omission of important events in the careers of Augustus and Tiberius. His explanation for this chronological lacuna is that the later additions to the supposed earlier version were intended to add only a few facts concerning Tiberius, without creating a thorough revision.

Pais's main contention is that the references to more recent matters were indeed added at a later date, but that most of the work was written earlier. Although Strabo mentions Tiberius and some occurrences which took place during Tiberius' lifetime in more than twenty different contexts, most of his references to contemporary events belong to the period after the death of Julius Caesar and during the reign of Augustus, until 7 BCE. This is especially surprising, notes Pais, because Strabo seems otherwise eager to glorify Augustus and Tiberius.

A further contention in Pais's argument is that Strabo was not acquainted with the Map of Agrippa. According to him, a writer focusing on geography and the description of the *oikoumene* was bound to be interested in such a map. The fact that Strabo does not mention it shows that he must have written his work before the map was displayed to the public.

Syme accepts Pais's general position, considering the *Geography* as composed of two strata written at different periods.[13] However he does not agree with the dates proposed by Pais and presents a suggestion of his own, according to which Strabo probably wrote the first draft by 3 CE and the revisions in 18 CE. These revisions included additions and also deletions of details from the first draft which were no longer relevant. Thus one would get the impression that Strabo ignored certain earlier events in his first draft as well, yet he might simply have deleted some of them in his later revision.

Neither Pais nor Syme discuss the date that Strabo began to write, but describe the composition as carried out 'by the year 7 BCE' (Pais[14]) or 'by 3 CE' (Syme[15]). They thus ignore a crucial point in understanding Strabo's process of writing and his methodology, for, as was said above, the issue of the duration of the work of composition is integrally related to our perception of Strabo as a scholar.

The argument that Strabo's silence about certain events may be used to indicate the time of writing is not convincing. First, it is quite likely that the selection of facts appearing in the *Geography* is to be attributed to his sources and the extent of his knowledge, which in turn depended on the quality and quantity of information that he collected. A fact not included in his sources or a hearsay piece of evidence which did not reach the place where he was writing (chapter 1, p. 14) could not find their way into his work.

Second, although it is possible to gain an impression about an author's tendency to insert personal reactions or opinions into his text, Pais's decisive judgment that 'Strabo takes every occasion to praise Augustus and even Tiberius',[16] sounds too forceful. According to this, Strabo would use every opportunity to glorify Roman power, and when he does not, Pais would evoke the existence of a second edition. However, the political message in the *Geography* is not at all self-evident. Generally speaking, Strabo does tend to be pro-Roman, as can be seen in his praise of the enormous territorial conquests, his emphasis on the peace and prosperity brought to the world and the glorification of Augustus (chapters 3 and 4). Nevertheless, he does not spare his disapprobation when it is justified in his eyes, accusing the Romans of oppression, decadence, theft of valuable works of art and extravagance in their manner of living (chapter 4, p. 119). It seems better, then, to conclude that Strabo does not in fact use every opportunity to praise the Romans, even if this entails the need to define his line of thought and to elucidate the contexts in which he prefers to glorify the Romans or otherwise.

Both Pais and Syme discuss what they consider to be 'important' or 'negligible' details from Strabo's point of view. However, modern scholars cannot establish precise criteria for assessing Strabo's rationale in editing his work. Apparently he chose details and facts reflecting his personal preferences, though sometimes, when he openly shares his deliberations with his audience, he takes account of the possible usefulness and benefit to his readers (below, p. 158).

Syme, as noted above, rejects Pais's comments on Strabo's suspicious silences, but does not refrain from using the same argument himself. However, it should be emphasized that the geographical treatise was not affected by historiographical ambitions, even though Strabo does insert some historical excursions. As we know, he wrote a *History* at a former stage of his life (chapter 2, p. 69), and his earlier inclinations undoubtedly had some influence on his later writings and on his way of thinking; besides, he certainly came across much geographical and ethnographical material while writing his *History*. Nevertheless, it is a misconception to seek historiographical accuracy and thoroughness in the *Geography*. The expressed aim of the treatise is to update knowledge of the *oikoumene*, using the new information obtained through the Roman conquests, for the benefit of a curious and pragmatic audience. This information is primarily topographic and ethnographic and not historiographic. It would seem, therefore, that one cannot draw far-reaching conclusions from the chronological lacunae in the work and from Strabo's omission of certain events.

On the whole, among the various interpretations discussed above, Niese's approach seems the more probable: Strabo wrote the work in one piece and there is no valid reason to assume the existence of two versions or editions. But as for the proposed date of writing, as I have shown, the dates offered by Niese (and one may include here also Aly's conjecture) are untenable as they stand. However, one may combine the earlier date of Niese's conjecture with the latest date mentioned in the *Geography* and so arrive at the years 18–24 CE. Niese's suggestion of the year 18 CE as the *terminus post quem* of the period of composition seems preferable on the basis of the various references to this year in the work. But since the latest event mentioned in the *Geography* is the death of Juba, king of Mauretania, in 23 CE (17.3.7, C 828 and chapter 1, p. 2), and taking into account that several months may have passed before Strabo heard of this death, we may safely assume that he wrote between the years 18 and 24. By this theory we may also ignore the objection addressed against Niese that it is unlikely that Strabo would have written such a lengthy work in only one year.

True, for this theory we shall have to accept that Strabo was of an advanced age at the time of writing, but at the same time we have no particular reason to doubt his ability to write or dictate when aged eighty to eighty-five years old. Moreover, one may assume that Strabo only began the actual writing in the year 18. It would seem that research, compilation of sources, and visits to sites were all carried out earlier in his life, even if Strabo did not at that time intend to write the *Geography*. The actual composition could certainly have been done in his last years.

The various books of the *Geography* are written consecutively, relying heavily on sources and editing them by way of association. Notes about contemporary events are usually inserted in their proper context. An important argument supporting a later date of composition is Strabo's evident familiarity with later sources. *Pace* Pais, one can show that he probably knew and used Agrippa's *Commentaries* and tablet. His citation of Roman miles and his references to 'the chorographer' and to a certain 'chorography' probably allude to the public project initiated by Marcus Agrippa to describe the *oikoumene* (chapter 4, p. 127). He possibly knew some details of Augustus' will and of his *Res Gestae* which was set up in front of his Mausoleum and in other public places after his death in 14 CE (chapter 3, p. 97). Allusions to the *Res Gestae Divi Augusti* may be traced both in the form of some general ideas expressed in the *Geography* and in certain details and figures of speech. Strabo notes the extent of the Roman conquests, mentioning nations and tribes, and thus constituting the only existing literary parallel to the list of geographical and ethnographical names included in the *Res Gestae* and perhaps in the *libellus* which was part of Augustus' will.[17] He mentions the Parthian hostages presented to Augustus and stresses the Parthian surrender to Rome (6.4.2, C 288), in a style similar to the description in the *Res Gestae* (32–3). Finally, he depicts the city of Rome at a stage of development that includes late buildings and sites (5.3.8, C 235–6 and chapter 3, p. 86). These details are an integral part of the context and not mere *retouches*.

Thus, the earliest date of the period of writing may be found in the only passage where Strabo gives an exact notation by fixing an accurate chronological interval between a known date in the past and the time at which he is writing. The latest date should be that of the most recent event mentioned in the whole work. Accordingly, it is likely that Strabo wrote his *Geography* towards the end of his life, probably in the years 18–24 CE, and descriptions which reflect earlier times are the result of his early sources and of his notes and are not indicative of the time of composition.

A Tiberian work chronologically, but an Augustan thematically, the *Geography* was not well known among ancient authors. Although Josephus and, later, Plutarch quote some parts of Strabo's historiographical work, there is no indication that they knew the geographical treatise. The earliest reference to this work mentioning Strabo by name occurs in the lexicon of Valerius Harpocration of Alexandria towards the end of the second century, which refers twice to short pieces of information from Books 8 and 10; the next is Athenaeus around 200 CE alluding twice to Book 3; Julian of Ascalon (probably fifth century[18]) discussed some measurements in light of Strabo; Procopius cited Strabo in a discussion of the Amazons *c.* 500, the Byzantine historian Jordanes mentioned Strabo's name about 550 and Byzantine scholars of the tenth century referred to the *Geography* at a time when the first manuscripts of the text are already attested. No Latin writer mentions the *Geography*, not even authors who would have been likely to take an interest in such a work, such as Pliny or Pomponius Mela. These findings, partial as they may be, show that although Strabo had in mind statesmen and intellectuals as his intended readers, thus apparently referring to both Romans and Greeks (below, p. 164), his work was read only by Greeks and, as far as we know, only about 160 years after its completion. Since circulation of texts in this period depended on the author's contacts and copies were distributed personally,[19] it seems that because Strabo composed his *Geography* very late in life and finished it shortly before his death, he did not have an opportunity to pass it about among his acquaintances and the work had to wait for later rediscovery. Although Strabo knew some Romans and was part of an intellectual circle formed in Rome (chapter 5), the work was most likely not distributed by him, and being written in Greek, it naturally appealed to Greek authors. The Roman authors either did not consider it worthy of quotation or, what seems more plausible, did not see the *Geography* at all. The papyrological findings show, however, that the text was available in second-century Egypt.

Strabo's influence on later geographical thought should not however be assessed merely on the basis of specific allusions to him by name, for his *Geography* may have influenced other geographers in its concepts and attitude and not necessarily through verbal quotation.[20] Thus, one interesting piece of evidence concerning Strabo's possible reception in the second century CE is a notion of Dionysius 'Periegetes' who probably lived in Hadrian's times and described the *oikoumene* in a pseudo-epic work written in hexameters. In his survey of Libya he notes that men say that the region is similar to a leopard skin.[21] This way of describing the country calls to mind Strabo's notion that 'Libya is – as others show, and indeed as Gnaeus Piso, who was once the governor of that country, told me – like a leopard's skin; for it is spotted with inhabited places that are surrounded by waterless and desert land' (2.5.33, C 130). Strabo's allusion indicates his own private chat with Piso but also 'others' as the origin for this simile. It may have reached Dionysius through another source, but as we do not possess such a source it seems rather interesting that such an impression, which indeed is in the nature of a personal observation rather than a scientific one, is echoed in Dionysius.

At about the same time Claudius Ptolemy, in his *Geography* encompassing the entire *oikoumene*, may have adopted Strabo's universal approach to geography as well as some particular ideas, for instance the clear distinction between chorography and geography, which although traditional, still is similar to Strabo's definitions (below, p. 154).[22] Ptolemy concentrated on listing map coordinates of cities, coastlines, rivers and other features of the landscape, according to longitudes and latitudes, so that a map could be constructed from the lists. He worked within the framework of his predecessors, and in this sense Strabo's universal approach may be included, but unlike Strabo he laid out the data in a numerical form.[23]

Geographers of the Middle Ages, dominated by Christian views of geography, generally ignored ancient Greek and Roman authorities, and were attracted by the concepts of the Scriptures. Thus, Strabo is hardly ever alluded to. At the beginning of the sixth century Priscian the grammarian seems to echo verbally a notion of Strabo's on Sybaris, and Cosmas Indicopleustes, the mid-sixth-century Alexandrian geographer, perhaps also used some part of the *Geography*. This is not enough to conclude for Strabo's popularity.

Similarly, there is no sign of a direct Strabonian influence on the Arab geographers, who in the ninth to eleventh centuries tended to translate other Greek geographical precedents, mainly excerpts from Plato, Aristotle and Ptolemy. The ninth-century Arab genre of *masalik wa mamalik* presents features similar to Strabo's approach in its global attitude, in its address to educated audiences of non-specialists and in its dual basis of literary sources as well as travels and autopsy. Like the Roman imperial period which influenced Strabo's geographical survey, this genre too was dominated by the Muslim empire of the Abbasid caliphate. The resemblance may however be ascribed to similar conditions rather than to actual influence.[24]

In about 1439 in Florence, the humanist Georgius Gemistus Pletho compiled and summarized various parts of Strabo's *Geography* and composed a work intended to emend and to clarify certain passages from it, mainly dealing with mathematical problems. This initiative in fact introduced to the Latin west the Strabo who until then had been known only in the Byzantine east. A few years later Guarino da Verona initiated a Latin translation of the *Geography* and the demand for more copies of the text increased. Directly arising from Pletho's undertaking and the resulting knowledge of Strabo's work, an extraordinary consequence ensued in the history of western geography, not only in theory but also in practice – the voyage of Christopher Columbus. Columbus's plan to cross the Ocean sailing westward to get to India was supported by several notions found in Strabo. These were indeed not Strabo's own ideas and were derived from his predecessors Eratosthenes and Posidonius, but his was the text read by Columbus. Thus one passage which influenced Columbus was Strabo's quotation of Eratosthenes:

> from the east to the west the inhabited world is longer . . . and it forms a complete circle, itself meeting itself, so that if the immensity of the Atlantic sea did not prevent us, we could sail from Iberia to India along one and the same parallel over the remainder of the circle.
>
> (1.4.6, C 64)

And another was his allusion to Posidonius:

> he suspects that the length of the inhabited world, being about seventy thousand stadia, is half of the entire circle on which it has been taken, so that, says he, if you sail from the west in a straight course you will reach India within the seventy thousand stadia.
>
> (2.3.6, C 102)

In such way the *Geography*, with Pletho's help, in fact had a central position in one of the greatest geographical discoveries in the history of the western world.[25] One of Strabo's unplanned achievements, then, was his recording of the ideas and notions of other authors whose writings are no longer accessible.

Strabo's geographical tendency was literary rather than scientific (except for the unavoidable reference to earlier scientific notions in Books 1 and 2), and stressed the universal rather than the particular. Similar descriptive tendencies are revealed in the cosmographies of the sixteenth and seventeenth centuries, following the Age of Exploration. Sebastian Münster, known to his contemporaries as 'the German Strabo', in his *Cosmographia Universalis* (1544), Philipp Clüver (Cluverius) in his compendium (1624), and Bernhard Varen (Varenius) in his *Geographia Generalis* (1650), encompassed all that was known at their time of various parts of the world. Varenius stressed the practical purpose of geography, for instance in his survey of Japan and Siam written for the merchants of Amsterdam. He also developed the idea of *general geography* vs. *special geography* as two parts of a whole, thus recalling to mind Strabo's distinction and synthesis between *geographia* and *chorographia* (below). The universalistic approach was finally abandoned in the nineteenth century when new geographical information became too abundant to be dealt with in a general survey and specialization became the rule.[26]

Three different periods and cultures responded to the *Geography*. Although not well received in Strabo's own time or immediately afterwards, it occasionally figures in second-century Egypt and particularly in Alexandria, then in sixth-century Constantinople and finally in the Renaissance, which displayed an enthusiastic new interest in the work. The appearance of printed editions at the beginning of the sixteenth century contributed to the dissemination of Strabo. Against the background of the new geographical and political connections established at the beginning of the modern age Strabo's *Geography* regained its reputation. It is noteworthy that Napoleon was interested in Strabo's information on Egypt and initiated a French translation of the work.[27]

PURPOSE AND VOCATION

Geography as a discipline had a centuries-old history, as Strabo himself was very well aware. He surveyed the earlier traditions thoroughly (chapter 2), and, while acknowledging that some of his predecessors had already done similar things, he still held that there was room for his project: 'I too am justified in having undertaken to treat this same subject, since it stands in need of so much correction and addition' (2.4.8, C 109).

But Strabo's contribution is not confined to mere 'correction and addition'. It presents a fresh approach to a traditional theme.

At the beginning of the *Geography* a distinction is made between geography and chorography (1.1.16, C 9–10).[28] Geography means, literally, description of the earth (*ge*) that is, the continents and seas in and beyond the *oikoumene*, and the size, position and nature of various countries. It is comprehensive and panoramic, since it describes an extended territory, and therefore benefits statesmen and generals who are interested in the wider picture. Within this extended framework various parts of the world are treated in different degrees of particularity according to the origin and point of view of the geographer, who would naturally elaborate more on regions closer to him and less on remote places (1.1.16, C 9).

Unlike the broad and general attitude of geography, chorography focuses on a certain region (*chora*) and includes many details and particulars. In the passage referring to the relativity of the description according to the attitude of the geographer, Strabo adds: 'It would not be remarkable even if one person were a proper chorographer for the Indians, another for the Ethiopians and still another for the Greeks and Romans' (1.1.16, C 9); that is, an elaborated description of a single region is quite common. This observation of Strabo's reflects the history of ancient geography up to his own time. From limited digressions in an historiographical context *à la* Herodotus, geography evolved into an independent subject matter through the influence of the historians of Alexander, in the form of monographs devoted to a single country, or, according to Strabo's definition, as chorographies.

In the second part of his extended two-book-long introductory remarks to his work, Strabo explains that in order to enhance scientific knowledge and political utility one's first and most important task is 'to try to give, in the simplest possible way, the shape and size of that part of the earth which falls within our geographical tablet (*geographikos pinax*[29])' and to present the nature of this part and its relation to the entire world, 'for this is the task proper to the geographer' (2.5.13, C 118). In this context the 'geographical tablet' could be a real tablet presenting the inhabited world, but it may also be Strabo's way of indicating the extent of the known world.

Both this notion and the previous definition imply that geography describes the known world in general outline and transmits simple cartographic details such as the position of sites, their names, the distances between them and their size, whereas chorography supplies the same details for a smaller territory and therefore does not refer to the relation between the particular – the region, and the whole – the world.

In view of this distinction it is noteworthy that in 8.3.17, C 346 Strabo defines his work as a chorography, applying this term to the survey of Greece which was indeed closer and especially familiar to him. Does this mean that the entire work is a geography, that is, a general description of the world, while some parts of it, better known to Strabo, have a chorographic character, that is, include additional ethnographic, historical and topographical details? Or does he mean to say that the whole work is a chorography?

Most of the *Geographies* written prior to Strabo had a somewhat limited orientation and scope. Eratosthenes, Hipparchus and Posidonius focused on scientific aspects and dealt mainly with astronomy and physics. Artemidorus was interested particularly in distances and coordinates and Polybius concentrated on historiography (chapter 2, pp. 46 and 59). But here lies one of Strabo's major innovations. The general framework of the treatise is that of a geography for it encompasses the known world and surveys its limits from end to end. But as far as the nature of the description is concerned, the work is a chorography, for Strabo attempts to supply facts and details which are beyond toponymic and cartographic annotations. The chorography of Greece, for instance, is part of the geography of the *oikoumene*. In this sense Strabo's work presents a new approach when compared with his predecessors, for it is neither a monograph on a certain theme, nor a chapter or a book taken from an historiographical survey, nor part of a scientific treatise, as he himself points out in 8.1.1, C 332. Strabo in fact joins together many chorographies and thus describes the entire inhabited world. The final result is an elaborated presentation, fresh and original in effect, and not only because of the updated information it contains.[30]

Strabo exemplifies this attitude by a metaphor from the domain of surgery:

> Just as, in surgery, amputation at the joints differs from unnatural piecemeal amputation, because the former takes off only the parts that have a natural configuration . . . whereas the latter follows no such course, and just as it is proper for us to use each kind of operation if we have regard to the proper time and the proper use of each, just so, in the case of geography, we must indeed make sections of the parts when we go over them in detail, and we must imitate the limb-by-limb amputations rather than the haphazard amputations. For only thus it is possible to take off the member that is significant and well defined, the only kind of member that the geographer has any use for.
>
> (2.1.30, C 83)

Thus the geographer's task is to discuss each part as if it were his main theme, that is chorographically, but to present all the parts as organs of one whole body of work. And if we look again at Strabo's remark that 'it would not be remarkable, even if one person were a proper chorographer for the Indians, another for the Ethiopians and still another for the Greeks and Romans' (1.1.16, C 9), we may infer that it would be indeed remarkable if the same person were to compose a chorography, and not a more general and limited geography, of the entire *oikoumene*.

Another characteristic of Strabo's approach is his encyclopaedic writing. The breadth of his descriptions is manifested not only in the geographical horizons of the *oikoumene*, but also in the variety of themes and topics interwoven in the various chorographies. He provides the reader with many details from various fields of knowledge, such as astronomy, geometry, mathematics, physics, medicine, botany, zoology, history, mythology, poetry, theology and different branches of philosophy. Each of Strabo's predecessors who took an interest in geography, beginning with Herodotus, also dealt with various other matters in addition to their specific focus, but Strabo consciously and deliberately intends to reveal a broader picture and to create an encyclopaedic work. This encyclopaedic wealth derives from his emphasis on the need for wide learning (*polymatheia*) among educated men in general and geographers in particular. It also has to do with the broad education (*enkyklios paideia*) given to upper-class Greeks and Romans, encompassing various branches of knowledge. Strabo himself was educated according to this approach which emphasized a wide range of themes and topics. It also complies well with the Roman emphasis on pragmatism, for it affects many aspects of various branches of knowledge.

Strabo's main purpose is to present the knowledge increased by recent Roman conquests. This consideration is apparent whenever he expands the survey of some matters or omits others, always having a practical purpose in mind. The principle helps him to determine when to elaborate and when to cut a story short. In 3.1.6, C 139 he says that descriptions of various regions in Iberia require special expansion, 'telling all that contributes to our knowledge of their natural advantages and prosperity'; in 8.7.3, C 385 he expresses his opinion that the Achaeans deserve an extended section in the survey for they are insufficiently known through other sources; in 10.3.5, C 465 he again notes his intention to improve on the descriptions of his predecessors and to add some facts previously unknown; in 14.1.6, C 635 he says that he is going to include in his survey some cities in Ionia omitted by Anaximenes of Lampsacus, thus specifically supplementing earlier sources; and in 15.1.4, C 691 he announces that the information he has on the island of Taprobane (Sri Lanka), is far richer than Eratosthenes' because it includes some information from other sources as well.

Strabo therefore is fully aware of one of his major achievements, that of updating and supplementing details and facts unknown to or omitted by his predecessors. In this task he moves between two extremes: his fear of omitting important information and at the same time his care not to digress or drift away from his main theme. His awareness of these two opposing dangers derives from a well-defined and well-planned scheme of writing.

Since he intends to update and supplement information and knowledge acquired prior to his work, he is afraid he might omit or ignore important items: 'I have already described them [sc. the Rhodians] before, but the number of the myths about them causes me to resume their description, filling up the gaps, if I have omitted anything' (14.2.7, C 654) and again:

these [sc. the historians' lies about Libya] I have already mentioned somewhere before, but I am again speaking of them, asking pardon for introducing marvellous stories, if perchance I shall be forced to digress into a thing of that sort, since I am unwilling wholly to pass them over in silence and in a way to cripple my survey.

(17.3.3, C 826)[31]

The intention to encompass all the facts and details omitted and neglected by his predecessors does not cause him to lose his focus and he tries carefully to maintain control over his survey and not to drift away: 'It is not permitted for me to linger over details, since they are so numerous, nor yet, on the other hand, to pass by them all in silence without even mentioning one or another of them in a summary way' (9.1.19, C 397).

He often says specifically that he will close a certain discussion in order not to expand it too far beyond the measure suitable for such a work, and on many occasions he expresses his awareness of his own digressions from the main theme, as these examples show: 'However, I am overstepping the bounds of moderation in recounting the numerous stories told about a country most of which is now deserted' (8.4.11, C 362). This implies that information on abandoned places is unimportant. And: 'I have decided to say by way of a brief digression from my geographical description' (14.5.2, C 669); 'Let me now return to Megasthenes and continue his account from the point where I left off' (15.1.45, C 707).

He sometimes apologizes to his readers for an apparently exaggerated elaboration on certain matters and feels that he needs to explain why he made it:

I have been led on to discuss these people rather at length, although I am not in the least fond of myths, because the facts in their case border on the province of theology.

(10.3.23, C 474)

I should ask the pardon of my readers and appeal to them not to fasten the blame for the length of my discussion upon me rather than upon those who strongly yearn for knowledge of the things that are famous and ancient.

(13.1.1, C 581)

In the case of famous places my reader must endure the dry part of such geography as this.

(14.1.9, C 636)

From these and other references it is evident that several matters of principle determine Strabo's decisions concerning the inclusion or exclusion of certain details. The general scheme of the survey is primarily determined by the work's projected utility and pragmatism. Therefore many things which are not

beneficial to the reader are superfluous, whereas the omission of vital information would damage the utilitarian effect of the whole. The examples quoted
above suggest that details of lesser benefit are matters pertaining to uninhabited regions (8.4.11, C 362; 8.8.1–2, C 388; 11.12.1, C 520), to dubious
mythological stories (10.3.23, C 479), or to ancient and chronologically
remote themes (13.1.1, C 581). Strabo phrases this orientation specifically:

> I must begin with Thessaly, omitting such things as are very old
> and mythical and for the most part not agreed upon, as I have
> already done in all other cases, and telling such things as seem to
> me appropriate to my purpose.
>
> (9.4.18, C 429)

Thus, all things which are distant from the reader, geographically, real-
istically or chronologically, do not benefit him and have no place in the
work.[32] Accordingly Strabo grades many matters in his survey according to
their compatibility or incompatibility with his purpose, using the terms
'worthy' (*axios*), for instance in 5.2.10, C 227, when a detail contributes to
the purpose of the work, or 'unworthy' (*ouk axios*), as in 3.3.3, C 152, when
it does not.

The importance of the details to be included in the work is determined
also by their size and their significance:

> I would not pass by anything important, while as for little things,
> not only do they profit one but slightly if known, but their omission
> escapes unnoticed, and detracts not at all, or else not much, from
> the completeness of the work.
>
> (6.3.10, C 285)[33]

Besides the main pragmatic consideration several other principles guide
Strabo's decisions to include or exclude certain facts. He emphasizes the
new information included in his work but at the same time he does not
wish to repeat famous and well-known themes already surveyed by earlier
sources (8.6.18, C 376); that is, he focuses on the novelty of his task.

Another principle has to do with Strabo's reverence towards Homer, for
he holds that anything mentioned by Homer ought to be considered. Hence
he elaborates on matters pertaining to the Homeric text, and specifically
says in 13.1.50, C 606 that 'the naming of it [sc. the winter torrent] by
the poet has made it worthy of mention'. Strabo's devotion to the Greek
tradition commits him to include earlier myths in the work, because they
are 'legends that have been taught us from boyhood', but also because
they affect the situation in the present (8.3.23, C 348).

Another important consideration in the choice of details and nature of
description derives from the place and time of composition, that is, in the

first years of Tiberius' rule in a Rome still deeply influenced by the atmosphere of the Augustan age (chapter 1, p. 15 and above, p. 150). This is clearly indicated for instance in the description of settlements in Campania: 'but I am thus going into detail, within due bounds, because of the glory and power of Italy' (5.4.11, C 250). Thus his decision to expand and go into detail here derives from the role of Italy in the formation of Roman domination, and this apparently minor piece of information, or at least one not more important than the description of any other place in the world, benefits from special elaboration for political reasons (chapter 4, p. 107).

Besides these principles of utility, fame, novelty, importance, relevance for the present, traditionalism and Roman glory, Strabo sometimes includes stories and anecdotes which do not seem to comply with any of these purposes, for instance the tale of the devoted sons who carried their parents on their shoulders, thus saving them from a volcanic eruption (6.2.3, C 269). These 'unneeded' stories may be explained in several ways. Some of them, especially the mythological, have to do with Strabo's inclination to the tradition in which he was educated. He may also have a hidden moralistic or didactic purpose, as the above story may imply, for the two brothers are an excellent example of honouring one's parents and may provide a moral. He also intended an additional and perhaps secondary benefit, wishing to entertain his readers and to present the material in an interesting and pleasurable way (chapter 2, p. 74).[34]

This may explain Strabo's inclusion of an amusing popular story about the people of Iasos who earned their living from fishing:

> When a singing harper was giving a recital, the people all listened for a time, but when the bell that announced the sale of fish rang, they all left him and went away to the fish market, except one man who was hard of hearing. The harper therefore went up to him and said: 'Sir, I am grateful to you for the honour you have done me and for your love of music, for all the others except you went away the moment they heard the sound of the bell.' And the man said: 'What's that you say? Has the bell already rung?' And when the harper said 'Yes,' the man said, 'Fare thee well,' and himself arose and went away.
>
> (14.2.21, C 658)

Strabo's primary practical purpose, accompanied by some entertaining and amusing features, accounts for his style of writing. Since the *Geography* is mostly a compilation of numerous pieces of information taken from various sources (below, p. 180), Strabo's task is to present them in a coherent and interesting way. He does this using a well-defined system for organizing the large mass of details (below, p. 166). His style therefore is somewhat didactic and presents the information in a way we may imagine an instructor in one of the philosophical schools would approach a popular audience, with touristic and exotic details of remote as well as familiar regions of the world. His clear words and coherent sentences lead the audience through countries and seas.[35]

All these factors in Strabo's attitude to his subject-matter result in a very unique approach. His universalistic and pragmatic goals determine the extent of his work and his encyclopaedic attitude affects the variety and number of details. Together with his Stoic inclinations, which are manifested in emphasis and terminology (chapter 2, p. 62), a unique Strabonian geographical description emerges. The result is a monumental composition. As Strabo himself puts it nicely:

> Just as in my historical work only the incidents in the lives of distinguished men are recorded, while deeds that are petty and ignoble are omitted, so in this work also I must leave untouched what is petty and inconspicuous, and devote my attention to what is noble and great, and what contains the practically useful, or memorable, or entertaining. And just as in judging of the merits of colossal statues we do not examine each individual part with minute care, but rather consider the general effect . . . so should this book of mine be judged. For it, too, is a colossal work (*kolossourgia*), in that it deals with the facts about large things only, and wholes, except as some petty thing may stir the interest of the studious or the practical man.
>
> (1.1.23, C 13–14)

The term *kolossourgia* appears only in Strabo and according to the context it seems to indicate the elaboration of the work and its numerous details as well as its size. The reader is meant to assess it according to general achievement and not in detail.[36]

Strabo's universalistic and encyclopaedic approach is thus nourished by his intention to benefit his readers. But who would benefit from a geographical survey, and whose needs and interests would such a work satisfy? To answer these questions, he refers both to ancient times and to present conditions, showing that the wisest of the ancient heroes were those who travelled widely and knew many places, and that at present

> the greater part of geography subserves the needs of states, for the scene of the activities of states is land and sea, in which we live. The scene is small when the activities are of small importance, and large when they are of large importance . . . the greatest generals are without exception men who are able to hold sway over land and sea, and to unite nations and cities under one government and political administration. It is therefore plain that geography as a whole has a direct bearing upon the activities of commanders . . .

for thus they can manage their various affairs in a more satisfactory manner, if they know how large a country is, how it lies, and what are its peculiarities either of sky or soil.

(1.1.16, C 9)

He gives some examples from the past for the correlation between familiarity with topography and military successes, through both defeat and triumph, such as the grand strategic error of Agamemnon and his fleet in taking Mysia for Troy, and the famous victory of the Persians at Thermopylae determined by information about a secret passage in the mountains. More up-to-date and current examples of the usefulness of geography are the Roman disasters in their campaigns against the Parthians, the Germans and the Celts, for these Barbarian peoples misled the armies and thus 'made the ignorant Romans believe to be far away what was really near at hand, and kept them in ignorance of the roads and of the facilities for procuring provisions and other necessities' (1.1.17, C 10).

Hence, practical and political benefit is Strabo's main concern and this is what determines the themes included in his survey and its entire extent and emphasis. This pragmatism stems from two sources: Polybius, who intended his work for politicians and generals but also emphasized the practical lesson of history for all men; and the Stoic school in its Roman context, accentuating the practical aspects of philosophy in everyday life.

Geography and the various branches of knowledge it incorporates pertain to rulers and to generals in the field, but also contribute to other matters such as hunting:

A hunter will be more successful in the chase if he knows the character and extent of the forest, and again, only one who knows a region can advantageously pitch camp there, or set an ambush, or direct a march.

(1.1.17, C 10)

This observation adds to the portrait of Strabo's intended reader who may be interested in hunting and thus belongs to the upper classes.[37]

Strabo's intended reader must be educated. He should be familiar with elementary geometry in order to be able to recognize straight and curved lines, a circle and a globe, and he must be familiar with some astronomical facts such as the seven stars of Ursa Maior and the difference between latitudes and longitudes on the globe. The reader therefore should not be simple (*haplous*) and ignorant (*agros*) for he would not be able to use the work and to benefit from it because of his inability to understand some of the discussions included in it (1.1.21–2, C 12–13).

Strabo's pragmatic orientation is towards a wide public including knowledge-loving men (*phleidemon*) or men with practical aspirations (*prag-*

matikoi) (1.1.23, C 14). Just as the ideal statesman has to be educated, so the potential reader should be interested in the world and in the various phenomena occurring in it.

> The geographer does not write for the native of any particular place, nor yet does he write for the man of affairs of the kind who has paid no attention to the mathematical sciences properly so-called, nor, to be sure, does he write for the harvest hand or the ditch digger, but for the man who can be persuaded that the earth as a whole is such as the mathematicians represent it to be.
>
> (2.5.1, C 110)

He therefore records details 'both for the purposes of science and for the needs of the state' (2.5.13, C 118).

Strabo's ideal audience is thus comprised of statesmen, men in high social positions, practical men and educated men. Who were the actual potential readers who answered to these ideal definitions at the time? May we identify them with a certain group of readers in terms of nationality or social status or is this definition a mere literary ideal?

Modern scholars have tended to join these questions with the problem of the place where Strabo composed his *Geography*, arguing that the venue determined his idea of intended readers. Thus scholars who assumed that Strabo wrote the *Geography* in Rome suggested that he had a Roman audience in mind. They based their notion on his specific address to statesmen and generals and on the Augustan context of the work in which the Romans are presented as the central political and military power. Within this conjecture some suggested that Strabo's Roman friends encouraged him to write the work, others that it was Augustus himself who backed this literary undertaking.[38] The basic assumption is reasonable for in Strabo's time statesmen and generals were mostly Romans and Strabo specifically designed his work for such men. But the implications for the intervention of Strabo's Roman friends or even Augustus himself, attractive as they are, have no real support from any source.

Pais, on the other hand, claimed that Strabo wrote in Amasia, that he envisaged a Greek audience and that he dedicated the work to Pythodoris queen of Pontus. He based this suggestion on his contention that Strabo used Greek and not Roman sources and that his work was known to Josephus and not to Pliny, representing Greek and Roman literature respectively.[39] However, this is a partial and inaccurate picture for, as we saw (chapter 3, p. 92), Strabo alludes to several, even if comparatively few, Roman sources and he reflects some parts of Roman history and the contemporary Roman political atmosphere. True, the work expresses a Greek cultural sense of superiority and is written from a Greek point of view accentuating various unpractical details which would hardly matter to any Roman general, such as myths and lists of scholars (chapter 2, p. 79). But this is only one aspect of the whole picture. The fact that Josephus cites Strabo whereas Pliny does not mention him, has nothing to do with the question of Strabo's intentions, for Josephus refers to Strabo's earlier historiographical work and not to the *Geography*. Thus, perhaps neither author knew the work. Moreover, an author may have hope for a certain audience, while such hopes are not always realized.

The attempt of both groups to make a connection between the place where Strabo supposedly composed his treatise and his intended readers seems rather awkward, for Strabo could surely have written the work in a certain place, being influenced by certain surroundings, yet intending it to be read by people of a different culture than the one immediately encircling him at the time of writing. Hence, a third conjecture, disregarding the question of the place of writing, seems to agree better with Strabo's own words. Dubois suggested that Strabo wrote for both Romans and Greeks for he dedicates his work to any public cultured and educated enough to understand the descriptions and the geographical explanations. His intention in forming a practical aid for Roman commanders was by no means to teach them how to administer the conquered regions but rather to supply them with information on various countries and nations even though the wars with them had been concluded long before. Thus the *Geography* was a sort of guidebook for the commander visiting the provinces, in which he could find some historical, ethnographical and zoological information.[40] Educated Greeks on the one hand and practical Romans on the other, answer to both of Strabo's expectations from his future readers.

In this sense the duality in Strabo's character reflects the duality in his intended audience and is clearly expressed in the duality of the themes. The work is Greek in its language, its traditional values and its scholarly orientation. Strabo expresses his sense of superiority over all cultures, including the Romans, who in his opinion are less refined and inferior in education. Even though he admires the political achievements of Rome in the Augustan age, he criticizes some of its aspects, usually on moral grounds. Thus when Strabo refers to his educated readers he probably has the Greeks in mind in particular. At the same time, the statesmen and generals who may benefit from the information in the work are presumably the Roman aristocrats who could read Greek. The very fact that Strabo chooses to illustrate the utility of geography for military affairs with an example from a Roman campaign, and the numerous examples from Roman history scattered throughout the entire work, implies an audience who would be able to apply the theories in practice.

The Greek nature of the work is understandable, for the author is Greek, but his audience is nevertheless larger and includes both Greeks and Romans. We may suggest Aelius Gallus and Strabo himself as exemplifying the two types of potential readers of the *Geography*, the one representing the Roman elite engaged in politics, military campaigns and administration, and the other standing for the intellectual Greek aspiring to knowledge and scientific enhancement.

This approach is apparent in Strabo's own words concerning the traditional treatment of the geography of Greece:

> This subject was first treated by Homer; and then, after him, by several others, some of whom have written special treatises entitled *Harbours* or *Coasting Voyages* (*Periploi*) or *General Descriptions of the Earth* (*Periodoi ges*), or the like, and in these is comprised also the description of Greece. Others have set forth the topography of the continents in separate parts of their general histories, for instance, Ephorus and Polybius. Still others have inserted certain things on this subject in their treatises on physics and mathematics, for instance, Posidonius and Hipparchus.
>
> (8.1.1., C 332)

He here distinguishes the different contexts of earlier surveys of the geography of Greece. These were *periploi*, *Histories* and scientific works. All described Greece, but none, except the *Periodoi ges*, did so in a general geographical context. While several were interested primarily in history or science, others focused on special topographical aspects, such as harbours or coasts. Therefore, Strabo's approach is new, for he combines a detailed description within a universal context, and, in relation to the older *Periodoi ges*, the novelty lies in the inclusion of new information.

ONE THEME – MANY UNITS

The *Geography*, based on Greek ethnographic traditions and at the same time presenting a new approach to the theme in its broad scope and encyclopaedic orientation, describes the entire *oikoumene*. Following the first two introductory books, each of the remaining fifteen concentrates on a certain region. Beginning in Book 3 with Iberia in the north-western part of the Mediterranean and moving towards the east and then to the south, in a circular survey around the Sea, it ends in Book 17 with Egypt, Ethiopia and Libya. Since earlier geo-ethnographic surveys were devoted to one region at a time, whether as part of a digression in an historiographical treatise or as part of a monograph on a certain country, Strabo's wider approach required a different model. He therefore followed the traditional order of the earliest *periegesis* of Hecataeus and of the *periploi* moving from west to east. But first he offered geographical, demographic and political reasons for beginning with Europe:

> I must begin with Europe, because it is both varied in form and admirably adapted by nature for the development of excellence in

men and governments, and also because it has contributed most of
its own store of good things to the other continents.

(2.5.26, C 126)

Although the *Geography* is based on many sources and pieces combined
together, Strabo's touch is apparent in the overall assembling of the details
into one carefully edited whole. The result is a unitary work, the interrelations between the various parts resulting from a calculated and defined
plan. This planning and unity may indicate also a relatively short time of
writing, for in spite of the length of the work and the enormous amount
and variety of detail included, the writer has all the parts in mind and
announces his descriptive plans in advance, according to a certain scheme.
This impression is based on several phrases and rhetorical means used
throughout the work.

There are many internal cross-references reminding the reader that a certain
detail was mentioned earlier or will occur later in the work. These expressions
use a general phraseology without alluding to a specific topic, for instance,
referring back: 'as was said' (10.2.1, C 450), 'it was said before' (12.3.5,
C 542), 'as I have said' (13.1.6, C 584), and also forward, which is more rare:
'I will mention' (7.5.7, C 316), 'I will say later' (12.3.9, C 544), 'I will clarify
right away' (16.1.25, C 747). The great majority of these references are
accurate, that is, they truly indicate that a theme has already been discussed
or is about to be discussed, and all are generally short-ranged, so to speak, in
that they refer to parts of the same book or are relatively near the reference
itself. In this way Strabo creates the sense of a whole continuous composition,
with connected parts, while showing that he has in mind what he has already
noted and knows what he is about to describe.

Beside these general cross-references, Strabo sometimes inserts more
detailed allusions mentioning the exact topic and occasionally even the place
where he had already touched on the same motif. To give only a few out
of numerous examples: 'Sinope is beautifully equipped both by nature and
by human foresight . . . and it has . . . wonderful pelamydes-fisheries, of
which I have already made mention, saying that the Sinopeans get the
second catch and the Byzantians the third' (12.3.11, C 545), thus alluding
to 7.6.2, C 320; 'The people of Priene serve as priests at this sacrifice, but
I have spoken of them in my account of the Peloponnese' (14.1.20, C 639),
referring to 8.7.2, C 384 which is in the book focusing on the Peloponnese;
and 'I have already discussed the levels of the bodies of water in my first
notes (*hypomnemata*)' (17.1.25, C 804), referring to the discussion in the
first of the two introductory books of the *Geography*, at 1.1.20, C 11. This
kind of reference is generally long-ranged, that is, it recalls themes discussed
in books preceding the one in which the allusion appears.

Strabo's use of expressions comparing phenomena, toponyms, topographies
and other details is another technique indicating his thorough awareness of

the entire survey so that he can easily find parallels in it. This too enhances the assumption of a relatively short time of composition and contradicts the suggestion that Strabo wrote the work over more than one decade. Several examples, representing many more, will suffice: turning the water of the Euphrates into canals in order to avoid flooding reminds Strabo of the same phenomenon occurring in the Nile (16.1.9, C 740); the size and character of the snakes in Arabia is compared to the Indian and the Libyan snakes (16.4.16, C 775); the volume of import and export in Alexandria is collated with the same in Puteoli (17.1.7, C 793); Egyptian temple reliefs resemble Etruscan and Greek ones (17.1.28, C 806).

Strabo's clear and defined plan of writing is apparent also in his summaries, mostly found at the beginning of each book, covering what was surveyed up to that point and what will come next.[41] These sections help the reader to follow the extensive work and give the impression that the author knows his goal in advance. For instance:

> Now that I have described Iberia and the Celtic and Italian tribes, along with the islands near by, it will be next in order to speak of the remaining parts of Europe ...
>
> (7.1.1, C 289)

and

> I began my description by going over all the western parts of Europe surrounded by the inner and the outer sea, and now that I have encompassed in my survey all the Barbarian tribes in Europe ... I shall give an account of the remainder of the geography of Greece.
>
> (8.1.1, C 332)

A similar outline appears at the beginning of each of the descriptive books, except for Book 6 where it is put in the middle (6.1.15, C 265) since the first part is a thematic continuation of Book 5 describing Italy. These summaries are more frequent in the later books, and this is understandable, for the longer the work, the greater the amount of information, and therefore the greater the need for such guiding sections, helping the reader to follow the course of the survey.

The general scheme of the description is based on the traditional geographical and ethnographic approach of the Greek historians and geographers, that is, first the country – its borders, its dimensions, its fauna and flora, and then its inhabitants – their history, their appearance and their customs. Each regional description therefore has a fixed plan, beginning with a delimitation of its geographical borders and a general survey of the territories included in it. Following this general opening, which often refers to the name of the region, Strabo gives a detailed and systematic account, always according to a geographical order influenced by local conditions, coastlines, river beds or other topographies (chapter 2, p. 40). Several times he stresses the order determined by natural conditions, for instance: 'I must tell about the Alps themselves . . . keeping the same order in my description as is given me by the nature of the country' (4.6.1, C 201); 'It is proper that I too, following the natural character of the regions, should make the sea my counsellor' (8.1.3, C 334); and 'such order and division is suggested by the nature of the regions' (12.3.42, C 563).[42] Then follow a great variety of details on local mythology, history, ethnography, botany, zoology and other matters.

Thollard has shown that Strabo's order of description is part of a systematic attitude determined by several guide-lines. These usually and primarily follow a linear pattern which facilitates the description of sites along the lines formed by coastlines and river beds (chapter 2, p. 40) or by roads. This linear order avoids the need to form a subjective order according to importance. In this sense the Homeric 'Catalogue of Ships' (below, p. 175) is also a sort of pattern which helps the author determine the order and the framework of the survey. Within each region the survey usually goes from east to west, continents before islands. As for the ethnographic element, the description generally begins with the more civilized and ends with the more Barbaric peoples. Thus there is a scheme and a system which is applied according to the particular condition of each region.[43] It should be born in mind that such aids are essential in organizing such an enormous and variated compilation of details.

Within this convention a unique tone may be discerned in each book, sometimes obvious, sometimes subtle. The division of the work into seventeen units corresponds to clear thematic divisions. Each book focuses on a different region, and each also has some stylistic characteristics. These derive from the natural differences between regions, requiring a distinct descriptive vocabulary, but also from Strabo's access to separate kinds of sources for each area (below, p. 180). In general, there are several themes which occupy his mind and constantly affect the nature of the survey in each section, according to circumstances. He is always aware of the political situation of the regions, and therefore refers to Roman dominance whenever applicable, as well as Parthian. He is also aware of major historical occurrences, for example Alexander's presence. As regards the more geographical themes he is impressed by peculiar phenomena. He sometimes incorporates wider discussions of ideas and concepts but always in the appropriate context and stimulated by a certain theme in the course of the survey. Ethnographic and geographic features therefore determine the special emphases in the books.

Strabo is aware of the impossibility of describing all regions with an equal amount of precision and an identical methodology. This disadvantage arises from the position of the geographer, clearly different if he is an Indian or a Greek, and in fact defines the difference between a chorography and a geography (above, p. 154). Political changes in the world also present some difficulties in acquiring information, for borders move, centres of power change and various leaders rule various regions. Moreover, even if the *oikoumene* were one empire or one state, its various parts would not be equally known, but the closer regions would be better known (1.1.16, C 9–10). Strabo's pragmatic considerations also affect the individual character of each book, since the goals and intentions of his audience – statesmen and philosophers – are distinctive to each region. Thus information relevant for India is certainly different from details pertaining to Asia Minor.

In view of these factors determining the special tendency of each book in advance, we should try to examine the particular constitution of each of the seventeen books of the *Geography*. This examination is not intended to summarize the books but rather to accentuate and highlight some themes which seem to stand out as their specific features. Strabo uses a construction similar to the one he employed in his earlier *History*. There he began his survey with four introductory books and in the geographical work as well the first two books form a separate unit of 'notes' (*hypomnemata*) (17.1.25, C 804; 17.1.36, C 809) serving as introduction. Books 1 and 2 are therefore particular in content and form. In them Strabo announces his intentions and goals, then presents the themes to be discussed in the work and refers to Greek precedents of geographical writing and thought.

The work opens with the declaration that geography in general requires wide learning and that it is a matter for a philosopher. Then Strabo explains the particular scope and purpose of his own geographical work (1.1.1–2.1, C 1–14). These opening remarks are followed by a presentation of Homer as the father of geography and then by a systematic survey of other geographers' perception of Homer, the extent of truth and knowledge in his poems, and various geographical themes in the epics (1.2.2–34, C 15–41). The discussion is constantly interwoven with allusions to Homeric scholars and interpreters, such as Aristarchus, Crates, Aristonicus, Demetrius and Apollodorus (chapter 2, p. 38). Then follows a thorough criticism of Eratosthenes, his methodology and his untruths (1.3.1–2.1.1, C 47–67); some critical notes on Hipparchus (2.1.1–5, C 67–9; 2.1.20, C 77 and so on); a general discussion on the credibility of various kinds of sources (2.1.8, C 70 onwards); a discussion of Posidonius' geographical notions (2.2.1, C 94 onwards) and of Polybius' opinions (2.4.1, C 104 onwards). From the presentation of their errors emerges the justification for Strabo's writing of a new geographical work. The last part of Book 2 (2.5.1, C 109 to the end) surveys some scientific matters pertaining to the shape and size of the *oikoumene* and involves mathematical and astronomical calculations, or more accurately a summary of previous calculations performed by Eratosthenes, Hipparchus and other predecessors. This is the only part of the *Geography* where Strabo discusses scientific geography, whereas the entire work is essentially descriptive.

The beginning of Book 3 is a transition from the introduction to the systematic survey of the *oikoumene*. The survey focuses on Iberia and some adjacent islands such as the Balearics. Against the background of the conventional pattern of geographical survey, the description of Iberia is unique in its emphases.

The Roman presence in Iberia and its cultural influence on the indigenous inhabitants is the central theme in this book. Many places in the region are introduced in a Roman context, when Strabo alludes to their foundation by Romans, such as Corduba by Marcellus (3.2.1, C 141), or to some nearby military actions. The relevance of some references and their importance is therefore determined by Roman campaigns, for instance the war between Pompey's sons and Caesar and Antony (3.2.2, C 141) and the actions of Sertorius in the Celtiberian War (3.4.10, C 161). This basic feature, dictated by Roman history and rule, brings in other connected themes. Strabo elaborates on the administrative system in the region, the various officials sent there and their number (3.4.19–20, C 165–7). He also stresses the Barbaric character of the inhabitants and the fact that some of them have adjusted to the Roman way of life (3.2.15, C 151 and chapter 2, p. 75 and chapter 4, p. 115).

Because of Rome's military and political interests in Iberia, this book abounds with strategic and military information. Strabo includes a detailed list of the weapons used by the Iberian tribes, for instance describing the Lusitanii:

> They have a small shield two feet in diameter, concave in front, and suspended from the shoulders by means of thongs . . . they have a dirk or a butcher's knife. Most of them wear linen cuirasses, a few wear chain-wrought cuirasses and helmets with three crests, but the rest wear helmets made of sinews. The foot soldiers wear greaves also, and each soldier has several javelins, and some also make use of spears . . .
>
> (3.3.6, C 154)

and

> The Iberians were once, virtually all of them, peltasts, and wore light armour on account of their brigand life . . . using javelin, sling and dirk. And intermingled with their forces of infantry was a force of cavalry, for their horses were trained to climb mountains, and whenever there was need for it, to kneel down promptly at the word of command.
>
> (3.4.15, C 163)

and the excellent slingers of the Balearic isles (3.5.1, C 168).

Another kind of strategic information especially emphasized is the record of rivers in the peninsula, their nature, their length and the extent to which they are navigable and permit penetration into the hinterland (chapter 2, p. 41). Strabo describes how high tide helps ships to enter the country through the estuaries. The tide pushes them inside, but when the water recedes the ships remain on dry land until the next tide refloats them (3.1.9, C 140; 3.2.4, C 143). Lists of harbours on the coasts of Iberia are also strategically and commercially useful (3.4.7, C 159) and Strabo further stresses the profitable potential of the country by elaborating on local products exported to Italy, such as grain, wine, olive oil, wax, honey, pitch, dyes, salted fish, wool, rams for breeding and so on (e.g. 3.2.6, C 144). Shipping access to the region therefore not only serves military purposes but is also useful for economic pursuits. The information may be derived from certain *periploi*. These details are useful for generals and statesmen who also have economic interests, precisely Strabo's intended readers (1.1.23, C 13 and above). Note also that in his report of the products exported he speaks particularly of Italy and thus points to the Roman focus of the entire work.

The general impression is that the Romans are still in a state of war in Iberia, or at least that this theme is very relevant to the survey. Although at the time of composition there was no active war front in the region, the pacification of Iberia continued up to Augustus' time so that the military theme is still very dominant while Strabo's sources are not necessarily updated. Strabo himself explains why the surrender took more than two hundred years. He says that the Romans fought in separate parts of Iberia and not in the entire region at once, since they had to deal with disunited tribes (3.4.5, C 158).

The barbarity of the inhabitants and the Roman conquests and military involvement are connected to another theme that pertains especially to this region. Strabo shows that Iberia is situated on the fringes of the *oikoumene* since the most western point of Europe and of the entire known world is located in it (3.1.4, C 137) and he indicates the limitations of knowledge about certain places (3.4.19, C 165–6).

Book 4 describes Gaul and its various parts (4.4.1–6, C 176–99), the British Isle, Ireland and Thule, the northern island identified as the Shetlands[44] (4.5.1–5, C 199–201), and the Alps (4.5.6, C 201). To some degree it includes topics similar to those of Book 3, since both discuss boundary regions of the Roman empire and represent the contacts of the Romans with the ferocious and barbaric nations of western and northern Europe. Here too the Roman presence is stressed and particularly the campaigns of Julius Caesar whose commentaries are one of the main sources for this part of the survey. In this book Strabo also alludes to the military ability of the Gallic and British tribes (for instance 4.4.1, C 195; 4.4.3, C 196; 4.6.2, C 202), but this is less central than in Book 3. Once again it can be attributed to Strabo's sources, such as Caesar, and to the state of active war obtaining not long before the time of writing.

Another central theme is the behaviour of the local tribes, whose customs Strabo defines as 'barbaric, wild, simple and strange': the Gauls hang their enemies' heads on horses' necks and then put them above their doors (4.4.5, C 198); the British cannot produce cheese and do not engage in agriculture (4.5.2, C 200); the people of Ireland eat their ancestors and commit incest (4.5.4, C 201); and the Vindelici are very cruel towards their enemies and murder pregnant women (4.6.8, C 206 and chapter 2, p. 77).

This book contains long lists of the names of various tribes, with reference to their position in the geographical layout but with no further description of their character and customs. For instance: 'above the Cavari are situated the Vocontii, Tricorii, Iconii, and Medulli' (4.1.11, C 185) and

> West of the Treveri and the Nervii dwell the Senones and the Remi, and farther on, the Atrebatii and the Eburones. And after the Menapii, on the sea, are, in their order, the Morini, the Belloaci, the Ambiani, the Suessiones, and the Caleti . . .
>
> (4.3.5, C 194)

and many more. This again is a feature which may derive from Strabo's sources.

Some of these regions are also situated at the boundaries of the *oikoumene* and therefore the available information on them is vague, for instance Ireland (4.5.5, C 201), and Thule which is even outside the boundaries of the *oikoumene* and all that is known about it derives from unreliable sources such as Pytheas of Massilia (4.5.5, C 201).

Books 5 and 6 are one thematic and geographical unit since both deal with Italy, from the north to Campania in Book 5 and southern Italy and Sicily in Book 6, including the Liparean islands, Malta and other islands between Sicily and Libya. They are similar in style and form. The historical dimension is very apparent in the Italian survey.[45] Strabo constantly alludes to the Italian past. He focuses on 'foundation stories' of various Italian cities including Rome itself, and emphasizes the Greek origin of many, established by Greek settlers and founded on a Greek cultural basis. Such are Pisa (5.2.5, C 222); Cosa (5.2.8, C 225); Rome itself (5.3.3, C 230); Elea (6.1.1, C 252); Lipara (6.2.10, C 275) and many more.

The emphasis on the Greek origins of the Roman people may derive from Strabo's pride as a Greek scholar, intending to show that the Roman 'superpower' of his time was founded on Greek culture and values.[46] Dionysius of Halicarnassus in his *Roman Antiquities* 1.4.1 and 1.5.4 also told his readers that Rome was founded by Greek settlers, thus trying to contradict the Greek prejudice about the unelevated beginnings of Rome. But Strabo also quotes the Roman historian Acilius as ascribing the origin of the city of Rome to the Greeks, commenting that the notion that Rome is an Arcadian colony is 'older and fabulous' (5.3.3, C 230). This trait may then derive from the tendency of the Romans themselves to rely on Greek precedents.[47] The preoccupation with the Greek origins of Italian cities causes Strabo to engage in a digression on the Pelasgians, their name and their dispersion, on the basis of notions in Homer and Hesiod as well as poets such as Aeschylus and Euripides (5.2.4, C 220–1).

The historical dimension is not confined to the Greek 'foundation stories', but is apparent also through Strabo's allusions to the Roman traditions on the foundation of Rome (5.3.2–3, C 229–30) and to Hannibal's presence in Italy, including an extensive discussion of his passage through northern Italy (5.2.9, C 226–7).

Another characteristic of the Italian survey has to do with local conditions, that is, the system of Roman roads.[48] In numerous passages Strabo uses the roads in order to simplify orientation and elucidate the description:

> As for the rest of the cities of Latium, their positions may be defined, some by a different set of distinctive marks, and others by the best-known roads that have been constructed through Latium, for they are situated either on these roads, or near them, or between them.
>
> (5.3.9, C 236)

For this he would have had to have an updated Roman source recording the layout of the Italian road system and this was possibly part of the lists included in Agrippa's project (chapter 4, p. 128). In Book 6, however, there are fewer allusions to Roman roads and a stronger emphasis on the transformation of what were originally Greek cities into totally Roman regions (6.1.2–3, C 253–4). These undertones are naturally connected to the historical background and conditions of southern Italy where Greek colonies were established already in the eighth century BCE and which was less central in relation to the region of Rome, and therefore had fewer roads.

The last part of the book (6.4.1–2, C 268–88) is devoted to the review of Rome's ascendance as an empire from the beginnings to the present. It is not an integral part of the geographical survey but stands out as an historical digression with political implications as a sort of summary of the description of Italy (chapter 4, p. 107).

Book 7 is not uniform in terms of its contents, which vary in emphasis according to the regions depicted. The first part, up to 7.4.8, C 312, describes the German tribes; the second part surveys Pannonia and Illyria; and finally, beginning with 7.7.1, C 320, it outlines Macedonia and Thrace, this last part being partly fragmentary.

The sections on the German tribes emphasize Roman military and political involvement in the region, which is also closely connected to the expansion of local information: 'These tribes have become known through their wars with the Romans' (7.1.4, C 291). Therefore the limits of conquest in these territories are also the limits of the known *oikoumene*. Strabo discusses Augustus' policies concerning the local tribes. The emperor preferred not to cross the Albis, and not to incite non-hostile tribes against the Romans. Had he done so, says Strabo, those tribes would have become better known to us, for our knowledge of the region ends with the Albis, beyond which hardly anything is familiar (7.2.4, C 294, quoted in chapter 4, p. 110). He admits: 'I cannot tell the precise boundaries' (7.3.1, C 295). The limits of knowledge (also in 7.3.17, C 306) have to do also with the extreme weather conditions (7.3.18, C 307). This awareness of the borders of empire and of knowledge is the pretext for a lengthy discussion of the credibility of ancient sources dealing with myths of boundaries and 'extreme' nations, and particularly with Homer's credibility (7.3.1–10, C 294–303). The fact that this is a border region determines its tones of both Barbarism and the Roman presence, as in Books 3 and 4.

Strabo speaks of military campaigns that occurred in his time, referring to Augustus, Tiberius and his brother Nero Drusus Claudius. In 7.1.3, C 290–1 he describes Drusus' conquests in the German region, the battles he initiated, a naval victory he gained and the exact place where he died in 9 CE. He also interweaves Augustus' relationship with the subjugated tribes and their leaders. Maroboduus stayed in Rome when young (7.1.3, C 290) and the tribes sent Augustus precious gifts with a request for Roman friendship (7.2.1, C 293). Tiberius' campaigns are alluded to in the context of an island on the lake between the Rhine and the Ister which formed his base in the naval battle against the Vindelici (7.1.5, C 292). The general emphasis is on the subjugation of the wild Germans and their surrender to Roman power: 'All were subdued by the Romans' (7.2.2, C 294).

The description of Pannonia, Illyria, Thrace and Macedonia includes a survey of coordinates, topographies and various tribes, and a broad discussion of the magnificent past of Greece in comparison with its present ruin and desolation (7.7.1–3, C 320–2; 7.7.9, C 327).

Books 8–10 all survey Greece but each has its own character. Book 8 describes western Greece and mainly the Peloponnese, 'the acropolis of Greece as a whole' (8.1.3, C 334). First Strabo gives a general introduction on Greece and its various parts and on its division according to dialects deriving from ethnic movements in early Greek history (8.1.1–2, C 332–4). The main emphasis in this book is on the ancient past of the region, connected to mythological situations and stories. This is manifested in allusions to genealogies of traditional Greek characters, for instance Nauplius in 8.6.2, C 368–9, and the identification of venues of famous mythological events, such as the site where Nestor was born (8.3.7, C 339), the temple where Telemachus found the people of Pylus sacrificing (8.3.16, C 344), and the place where Bellerophon caught the winged horse Pegasus (8.6.21, C 379). The centrality of Homer as a source also determines some of the discussions which focus on understanding the text and identifying sites mentioned by him. At the same time, the Roman presence is ignored or rarely mentioned.

Book 9 focuses on central Greece, that is, Attica, Boeotia, Phocis, Locris and Thessaly. The basis for the description is clearly the Homeric 'Catalogue of Ships'. The order of the geographical survey and the cities mentioned in it are determined by the list of the forces in the Trojan War as it appears in the second book of the *Iliad* (chapter 2, p. 36). This is a clear case of a source determining the order of description: 'As for the remaining cities, it is not worth while to mention any of them except those which are mentioned by Homer' (9.4.5, C 426) and 'here, too, [sc. Thessaly] there will be an enumeration of famous names of cities, and especially because of the poetry of Homer' (9.5.3, C 430 and many more).

Other historical events also function as a background for the survey, mainly the Persian presence in central Greece (for instance 9.4.16, C 429), the Macedonian campaigns (9.5.10, C 433), and the actions of the people of Thebes (e.g. 9.2.5, C 402–3).

Book 10, the third on Greece, describes Euboea, Aetolia, Acarnania and Crete, and then the Cyclades and the Sporades. The Homeric epic is still the basis of description and identification of sites (for instance 10.1.3, C 445) and Strabo adds long discourses on Homeric interpretations (10.2.10–12, C 453–5). Twice he digresses from the systematic survey and engages in long discussions, and in both cases he apologizes for the digression and explains why he decided to include it in the *Geography*. First he has a broad discussion of Greek rites and religious ceremonies involving music. To this he attaches quotations from poets such as Pindar (10.3.13, C 469) and Hesiod (10.3.19, C 471), as well as from the tragedies of Aeschylus (10.3.16, C 470), Sophocles (10.3.14, C 470) and Euripides (10.3.13, C 469). The context for this digression is the Aetolian tribe of the Curetes and the theological component of their history. Strabo drifts into a relatively long survey of the rites in various Greek cities and into a general meditation on myth and religion. But he is fully aware that this is a digression from the original plan and therefore makes a reference to this fact at the beginning (10.3.8, C 466) and at the end of the passage (10.3.23, C 474).

The second digression (10.4.16–22, C 480–4) deals with the ancient Cretan constitution, Strabo saying: 'I have assumed that the constitution of the Cretans is worthy of description both on account of its peculiar character and on account of its fame' (10.4.22, C 484).

What determines the special traits in this book are the geographical details of the region – a people or an island – which due to special historical circumstances make Strabo expand the discussion.

Books 11–14 form another geographical unit divided into sub-units. These four books all describe Asia Minor, each concentrating on a separate part of the region and therefore with its own descriptive character. Book 11 surveys the eastern part of Asia and the south-eastern parts of the Black

Sea up to Media and Armenia. Several themes are perceptible in the background of this part of the survey and influence its special character. First, the story of Jason, Medea and the golden fleece which is associated with ethnographic and toponymic phenomena, for instance the Caucasian tribes' habit of collecting gold on fleeces (11.2.19, C 499); the existence of memorials and temples devoted to Jason throughout Armenia (11.4.8, C 503); the dress style of the Medes introduced by Medea (11.13.10, C 526); the canal built by Jason to connect the Araxes and the Caspian Sea (11.14.13, C 531); and the notion that the Medes and the Armenians are the descendants of Jason and Medea (11.14.14, C 531). This myth, together with the stories about the Amazons, brings Strabo to discuss the distinction between truth and myth (11.5.3, C 504).

Another central theme is the historical presence of Alexander the Great. Strabo complains about the geographical and historical distortions concerning these regions found in the writings of Alexander's contemporaries who were motivated by flattery (chapter 4, p. 111). In spite of this criticism, much information is still based on Alexander's actions, mainly in the eastern parts of the region (for instance 11.11.4, C 517–18 and many more). Strabo's sources for this part of the survey are in fact often the historians of Alexander.

A third determinant, so to speak, of the nature of the description is the political balance of world power. Strabo describes the Parthian power and its relation to Rome. Although he thinks that Rome is the leading political and cultural power in the world, he is still aware of the fact that on the edges of the Roman empire there are other forces which are not subject to Roman rule (chapter 4, p. 113). This is apparent especially in this book, which surveys the regions ruled by the Parthian empire.

Book 12 surveys the central part of Asia Minor including Cappadocia and Pontus up to Phrygia and Mysia. Strabo's personal background is accentuated through his autopsy of various parts of his homeland and neighbouring territories (chapter 1, p. 18). The relations of his ancestors with the Pontic kings (chapter 1, p. 5) seem to influence him to elaborate on the royal house of Pontus past and present. Thus he surveys Mithridates Eupator's actions and often refers to the royal family, as for instance in 12.3.1, C 540–1. He also alludes to the political conditions of his time, dominated by the Roman presence (12.2.11, C 540; 12.3.9, C 544 etc.) and by Queen Pythodoris' rule over part of the region (12.3.29, C 555–6; 12.3.37, C 559–60). There is one central digression on the Homeric text and its reliability, assessed through Strabo's fierce confutation of Apollodorus' notions (12.3.20–7, C 549–55).

Book 13 describes the region around Troy, that is, the Troad, Lydia and the adjacent islands such as Lesbos. The dominant theme influencing the special tendencies of this description is naturally the Trojan War as described by Homer and as understood by his commentators and by Strabo himself (chapter 2, p. 37). The Homeric epics help Strabo to recognize the area around Troy and the topography helps to understand various details in the *epos*. Therefore there are long and exhaustive discussions in this book about the Homeric text, including an analysis of strategic moves in the ancient war, of local topography and of various other textual problems, for instance 13.1.2, C 582; 13.1.7, C 584–5; and many more.

The western part of Asia, that is Ionia, Caria, Pamphylia, Cilicia and the islands Samos, Chios, Rhodes and Cyprus, is described in Book 14. This abounds with lists of scholars born and active in the region, almost every city in the survey having a short list attached of native-born scholars from various fields (chapter 2, p. 79). This probably has to do with the background of Ionia as an important cultural centre since the sixth century BCE. The historical context is also emphasized in this book, with constant allusions to the actions of the Persians, Alexander and the Romans.

The description of India in Book 15 is heavily influenced in content as well as in style by the knowledge derived from the campaigns of Alexander the Great as described by his historians. This book is in fact a series of quotations almost without any Strabonian connecting passages. The general impression is of associative writing and of very simple, unrefined and barely edited stitching together of various quotations. A clear and systematic descriptive plan is less felt here because the survey is cut into pieces. The progress of Alexander's campaigns in the eastern region forms the background of the description, for instance: 'after the Cophes he went to the Indus, then to the Hydaspes, then to the Acesines and the Hyarotis, and last to the Hypanis' (15.1.27, C 697).

Since the rivers in India and particularly the Ganges and its tributaries are very dominant in the life of the inhabitants and in the nature of the country, Strabo, or rather his sources, engage in constant comparisons with conditions in Egypt and with the Nile itself in terms of the nature of the river and also the fauna and flora (15.1.19–26, C 692–7). The latter part of the book, beginning in 15.2.1, C 720 and surveying the Persian regions west of India, proceeds in Strabo's usual style of description, probably because the information derives from his regular sources and is more abundant. As far as political power is concerned, Strabo refers only to the Persian region which is partly dominated by the Parthians (for instance 15.3.3, C 728) and there is no indication of any Roman domination in the far east, other than the Indian recognition of Augustus' dignity (chapter 3, p. 101).

Mesopotamia, Syria, Phoenicia, Judaea, the Persian Gulf and Arabia, are the theme of Book 16. Here Strabo refers constantly to Alexander's presence in these regions (for instance 16.1.9, C 740) and to the contemporary political map formed according to the division of power between Rome and Parthia (chapter 4, p. 113):

> The Euphrates and the land beyond it constitute the boundary of
> the Parthian empire. But the parts this side of the river are held

by the Romans and the chieftains of the Arabians as far as Babylonia, some of these chieftains preferring to give ear to the Parthians and others to the Romans, to whom they are neighbours.

(16.1.28, C 748)

A dominant historical event is Gallus' campaign in Arabia, which is described in detail, perhaps according to information derived directly from the general, in 16.4.22–4, C 780–2. There is also a digression on the roles of prophets and on man's submission to God (16.2.38–9, C 761–2).

In terms of ethnography, a peculiar feature in the latter part of this book is that the nations living near the Persian Gulf are defined according to their nutrition. Thus Strabo speaks of tribes who eat roots, seeds or meat, people who milk bitches, and others who eat elephants, birds, locusts, fish and turtles (16.4.9–14, C 771–3). He is also impressed by peculiar natural phenomena such as the feature he calls Lake Sirbonis but is obviously the Dead Sea and its environs (16.2.42–4, C 763–4), and striking beasts, such as elephants, lions, leopards, rhinoceroses, camelopards (that is, giraffes), monkeys, wild carnivorous bulls, hyenas and giant snakes (16.4.15–16, C 774–5).

Book 17 completes the survey of the *oikoumene* in Africa, describing Egypt, Ethiopia and Libya. The Egyptian survey is clearly affected by Strabo's own visit to the country at the time of Aelius Gallus' mission as Roman governor. He visited many of the sites in person and his presence is felt more than in any other book of the *Geography* (chapter 1, p. 20). Because of his close relationship with Gallus Strabo was also acquainted in some detail with the administrative and military system of Roman rule in Egypt (17.1.12–13, C 797–8). The Roman presence is introduced mainly through the exploits of Caesar, Antony and Augustus (17.1.10, C 795). In the geographical description, the Nile and the yearly inundation which had fascinated geographers since Herodotus are very dominant, as they affect every aspect of the social and economic life of the inhabitants, as well as the nature of the plants and animals (17.1.3–4, C 786–9). These three features – autopsy, the Nile and the Romans – determine the nature of the Egyptian survey. In one particular context, that of the temple of Ammon, Strabo digresses into a more general discussion on oracles and divination in past and present, as used by Alexander and among the Romans (17.1.43, C 813–4).

Then he goes on to complete the African survey, first with Ethiopia and then leaping to northern Africa, that is Libya, where, as in the survey of Europe, he goes from west to east, including for instance Mauretania (17.3.2, C 825), Carthage (17.3.13, C 832) and Cyrene (17.3.21, C 837). A dominant factor in the description of these parts is again Strabo's awareness of the extreme position of these countries with respect to the borders of the *oikoumene* and therefore the limits of our knowledge of these regions:

We may conjecture that all lands lying in unbroken succession on
the same parallel of latitude are similar as regards both climate and
plants, but since several deserts intervene, we do not know all these
regions. Similarly, the regions above Ammon and the oases as far
as Ethiopia are likewise unknown. Neither can we tell the boundaries either of Ethiopia or of Libya, nor yet accurately even those
of the country next to Egypt, much less of that which borders on
the Ocean.

(17.3.23, C 839)

The survey of the *oikoumene* ends in fact with these very comments in
17.3.23, C 839, but a concluding digression follows on the ascendance of
Roman power and rule over extensive parts of the *oikoumene*. As Strabo felt
it necessary to add a brief laudatory passage at the end of the survey of the
Italian peninsula in Book 6 (above, p. 173), here too he finds a justification
for outlining the division of the *oikoumene* into provinces according to the
administrative measures formed by Augustus (17.3.24, C 839 and chapter
4, p. 109). He therefore specifies in detail the provinces of the Roman
people and the provinces controlled directly by Caesar Augustus, thus adding
a sort of Augustan frame to the broad description of the entire world.

Three main factors seem to influence the character of the various descriptions and determine their tendencies and accentuations. First, the physical,
topographical and ethnographical conditions of the region: rivers in Book 3,
tribes in Book 4, the road system in Books 5 and 6, the boundaries of the
oikoumene in Book 7, islands in Book 10, numerous scholars in Book 14.

Second, the nature of the sources: Roman sources in Books 3 and 4,
periploi in Books 8 and 14, the Homeric 'Catalogue of Ships' in Book 9,
Strabo's autopsy in Books 12 and 17, Homer and Demetrius of Scepsis in
Book 13, the historians of Alexander in Books 11 and 15.

Third, pragmatism and utility: weapons and strategic information for
military and commercial purposes in Book 3, tribal names and settlements
in Book 4, the political situation in Books 3, 6, 7, 11 and 12.

Geographical conditions and the nature of the sources are given factors
with which Strabo had to deal and shape his description accordingly.
However, the pragmatic emphases are his own and are the product of his
own considerations, control and decisions.

The result is a unitary colossal work (in Strabo's phrasing) which at the
same time has smaller units of a particular descriptive nature. As already
remarked, Strabo himself is aware of the fact that various parts of the world
are presented in different degrees of elaboration according to the point of
view and origin of the geographer (1.1.16, C 9–10). Therefore it is not
surprising that in his own description three regions have especially broad
treatment: Italy in Books 5 and 6, Greece in Books 8–10, and Asia Minor
in Books 11–14. The structure of the entire work seems therefore to reflect

the portrait of the writer: born in Asia Minor, growing up and educated as a Greek and admiring Rome.[49]

SOURCES

Major work as it is, encompassing so many details from various fields of knowledge, from astronomy to zoology, the *Geography* was necessarily founded on numerous sources. Strabo himself mentions them in part. Some are central to his whole orientation and scholarly profile, such as Homer, Polybius and Posidonius and the geographers Eratosthenes, Hipparchus and Artemidorus (chapter 2). Others are Roman, for instance Fabius Pictor, Cicero, Caesar and Asinius Pollio (chapter 3). Beside these there may be sources implied indirectly, namely Augustus' *Res Gestae* and Agrippa's project (chapter 4). Strabo does not specify his sources each time he relies on them, although most of the details in the work do not and indeed cannot derive from his own experience, for instance historical facts or descriptions of remote places such as India. The fact that Strabo needed to use many sources of information does not turn him into a mere compiler of literary excerpts,[50] for, as we saw above, the colossal work is organized according to a defined plan. The author decided whether or not to use various pieces of information and applied his sense of criticism, manifested in the final assembly of the material. Therefore, although he constantly and rightly relies on other authors, he is independent and focused on his own aims, which do not necessarily include originality (above, p. 156).

Modern studies of Strabo's sources date mainly from two periods. Some are more than a hundred years old and others were published relatively recently in the last decades. Just as there are several basic sources for the entire survey which Strabo uses extensively whenever he finds them appropriate, there are also general studies of his use of these sources which do not specifically focus on a certain book. Such are Heeren (1823) who gives a general survey of the sources; Niese (1877) on Apollodorus' commentary on the Homeric 'Catalogue of Ships' as one of Strabo's sources; W. Fabricius (1888) on Theophanes of Mytilene and Dellius as sources and also on Artemidorus; Zimmermann (1888) and Munz (1929) on Posidonius and Strabo; Dubois (1891b) on Polybius and Strabo; and Däbritz (1905) on Artemidorus as Strabo's authority. Ambaglio (1988) examined Strabo's use of various Greek sources, mainly the historians.

Another characteristic of modern Strabo research is the tendency of scholars to concentrate on books of the *Geography* which relate to their own culture and geographical region, thus for example, as we shall see below, some Spanish scholars deal with Book 3 and the Italians with Books 5 and 6.

One of the primary determinants of the individual character of each book in the *Geography* is the different nature of the sources available on each region. Therefore, alongside the special topics and perhaps the literary style of every book, one can detect the typical source or sources dominant in it. Various modern studies of Strabo's individual books as well as of his sources comment on this feature.[51]

One of the problems connected with the question of sources, which is relevant to most ancient authors, is the fact that there were no conventional rules for making references to the texts one used; that is, it was widely accepted that one cited other authors without having to mention them. This general ancient habit becomes more complicated in the *Geography* because of the variety of subjects and broadness of theme, necessarily requiring numerous sources of information. We may assume that Strabo does not always mention his sources, though it is difficult to recognize any method or consistency.[52] In the introductory remarks he highlights his most admired sources, mainly Homer, Polybius and Posidonius, whom he uses extensively throughout, even though he does not mention them by name in each and every excerpt.

Because of this complexity, and because Strabo compiles many pieces of information from various periods, taking special pride in his ability to add to his predecessors' knowledge, the central question concerning his use of sources is whether he used them directly or through an intermediary source, and, more specifically, whether the compilation of various pieces of information was made by him or by the latest source quoted. Some modern studies refer extensively to this question and offer suggestions which vary according to the source or the specific book under discussion. Generally, there seems to be no reason to dismiss the possibility that Strabo read most of his sources directly, as his style of referring to them indicates. As a rule it is best to try and locate Strabo's sources among known literary authors or other recognized informants such as monumental inscriptions. Conjectures of some vague nature, such as Lasserre's anonymous 'panegyrist' as Strabo's source for the laudatory passages on Augustan peace and prosperity in Books 3 and 4,[53] only create excessive problems. However in this section I do not intend to engage in a thorough *Quellenforschung*, which would, as one can imagine, require an extremely lengthy discussion far beyond the scope and the purpose of the present book. I shall, however, propose a brief survey of the major authorities Strabo used in each book as well as indicate some modern studies relevant to various aspects of the theme.

Since Books 1 and 2 are basically a systematic critique of the ideas of Strabo's predecessors, except for the first part which covers his own purpose and orientation, and the last part which briefly surveys the subject-matter, the *oikoumene*, the sources are in fact the theme. Therefore he thoroughly examines Homer, Eratosthenes, Hipparchus, Posidonius and Polybius. He does however use some other sources, especially in the course of the Homeric discussion where he introduces some of the commentators' notions. Various themes pertaining to the *prolegomena* appear in Aly (1957) 372–97 while

Biraschi (1984) and Jacob (1986) present a general survey of the first two books. A discussion of the contents of the first two chapters of Book 1, and of Strabo's use of sources there, is to be found in Floratos (1972), esp. 16–77.

Iberia, which Strabo did not visit himself, required an extensive use of sources in Book 3 of the *Geography*. Typically, here too Strabo relies on his most admired Greek sources, as he does throughout the work. Thus he finds clues for Iberia in Homer (for instance 3.2.12–14, C 149–50) and points out information based on Polybius' investigations (for instance 3.2.10, C 148). He also indicates two persons who visited the region and gave a description based on their experiences. These are Artemidorus (for instance 3.1.4, C 137), who may be the author behind the *periplous* around the coast of Iberia which emphasizes its navigable rivers and convenient harbours (3.1.7, C 140; 3.2.3, C 142); and Posidonius (for example 3.1.5, C 138), on whose travels broad parts of Book 3 are based, for instance his visit to Gades (3.5.3–10, C 168–75). One Roman source, Silanus, is mentioned in this book (3.5.7, C 172). However, through an analysis of linguistic and thematic components of Book 3, Aly (1957) 109–14 suggested that Strabo also used another Roman source, Tanusius Geminus. This book does indeed reflect some Latin background in the form of Latin words (chapter 3, p. 88), distances expressed in Roman miles (chapter 4, p. 128) and relative elaboration on the actions of Sertorius in Spain. It is however difficult to identify the exact Roman source, whether Tanusius, Silanus or Agrippa's *Commentaries*. Still, the two latter have more to speak for them, since Strabo mentions Silanus specifically and since toponyms and distances seem to be the typical information included in Agrippa's lists. General studies on the sources of Book 3 are Zimmermann (1883), Ruge (1888) 2–46, Morr (1926), Aly (1957) 109–34 and Lasserre (1966) 4–15. Commentaries on Book 3 are García Bellido (1945) and Schulten (1952). Thollard (1987) discussed particularly the aspect of Barbarians in this and the following book and Alonso-Núñez (1992) has recently treated Strabo's description of the northern part of Iberia. As one can see, the theme has special appeal for Spanish scholars, such as Plácido Suárez (1987–8); Domínguez Monedero (1988); Cruz Andreotti (1994) and recently Cruz Andreotti (1999), with a particular discussion of sources by Trotta (1999).

A central source for Book 4 on Gaul, Britain and the Alps is Julius Caesar's commentaries of the *Bellum Gallicum* (4.1.1, C 177), whose opening sentences are echoed in Strabo's notion about the threefold division of Gaul. Klotz (1910) 69–75, observed that Strabo used in addition a later and more updated source, identified it as Timagenes of Alexandria and claimed that Strabo knew Caesar's work as well as some notions of Artemidorus and Posidonius through Timagenes and not directly. Since we know that Strabo used the works of Artemidorus and Posidonius for information on other regions, and since in this book too he seems to quote them directly, for instance Posidonius (4.1.7, C 182) and Artemidorus (4.4.6, C 198), it is unnecessary to assume the existence of an intermediary source. As for Caesar, Strabo probably had enough knowledge of Latin to be able to read the *Commentaries* (chapter 3, p. 93). One particular authority for this book and especially for the unknown regions near Thule (northern Britain, possibly the Shetlands[54]), is Pytheas of Massilia who 'is obviously more false concerning the districts which have been placed outside the inhabited world', yet is quoted on the climate, the agriculture and the nutrition of the inhabitants (4.5.5, C 201). Pytheas appears again as Strabo's source for the northern parts of Europe in Book 7 (below).[55] A partial commentary on Book 4 is Dirkzwager (1975) on 4.1.1–14, C 176–89. Various themes in this book are discussed in Aly (1957) 281–309. Law (1846) examined Strabo's description of the Alps. Wilkens (1886) 1–60 and Lasserre (1966) 106–16, discuss generally Strabo's sources in this book. Clavel-Lévêque (1974) focused on Strabo's style and concepts in the description of Gaul and its inhabitants, and Thollard (1987) applied his analysis of the theme of Barbarians to this book as well.

Books 5 and 6 form one thematic unit describing the Italian peninsula from north to south, including Sicily in the last part of Book 6. The sources are Strabo's usual ones for the entire survey, such as Ephorus, Artemidorus and Posidonius. Parts of the description are based on Strabo's autopsy, since this is the first region covered in the survey which he visited himself. On certain themes, for instance the digression on the Pelasgi, he quotes some poets such as Pindar (5.4.9, C 248). A major source for southern Italy is Antiochus of Syracuse (for instance 6.1.1, C 252), discussed in Moscati Castelnuovo (1987) 237–46. Strabo probably chose him because Antiochus was a native Sicilian, as he tends to choose natives as sources for other regions, for instance choosing Demetrius of Scepsis for the Troad in Book 13. Some details rely on the Chorographer, probably referring to the project of Agrippa (chapter 4, p. 128). Modern research has again made general assessments of various aspects of Strabo's survey of Italy. These are Aly (1957) 211–79, and the relatively recent Greco (1986), Biffi (1988), esp. xxxvii–xli on the sources, Maddoli (1988), Musti (1988) and Weiss (1991). Specific studies of the sources are Lasserre (1967) 10–28 on both books, Steinbrück (1909) on Book 5, and Hunrath (1879) and Sollima (1897) on Book 6. Greco (1986) 121–34 focused on Magna Graecia. Massaro (1986) 81–117 emphasized the temporal aspect of Strabo's Italian survey.

Strabo's sources for Book 7 are partly his usual and most frequently used ones, such as Homer and his interpreters, and the *periploi* of Artemidorus and Posidonius. He does, however, add some particular sources for this more northern part of Europe such as Pytheas of Massilia (7.3.1, C 295), the historians of Alexander, Eudoxus of Cnidus and Hecataeus of Miletus (7.7.1, C 321), both the latter visited these regions. Discussions of the sources are those of Heilmann (1885), von Stern (1917) and recently Baladié (1989) 13–41. Lulofs (1929) focused on the Scythians as described by Strabo.

There are two central sources for the information in Book 8, both determining the scope and nature of the description. The most apparent is Homer (chapter 2, p. 36), who is mentioned in almost every chapter, since he was the first to deal with the geography of Greece (8.1.1, C 332), and because Strabo was educated on him from childhood (8.3.3, C 337). Therefore he identifies various sites by consulting the Homeric epics. These references are accompanied by discussions on Homeric interpretation according to Demetrius of Scepsis and Apollodorus (for instance 8.3.6, C 338–9), and by digressions on poetic expressions (8.3.8, C 340–41 and many more). Another central source influencing the descriptive framework and its character is the *periplous*. Strabo mentions 'those who write *periploi*' as his sources (8.3.20, C 347) and specifically claims to follow the coastline as did Ephorus (8.1.3, C 334). There are numerous examples of this usage, for instance 8.3.27, C 351. Since one of the central themes in the description of the Greek region is mythology, Strabo also consults many poets, such as Hesiod (8.3.11, C 342), Stesichorus (8.3.20, C 347) and Tyrtaeus (8.4.10, C 362). His own visit to Corinth (8.6.19–21, C 377–9) is important for his information, although it does not prevent him from using written material as well (chapter 1, p. 20). Discussion of Strabo's sources for some excerpts of this book appears in Bölte (1938), and Baladié (1978) 19–32 and (1980) has surveyed the sources of the entire book, as well as Strabo's description of the Peloponnese. Other studies discuss some Strabonian issues pertaining to the entire Greek region as they appear in Books 8–10. These are Niese (1877), Wallace (1979b) and Biraschi (1994a).

The rest of the description of Greece, in Books 9 and 10, is also heavily based on Homer and particularly on the 'Catalogue of Ships'. In the background stand also Ephorus (9.2.2, C 400) and a *periplous* (9.2.21, C 408). In Book 10 the Homeric authority together with commentators such as Apollodorus, who wrote on the Homeric 'Catalogue', and Demetrius, are supplemented by the dominant sources of Ephorus, Artemidorus, and Posidonius. A brief survey of the sources of Book 10 appears in Lasserre (1971) 8–16. Funke (1991) has surveyed the description in Book 10 and its indebtedness to Homer. Aly (1957) 331–71 devoted a chapter to various themes in the whole description of Greece in Books 8–10.

Since Book 11 describes the northern parts of Asia Minor where Alexander waged his first campaigns, the historians of Alexander are especially dominant in this context. Apart from his usual sources, here Strabo uses some relatively recent ones, among whom are Theophanes of Mytilene, who visited these regions with Pompey and is the source for the survey of the Armenian region based on his visits (for instance 11.2.2, C 493). Lasserre (1975) 7–29 and Neumann (1881) give a general discussion of the sources of this book. Lünemann (1803) compared Strabo's Caucasian description with those of later seventeenth-century geographers, Kauchtschischwili (1978) examined Strabo's description of Asian Iberia beside the Caucasus, and Aly (1957)

86–108 discussed some aspects of Book 11, as he does with all the other books of the *Geography*.

Book 12 focuses on the regions in and around Strabo's homeland and therefore is partially based on his own presence there (for instance 12.2.3, C 535; 12.2.4, C 536; 12.3.39, C 561), even when he does not mention it specifically (chapter 1, p. 23). This fact does not prevent him from using various sources that are surveyed in Lasserre (1981) 12–35. General discussions of Strabo's treatment of Asia Minor appear in Aly (1957) 25–34 and Syme (1995).

Again, the theme of Book 13 is related to the sources in that they determine the nature of the description and the region requires this particular kind of sources. Since the focus here is the regions around Troy, Strabo naturally relies heavily on Homer. Another central source, connected to the Homeric context, is Demetrius of Scepsis. The fact that Demetrius came from Scepsis, which is not far from Troy, adds to the scholar's credibility for he knew the region and saw it even as a child (chapter 2, p. 38). A discussion and commentary on Strabo's description of the Troad is found in Leaf (1923) and some comments on its themes appear in Aly (1957) 310–30.

Book 14, focusing on the islands adjacent to Ionia and Pamphylia, is another indication of topography apparent in the nature of the sources, for a *periplous* is very dominant here (chapter 2, p. 42). Aly (1957) 34–68 refers to various topics pertaining to this part of Strabo's survey.

Strabo apologizes at the beginning of Book 15 on India for having to use the writings of Alexander's historians, which are not highly reliable. He also discusses the problem of the sources on India (15.1.2–10, C 685–8). He comments:

> It is necessary for us to hear accounts of this country with indulgence, for not only is it farthest away from us, but not many of our people have seen it, and even those who have seen it, have seen only parts of it, and the greater part of what they say is from hearsay, and even what they saw they learned on a hasty passage with an army through the country ... moreover, most of those who have written anything about this region in much later times, and those who sail there now, do not present any accurate information either.
>
> (15.1.2–3, C 685)

This book presents a special problem for Strabo and it therefore also has its own character in terms of style, or better, the lack of it. Since early times, information on India was mysterious and vague. This situation reached a turning point with the first organized campaign to this remote country, undertaken by Alexander the Great. For the first time a systematic description of the region appeared in a series of geographic and ethnographic monographs written by his companions. The records of Nearchus, Onesicritus, Cleitarchus and Aristobulus therefore comprise the contents of Book 15. The problem of the credibility of these sources, whose words were corrupted by flattery, disturbs Strabo, who discredits them (chapter 4, p. 111). At the same time, however, they are the only sources supplying a thorough and extensive survey of India. Therefore, this book is in fact a series of quotations almost without any authorial connecting passages. Many topics are repeated in various parts of the book, for the text is organized according to sources and not according to themes, so that Strabo quotes Nearchus, and then Aristobulus, and then Onesicritus, and then Cleitarchus, while both Nearchus and Onesicritus comment on the Indian elephants. Discussions of Strabo's sources in this book are those by Vogel (1874) and recently Engels (1998a) 146–52. Other aspects are discussed by Aly (1957) 135–56.

The dominant sources for Book 16 on Syria and Palestine are Eratosthenes (16.1.12, C 741), Posidonius, who was originally from Apameia in Syria (16.1.15, C 743); and Artemidorus, who supplies Strabo with distances between sites (16.2.33, C 760). Others are used for minor details, such as Nearchus and Orthagoras (16.3.5, C 766), Aristobulus (16.1.11, C 741) and Polyclitus (16.1.13, C 742). Modern research seems to find particular interest in the sections devoted to Jews and Judaea; such are Stern (1976), Bar-Kochva (1997) and Ludlam (1997). Aly (1957) 157–210 refers to Gallus' Arabian campaign and to the section on Moses.

The Egyptian survey in Book 17 is influenced by Strabo's own visit as Aelius Gallus' companion. Therefore his autopsy is apparent in various parts of the description (chapter 1, p. 20). He also relies on the impressions of his predecessors who visited or stayed in Egypt, such as Eratosthenes (17.1.2, C 785) and Polybius (17.1.12, C 797), or saw other parts of northern Africa, such as Posidonius (17.3.4, C 827; 17.3.10, C 830). Since Book 17 surveyed not only Egypt but also Ethiopia and Libya, Strabo had to rely on other sources as well for these regions. On the description of Libya see the study of Strenger (1913). Vogel (1884) studied the sources for this book; Ruge (1888) 71–101 discussed especially Eratosthenes and Artemidorus; and Aly (1957) 69–85 refers to various themes related to Book 17.

THE IDEAL GEOGRAPHER

Not just any person can be a geographer. He who presumes to engage in geography should acquire a broad and encyclopaedic education encompassing various fields of knowledge and 'much learning (*polymatheia*)' (1.1.12, C 7). The ideal geographer should therefore be first and foremost a philosopher, as any competent scholar and scientist should be (1.1.1, C 1). The geographer should arrive at proficiency in astronomy in order to identify the heavenly bodies and to recognize eclipses, and at knowledge of geometry in order to be able to describe shapes, sizes and distances between various sites (1.1.12–3, C 7). These are necessary in order to observe the natural differences between various countries and to fix the position of sites in the inhabited world, the *oikoumene*, for there is a difference between the appearance of large plains as plane surfaces according to the senses and their actual layout with reference to the celestial bodies. Therefore 'the person who attempts to write an account of the countries of the earth must take many of the physical and mathematical principles as hypotheses and elaborate his whole treatise with reference to their intent and authority' (2.5.1, C 109).

Knowledge of terrestrial matters which do not pertain to celestial bodies but deal with the *oikoumene* and its character is also required in geography. Therefore one should have a wide understanding of the 'history' of animals, that is, of the zoology and also the botany of land and sea (1.1.15–6, C 8). The arts, mathematics, physics, as well as history and mythology, also pertain to geography (1.1.19, C 11).

All these should be included in a good geographical survey, always focusing on useful and true information. The purpose of the geographer should be the benefit and utility of the reader. He therefore should have in mind a fixed plan of description and try not to deviate from it unless the reader's needs or curiosity require an extended discussion on certain matters. The work of the ideal geographer should therefore be confined to the physical limits of the *oikoumene* and to the conceptual limits of the theme defined according to the audience. At the same time he should be aware of political changes in the world which shift borders and some-times extend the limits of the *oikoumene* itself, thus revealing new and previously unknown regions. The ideal geographer's readers must also have the 'encyclopaedic training (*enkyklios agoge*) usual in the case of free men or of students of philosophy' in order to be able to understand geographical matters and to form an opinion about them (1.1.22, C 13).

Although he was hardly an expert mathematician or the best of zoolo-gists, Strabo undoubtedly succeeded in giving a thorough survey relating to many realms of knowledge. Relying on centuries of Greek geography and ethnography, he produced a *magnum opus* presenting a new attitude to the entire *oikoumene*. He did this with his special approach and style of pragmatism, universalism and Stoicism.

NOTES

1 STRABO'S BACKGROUND AND ANTECEDENTS

1 Olshausen *DNP* s.v. Amaseia col. 571.
2 Suda s.v. *Straton* (sic) Σ 1155 (Adler).
3 For the entire discussion see Niese 1878: 38–40; 1883: 567–75.
4 Pothecary 1997.
5 On the date see *PIR²* J 65.
6 Amasia – Pais 1908: 414–17; Rome – Niese 1878: 36–7; Ridgeway 1888.
7 Honigmann *RE* s.v. *Strabon* (no. 3) col. 84.
8 Strabo surveys Pontus in Book 12 of the *Geography* and constantly refers to historical and political matters: 12.3.1–41, C 540–63. The best modern surveys of the history of the Pontic kingdom and its dynasty are Sullivan 1980; McGing 1986; Syme 1995: 111–24; 289–301; Bosworth and Wheatley 1998.
9 On the Hellenistic character of the Pontic court, see Olshausen 1974; McGing 1986: 89–108.
10 Archaeological findings from Amasia are discussed in Cumont and Cumont 1906: 136–84; Anderson, Cumont and Grégoire 1910: 109–10; 114–18; Price and Trell 1977: 91–3.
11 Polyb. 5.43.1.
12 Jos. *AJ* 13.284; 14.34, 104, 111, 114, 137; 15.8; Suda s.v. *Straton* (sic) Σ 1155 (Adler).
13 Note that in 10.4.10, C 478 the *LCL* translation is twice in error, once in saying that Strabo's grandmother was Lagetas' sister, though the text reads *thygater*, and also in saying that Lagetas was the one who revolted, whereas *ekeinos* clearly refers to Dorylaus; the story with exactly the same wording is repeated in 12.3.33, C 557 where the context undoubtedly suggests Dorylaus.
14 Pais's attempt to recover this part of the family by emending parts of the text seems baseless and unnecessary. See Pais 1908: 410 n. 3. It is interesting to see the similar background of Strabo's contemporary Pompeius Trogus; see Alonso-Núñez 1987.
15 App. *Mith.* 17; 49; Plu. *Luc.* 17.3; *Sull.* 20.2–3; Memnon *FGrH* 434 F 1. cf. Willrich *RE* s.v. Dorylaos (nos. 2, 3) col. 1578; *DNP* s.v. Dorylaos (nos. 1, 2) col. 797; McGing 1986: esp. 38–9.
16 Plu. *Luc.* 17. 3 trans. B. Perrin (*LCL*) slightly adapted.
17 See Katherine Clarke's observation that this is conventional in geographical writings in contrast to historiography, Clarke 1997.
18 Suda s.v. *Straton* (sic) Σ 1155 (Adler); Plu. *Luc.* 28. On Strabo's historiographical project see chapter 2, p. 69.
19 Kajanto 1965: 19; 63–4; 239.
20 Bowersock 1965: 128–9.
21 Bowersock 1965: 128 n. 7.
22 Glover 1969: 227.

23 On Aristodemus see Suda s.v. *Iason* I 52 (Adler); *FGrH* 22 F 1a, b; Schwarz *RE* s.v. Aristodemos (no. 30) col. 925; Robert 1940: 146, 148. On the special scholarly atmosphere in Nysa, see Ruge *RE* s.v. Nysa (no. 10); Robert 1940: 144–8. On Sostratus' geographical work see *FHG* 4, 504–5.

24 Cf. Robert 1940: 148.

25 Richards 1941: 82. Sihler 1923: 136–7 suggests Tarsus. On Xenarchus, see Moraux *RE* s.v. Xenarchos (no. 5) col. 1422.

26 On Tyrannion see Suda s.v. *Tyrannion* T 1184 (Adler); Wendel *RE* s.v. Tyrannion (no. 2) col. 1811.

27 Cf. Plu. *Sull.* 26.1. On this library see Lindsay 1997a.

28 Cic. *Att.* 2.6.1 trans. E.O. Winstedt (*LCL*); cf. *Att.* 2.7.1 and Shackleton-Bailey 1965 ad loc. For indications that Cicero might still have written a geographical work, see Geiger 1985: 77.

29 Horace L. Jones, the English translator of the *Geography* in the *LCL*, suggested that Andronicus of Rhodes was another teacher of Strabo (*LCL* vol. VII, p. 270–1 n. 2), probably because he was the teacher of Boethus who was Strabo's fellow-student (below). We would, however, expect Strabo to say so specifically. Cf. Lindsay 1997a: 296–7.

30 Ath. 14. 657 F.

31 See discussion in Schweighaeuser 1805: 645–6.

32 On this literary feature see p. 79.

33 This is probably where he met Strabo. Pais 1908: 417 and Sihler 1923: 137 suggest Tarsus. On Athenodorus see Hülser *DNP* s.v. Athenodoros (no. 3) col. 203; *FGrH* 746; Bradford Welles 1962: 54–6; Cic. *Att.* 16.11.4; 16.14.4; Dio Cass. 56.43.2; Dio Chr. 33.48; Zos. 1.6.2. On his relationship with Augustus see Grimal 1945; 1946. Strabo mentions another Stoic Athenodoros of Tarsus, called Cordylion, who was the supervisor of the library in Pergamon. He lived for a while with the younger Cato, who eventually slew him (14.5.14, C 674 and chapter 5). On the distinction between the two Athenodoroi, see Geiger 1971: 170.

34 On Strabo's description of Petra based on Athenodorus' impressions see G.R.H. Wright 1969: 113–16.

35 On Boethus and his philosophy, see von Arnim *RE* s.v. Boethos (no. 4) col. 601; Gottschalk *DNP* s.v. Boëthos (no. 4) col. 725; *SVF* 3, 265–7; Dobson 1914; Huby 1981.

36 On the distinction between three poets with the same name and the identification of Strabo's friend, see Gow and Page 1968: II, 263–4; Degani and Heinze *DNP* s.v. Diodoros (no. 9) col. 590.

37 Polyb. 12.28.5; Cic. *de Orat.* 1.5, 9–12, 69–73, 128, 210–21, 256; Vitr. 1.1–18, cf. Strabo's allusion to the knowledge required from an architect as compared with a geographer: 1.1.13, C 7; 2.5.1, C 109.

38 Varro, *Opuscula*, F. Ritschl (ed.), 3, 352–402. Medicine and architecture were not part of the classic course of education and were not included in the seven arts which became canonical in medieval society. See Marrou 1965: 266–7; 481–4; Wagner 1983.

39 Cf. Smyth 1956: 75 D; 3015.

40 Niese 1878: 36–7.

41 Häbler 1884.

42 Pais 1908: 414–17; 427.

43 Anderson 1923: 11–13.

44 So indicates Ridgeway 1888: 84.

45 Cf. Niese 1878: 44 and Pais 1908: 419–20.

46 Waddy 1963: 296–8.

47 For suggestions of his routes, see Pais 1908: 419; Waddy 1963: 298.
48 See discussion of the topography and the sight revealed to Strabo, in Wallace 1969.
49 For the date see Jameson 1968: 78–9.
50 Armayor 1985: 85–99 shows that this description is not based on autopsy, which may indicate that although present in the place, Strabo preferred to attach an already extant, though inaccurate, written survey.
51 Pais 1908: 419. His theory about Strabo's eastern aspirations does not seem to comply with other evidence, which portrays Strabo as a Greek Augustan scholar.
52 Pais 1908: 419 n. 6 suggested Berytus and Ascalon, based on the fact that both cities are situated on the sea route from Alexandria to Isus and thence to Amasia via Comana. The description of Berytus is, however, restricted to distances (14.6.3, C 683) and historical facts (16.2.19, C 756) and Ascalon is noted briefly as a small town, a good onion market and the birthplace of Antiochus the philosopher (16.2.29, C 759). All these details may derive from a literary source and do not in themselves support Pais's assumption. Similarly his suggestion that Strabo met Nicolaus of Damascus in Syrian Antiochia (Pais 1908: 412, 428) has no support in the short description of the city (16.2.4–5, C 750) and seems to arise from Pais's misinterpretation of the location of Nicolaus' meeting with the Indian embassy to Augustus as the venue of a meeting between himself and Strabo. The baseless conjecture that Strabo had some contact with Herod, supplying the king with advice and Roman news, is made by Roller who seems to misunderstand Strabo's travel declaration as a presentation of a whole area, whereas Strabo only indicates the most extreme points he reached. See Roller 1998: 22, 32, 49, 56–7, 64–5, 91, 115, 165.
53 Cf. the description of other cities certainly visited by Strabo, such as Rome, Alexandria and Corinth.
54 *LSJ* s.v. *deiknymi* 3.
55 Sihler 1923: 136–7; Pais 1908: 417, 419.
56 Cf. Leaf 1916: esp. 26, 31; 1923: xxviii–xxxi.
57 Cf. Strabo's notion of the exports from Turdetania to Dicaearchia and Ostia, measured also by size and number of ships, 3.2.6, C 145.
58 Niese 1878: 44 and Pais 1908: 418 claim that Strabo did not visit Sicily and Southern Italy.
59 Wallace 1972; 1979a; 1979b: 3–4.
60 Weller 1906.
61 Waddy 1963: 298–300.
62 Cordano 1994: 187–98 holds that Strabo knew Cnossos but not other Cretan cities.
63 Pais 1908: 419 n. 6.

2 STRABO AND THE GREEK TRADITION

1 Alexander was probably influenced by Aristotle. See N.J. Richardson 1992: 36.
2 Cf. De Lacy 1948; Biraschi 1984: 132–7; Long 1992: esp. 51–7; 64–6.
3 On these earlier discussions and the position of Strabo see Schenkeveld 1976: 52–6 cf. N.J. Richardson 1992. Analyses of various aspects of Strabo's scholarly relations with Homer are to be found in Neumann 1886; Floratos 1972; Biraschi 1984; 1994b.
4 For the place of Homer in Eratosthenes see Berger 1964: 19–40.
5 Cf. *FGrH* 87 F 83; Edelstein and Kidd 1972: F 216; Theiler 1982: F 1. On the extent of the influence of Polybius, Eratosthenes, Hipparchus and Posidonius on Strabo in other geographical matters see below pp. 53.

6 See Visser 1997 on the 'Catalogue'. Wallace 1970 and 1979b: 2 show that Strabo alludes to all the cities of the 'Catalogue' (almost 200) except two.

7 Göbel *RE* s.v. Menekrates (no. 27) col. 801.

8 On Strabo's use of Demetrius see Leaf 1916.

9 Cohn *RE* s.v. Aristarchos (no. 22) col. 862; Montanari and Heinze *DNP* s.v. Aristarchos (no. 4) col. 1090.

10 Kroll *RE* s.v. Krates (no. 16) col. 1634.

11 Schwarz *RE* s.v. Apollodoros (no. 61) col. 2855; Montanari and Heinze *DNP* s.v. Apollodoros (no. 7) col. 857.

12 Some of Strabo's longer discussions on Apollodorus appear in 12.3.24–7, C 552–5 and 14.5.22–9, C 677–81. On the difference between geography and chorography see chapter 6, p. 154.

13 Cohn *RE* s.v. Aristonikos (no. 17) col. 964; Montanari and Heinze *DNP* s.v. Aristonikos (no. 5) col. 1119.

14 Gabba 1982 presents this inclination as part of a general revival in literature at the time of Augustus. This suggestion, however, does not seem to explain similar inclinations of Strabo's predecessors long before the Augustan age.

15 For the nature of these accounts and information on specific *periploi* see Güngerich 1950; Janni 1984: esp. 41–9; 120–30; Dilke 1985: 130–44; Diller 1986: 102–46.

16 Dilke 1985: 130.

17 In some exceptional cases Strabo gives distances in other measures such as Roman miles (chapter 4, p. 128), Egyptian schoeni (for instance 17.1.24, C 804) and Persian parasangs (11.11.5, C 518).

18 The use of rivers is similar to the use of Roman roads as a linear basis for geographical descriptions mainly in the Italian region. See 6, p. 173.

19 Cf. Baladié 1980: 225–64.

20 See, however, the sailing terminology, for instance in 17.1.4, C 788–9 and 17.1.6, C 791, not all deriving from Strabo's personal experience, as the sailing beyond the Straits of the Pillars of Heracles (Gibraltar) in 17.3.2, C 825.

21 Artemidorus: Brodersen *DNP* s.v. Artemidoros (no. 3) col. 50; *GGM* I, 574–6; Posidonius: Edelstein and Kidd 1972: T 56. On both authors see below pp. 59 and 60.

22 In this particular context he refers to a site which does not appear in their writings, but we can infer from this that otherwise he used them as his source.

23 Dilke 1985: 133 holds that the concept preceded the practical experience. Early sailors had the notion of a surrounding Ocean and thought it possible to circumnavigate the inhabited world. Thus the concept encouraged exploration.

24 Indications of the borders of the *oikoumene* in the *Geography*: 1.1.13, C 7–8; 1.2.24, C 31; 2.1.1, C 67; 2.1.13, C 72; 2.1.17, C 74; 2.5.7–8, C 114–15; 2.5.14, C 119; 2.5.33–4, C 131–2; 3.1.4, C 137; 3.5.5, C 170; 4.5.5, C 201; 7.2.4, C 294; 11.6.2, C 507; 16.4.4, C 769; 16.4.14, C 774; 17.3.1, C 825; 17.3.23, C 839.

25 Wijsman 1998.

26 Cf. Heidel 1976: 12–19; 26–55. On the special problem involved in the description of nations who dwell by the edges of the world see Nicolai 1984: 118.

27 2.5.6, C 113; 2.5.13, C 118; 2.5.9, C 116; 2.5.16, C 120; 11.11.7, C 519. Strabo refers to Posidonius' different opinion on the position of the *oikoumene* on the globe: 2.3.6, C 102.

28 The length and width of the *oikoumene* and their calculations: 1.4.2, C 62–3; 1.4.5, C 64; 2.1.13, C 72; 2.1.30, C 83; 2.3.6, C 102; 2.4.3, C 106; 2.4.7, C 108; 2.5.6, C 113; 2.5.9, C 116; 11.11.7, C 519.

29 Further discussion on the boundaries between the continents appears in
11.1.4–5, C 491. On the measures of the continents, see 2.4.7, C 108.

30 On the zones see 1.2.24, C 31; 2.1.17, C 74; 2.2.1–3, C 94–8; 2.3.7, C 102–3;
2.5.3, C 111; 2.5.5, C 112. On the climate affecting habitation, see 2.3.1,
C 96–7; 2.5.26, C 127; 3.1.1, C 137; 7.2.4, C 294. On precedents for the
concept of climatic zones see discussions in Diller 1934; Dicks 1955; 1956;
Aujac 1972; Heidel 1976: 19 n. 42.

31 There are some fragments of the *History* (*FGrH* 91), to be discussed below,
p. 70.

32 Strabo does not appreciate Herodotus' inclusion of myth within history and he
shows more than once that Herodotus was unreliable, see 1.2.35, C 43; 11.6.3,
C 508; 11.14.13, C 531; 12.3.21, C 550; 13.2.4, C 618; 17.1.52, C 818–19.
Cf. Prandi 1988a. On the precedence of Hecataeus of Miletus who wrote a
periodos ges which also influenced Herodotus see p. 48.

33 On Polybius' personality and works see Walbank 1957: 1–35; 1972: esp. 1–31,
and on Strabo's attitude towards him see Dubois 1891b.

34 Therefore I see no reason to adopt the suggestion of Sihler 1923: 138 that the
idea to continue Polybius was initiated by Augustus himself who transmitted
it to Strabo through Athenodorus. There is no evidence for a direct relation
between Augustus and Strabo, even through an intermediary.

35 Trans. W.R. Paton (*LCL*).

36 See also 3.31.3–13. Strabo similarly uses an analogy from the world of medicine
to expound the essence of geography in 2.1.30, C 83 quoted below, chapter 6,
p. 156.

37 The expression 'pragmatic history' in Polybius: 1.35.9; 3.47.8; 6.5.2.

38 On the practical orientation of the Romans in the field of geography see Bekker-
Nielsen 1988 and see Crinagoras' specific demand for a *periplous* in order to
travel, chapter 4, p. 123.

39 See also 3.1.4–8; 3.32.1–10; 5.33.1–8.

40 Cf. Alonso-Núñez 1987 and chapter 5.

41 Cf. Walbank 1948: 170–2; 1972: 125–6.

42 For a brief survey of the history of ethnography prior to Strabo see Prontera
1984a; Oniga 1995: 11–36.

43 To this end he travelled widely: 3.48.12. Strabo is also aware of the new
geographical horizons expanded by the Roman and Parthian conquests, see
chapter 4, p. 107.

44 For instance, Polybius refers his readers to additional information on the
barbarian tribes of western Iberia in 3.37.11: 'I shall speak more particularly
on a subsequent occasion'.

45 On Book 34 see Pédech 1956; Walbank 1979: 563–639; Polyb. *LCL* vol. 6.
Many of the surviving fragments of the thirty-fourth book are to be found in
Strabo's *Geography*.

46 Cf. Prandi 1988b.

47 Note that Strabo follows Ephorus methodologically in his reliance on the coastline as a 'counsellor', 8.1.3, C 334 quoted above, p. 40.

48 Pédech 1956: 5–7. On chorography see chapter 6, p. 154.

49 Walbank 1948 shows that in this way Polybius combined Greek literary traditions with Roman practical inclinations.

50 1.1.5; 4.2.3–7; 4.11.1; 6.11–41. On Polybius' attitude towards Rome and on
his influence on his followers see Momigliano 1975: 23–30.

51 Their different point of view is manifested also in the slightly different model
of the mixed constitution as applied to the Roman political situation, see below,
p. 66 and cf. Alonso-Núñez 1983.

52 A systematic survey of the scientific components in the *Geography* such as measurements, coasts and seas, hydrology, orography, climate and various branches of geography was offered by Calzoni 1940, who concluded that despite some faults and inaccuracies, Strabo aspired for precision. Aujac 1966 set Strabo against the background of the science of his time. On his typical ancient concept of space see Gonzáles Ponce 1990 and on his indebtedness to cartographic traditions see Engels 1998b: 63–114.

53 Physics is an *arete* (2.5.2, C 110) that is, an independent branch of science with its own rules and set of proofs. On the Stoic inclination behind this definition see below, p. 62.

54 According to Strabo, expertise in the sciences sometimes derives from practical needs. Geometry was born in Egypt to measure portions of land because the Nile inundations moved the boundary-marks (17.1.3, C 787). Astronomy and arithmetic developed mainly in Phoenicia and especially among the Sidonians because they were engaged in commerce and in night-time navigations (16.2.24, C 757).

55 See, for instance, unusual animals: 3.2.7, C 145; 4.6.10, C 208; 7.4.8, C 312; 15.1.37, C 703; 15.2.12–13, C 725–6; 16.4.15–16, C 774–5. And exceptional plants: 3.2.7, C 145; 3.5.10, C 175; 12.7.3, C 570–71; 15.1.21, C 694; 16.2.41, C 763.

56 3.4.15, C 163; 5.3.10, C 237; 6.1.14, C 264; 9.3.3, C 418; 12.7.2, C 570; 16.2.41, C 763; 16.4.18, C 777.

57 5.3.1, C 228; 5.3.6, C 234; 5.3.11, C 238; 5.4.5, C 244; 5.4.9, C 248; 6.1.13, C 263; 8.3.19, C 347; 10.1.9, C 447; 14.5.12, C 673.

58 On Eratosthenes and his writings see *FGrH* 241; Knaack *RE* s.v. Eratosthenes (no. 4) col. 358; Tosi and Heinze *DNP* s.v. Eratosthenes (no. 2) col. 44; Fraser 1970; 1972: 525–39.

59 This might also be the feeling behind the previous definition of Eratosthenes as 'mathematician among geographers, and geographer among mathematicians', as the context shows. It presents him in an unfavourable light because he does not achieve excellence either in mathematics or in descriptive geography and therefore can be criticized in both fields. The whole picture complies with the name '*beta*' attached to Eratosthenes, implying his mediocrity, see Suda s.v. *Eratosthenes* E 2898 (Adler) and cf. Fraser 1972: 777.

60 2.1.1, C 67 and further. On Hipparchus see below. Gabba understands the criticism of Eratosthenes as part of a general trend with political significance in the Augustan age to praise the classical models and to criticize the literature written after Alexander, which is manifested also in the literary approach of Dionysius of Halicarnassus, see Gabba 1982: 60; 65.

61 On Hipparchus see Rehm *RE* s.v. Hipparchos (no. 18) col. 1666; Hübner *DNP* s.v. Hipparchos (no. 6) col. 568; Dicks 1960: esp. 1–18; 31–7.

62 The fragments: Dicks 1960: 57–103.

63 Dicks 1955; 1956.

64 On Artemidorus see Berger *RE* s.v. Artemidoros (no. 27) col.1329; Brodersen *DNP* s.v. Artemidoros (no. 3) col. 50.

65 On Posidonius see Reinhardt *RE* s.v. Poseidonios (no. 3) col. 558. Fragments of his various works appear in *FGrH* 87; Edelstein and Kidd 1972; Theiler 1982; Kidd 1988.

66 Cf. 2.2.1, C 94. On Posidonius' works as Strabo's sources, see Munz 1918; Grilli 1979.

67 On Posidonius' ideas concerning the zones as compared to his predecessors see Diller 1934.

68 Pédech 1974a.

69 Plu. *Luc.* 28.7; *Caes.* 63.3.

70 s.v. *Straton* (sic) Σ 1155 (Adler).

71 s.v. *Amaseia.*

72 For a survey of his Stoic inclinations see Aujac 1983.

73 Translated 'our school' in *LCL.*

74 Jones (*LCL*) translates the plural '*hemeis . . . zetoumen*' in 1.2.13, C 23 as 'we in our School demand'. The addition 'in our School', presumably implying the Stoics, seems unwarranted.

75 Cf. Aujac 1969; Long 1974: 118–20.

76 On this genre and the Stoics see *SVF* 3.544; 547; 599.

77 Cf. Aujac 1983: 20–3.

78 Cf. Aujac and Lasserre 1969: xxi–ii; Sandbach 1975: 69; 79–80; Aujac 1983: 19–21.

79 Cf. Reesor 1951: 10–11; Aujac 1983: 25.

80 Rist 1969: 37–53; Long 1974: 206–7; Sandbach 1975: 147–8.

81 On these ideals see Cic. *Fin.* 5.23; 87; Hor. *Ep.* 1.6 (Mayer 1994: 143–4); Diog. Laer. 9.45.

82 Pédech 1974b: 137–8; 142 and nn. 24–5.

83 Cf. Sen. *Nat.* 2.45.1–3; Glover 1969; Stern 1976: vol. 1, 305–6.

84 Cf. Aujac and Lasserre 1969: xxi.

85 On the Stoic ideas of Posidonius see Capelle 1932: 98–104; Reesor 1951: 51–5; Strasburger 1965: 46–51. On his political and historic ideas see Alonso-Núñez 1994. On Posidonius' view as it is communicated by Diodorus of Sicily see Desideri 1972. His influence on Strabo was discussed by Zimmermann 1888.

86 Some of the non-Stoic ideas in the *Geography*, particularly Academic and Peripatetic, are surveyed in Aly 1964.

87 This is in contrast to Augustus who claimed to be restoring republican institutions, see *RG* 1; 34; Vell. 2.89; Tac. *Ann.* 3.28; Suet. *Aug.* 28.

88 Cf. Aujac 1986.

89 And also 12.3.23, C 551: a discussion of Demetrius' interpretation of the Homeric allusion to the Halizoni and the Chalybians in Cappadocia. Strabo uses rhetorical questions in summarizing Demetrius' opinion and answers them by '*ne Dia*', thereupon continuing the discussion.

90 Cf. Lindsay 1997a.

91 s.v. *Polybios* P 1941 (Adler).

92 Pédech 1974b: 129.

93 Ridgeway 1888: 84 *pace* Engels 1998a: 144.

94 See Plutarch's reference specifically to the *Hypomnemata* which alluded to the Roman war against Tigranes, king of Armenia, Plu. *Luc.* 28.7 = *FGrH* 91 F 9.

95 Pédech 1974b: 129–30.

96 Pédech 1972: 397; Diller 1975: 3; Lasserre 1983: 869–70; Ambaglio 1990: 381; Engels 1998a: 135.

97 These were probably influenced by Ephorus and Polybius, see above, p. 48, on Polybius and cf. Prandi 1988b on the influence of Ephorus on Strabo's *Histories*. On Strabo's sources for his historical notions in the *Geography* see Ambaglio 1988.

98 These are the fragments as they appear in Jacoby *FGrH* 91. Ambaglio 1990 translated them into Italian and added a commentary. Otto 1889 had a maximalist attitude and also included historical allusions from the *Geography*. On these different compilations see Engels 1998a: 136–7.

99 Cf. Diller 1975: 7.

100 The contexts in Josephus are obviously connected to Jewish history; however, when he quotes Strabo or refers to his work, it is possible in most cases to infer the original Strabonian context at least in a general way. Therefore the method for evaluating the fragments in Josephus, should be, I think, to set aside Jewish context which was Josephus' interest and to focus as much as possible on what is probably pure Strabonian writing. On Strabo as Josephus' source see Albert 1902.

101 Cf. Pédech 1972: 397.

102 Cf. chapter 5 and Alonso-Núñez 1987. On these grounds Strabo's portrait as an historian who was particularly interested in Judaean affairs and who also visited Herod's court has no support in the sources and does not comply with his image as a Greek Augustan scholar *pace* Roller 1998: 22, 32, 56–7, 64–5, 91, 115.

103 Pédech 1972 and Lasserre 1984.

104 On his difficulties in choosing between sources see 8.3.31, C 356; 9.5.22, C 443; 10.2.24–6, C 461–2.

105 On the main myths in Strabo and their most common contexts see Bassi 1941–2.

106 Pédech 1974b and Engels 1998a: esp. 139–46; 168–71.

107 Cf. Dueck 1999b.

108 He does mention several Latin sources but briefly and sporadically, see chapter 3, p. 92 and cf. Aujac and Lasserre 1969: xiv–xv.

109 On Strabo's definition of culture vs. savagery see Sherwin-White 1967; Clavel-Lévêque 1974; van der Vliet 1977: 317–19; Thompson 1979: 213–29; van der Vliet 1984; Thollard 1987. On the Greek attitude towards strangers and its historical development see Haarhof 1948: esp. 27–40; 51–9; Baldry 1965; Momigliano 1975: 7–8; 17–19; Müller 1993.

110 Compare the version in Plu. *Mor.* 329 B-D (=*De Fort. Alex.* 6) and cf. Baldry 1965: 119–21; 167–71.

111 Cf. an earlier reference to the same dispute of Thucydides and Apollodorus on the question whether or not Homer had already made the distinction between Hellenes and Barbarians in 8.6.6, C 370. For another allusion to the different pronunciation of names by Greeks and Barbarians see 16.4.27, C 785. On the notion of 'Barbarian' in other authors, both Strabo's predecessors and contemporaries, see Thollard 1987: 27–39.

112 Bowersock 1992 concludes that in Strabo's time there were signs of a revival of Greek culture in Italy and thus this passage is anachronistic, but in view of other notions of Strabo, specified below, it seems that he did see the Romans as a sort of Barbarians. See also the importance ascribed to the Greek origin of the Alexandrinians in 17.1.12, C 797.

113 See discussion in Desideri 1992.

114 Aujac and Lasserre 1969: xv–xvi.

115 Trans. A.T. Murray (*LCL*).

116 On this determinism and on Strabo's concepts see more detailed discussion in van der Vliet 1984: esp. 44–75; Thollard 1987: esp. 12–26.

117 Thollard 1987: 59–84.

118 Däbritz 1905: 52–69 traces these lists to an Alexandrian habit and says that Artemidorus is Strabo's source. On this phenomenon see Stemplinger 1894 and Aujac 1983: 28.

119 This feature is of course very dominant in Pausanias' description of Greece, on which see Arafat 1996: 43–79 and Habicht 1998: esp. 131–2.

120 Strabo's interest in art may have figured also in his historiographical work, see *FGrH* 91 F 14.

121 For Plutarch's similar view see Swain 1990 and cf. Crawford 1978.

122 Aujac and Lasserre 1969: xv–xvi.

123 See Polybius' comparative survey of the construction of military camps by Greeks and by Romans in 6.42.

124 Dionysius of Halicarnassus likewise tried to show his Greek readers of the *Roman Antiquities* that Rome was founded by Greek colonists (1.4.1; 1.5.4), his aim being to refute the Greek prejudice which depicted Rome as built on poor foundations. Cf. Plu. *Cam.* 22.2 (Heraclides of Pontus); Dion. Hal. *AR* 1.72.3–4 (Aristotle).

125 The respect and benefits were sometimes the result of personal ties between Roman commanders and Greek individuals, mostly intellectuals. Thus the Roman spared some Greek cities as a token of personal friendship, for example Pompey sparing Mytilene for the sake of Theophanes (13.2.3, C 617) and Julius Caesar sparing Cnidus for the sake of Theopompus (Plut. *Caes.* 48.1). On this phenomenon see Crawford 1978: 197–207 and chapter 5 below. On the meaning of the term *eleutheria* for the Greeks and for the Romans see Ferrary 1987: 3–218.

126 And compare with the situation in Cappadocia where the people could not handle their freedom and autonomy and asked the Romans to appoint a king for them, 12.2.11, C 540.

127 Lasserre 1977; 1983: 889–96.

3 STRABO AND THE WORLD OF AUGUSTAN ROME

1 Cf. Pais 1908: 410 and n. 5.

2 Date according to Pais 1908: 411 and n. 2 and cf. Coleman 1990: 53: 'Late thirties'.

3 Niese 1878: 42–3 suggests that this was Strabo's first visit.

4 On this date see Jameson 1968: 78–9.

5 Pais 1908: 413.

6 Tac. *Ann.* 2.41.

7 Pais 1908: 412–13 holds that Strabo saw him in Egypt, but there is no support in the text for this contention.

8 None of these experiences can be definitely dated. Strabo says that he saw the 'Dionysus' before the temple was burnt (8.6.23, C 381), an event occurring in 31 BCE (Dio Cass. 50.10.3). Pais 1908: 411 holds that Strabo's allusion to the fire proves that he was in Rome at the time, but he could have seen the painting at any prior date. Note that Strabo indicates that Polybius saw the same painting together with other works of art plundered by Roman soldiers after the destruction of Corinth. Perhaps he read about it in Polybius, was impressed and went to look for it in Rome. On the temple see L. Richardson 1992: 80–1 and Steinby 1993: 260–1.

9 On Strabo's description of Campus Martius see Wiseman 1979 and Jaeger 1995.

10 Although the construction began in 28 BCE, the fact that Strabo refers to Augustus' own tomb may indicate the time of writing, cf. various opinions in Ridgeway 1888: 84; Aly 1957: 211; Richard 1970: 375–6.

11 *LSJ* s.v. *Mausoleion*; *OLD* s.v. *Mausoleum* 2 and cf. Aly 1957: 211; Richard 1970: 371–5.

12 On Gallus see Wellmann *RE* s.v. Aelius (no. 59) col. 493; Eck *DNP* s.v. Aelius (no. II 11) col. 172.

13 Cf. also Jos. *AJ* 15.317; Plin. *Nat.* 6.160; Dio Cass. 53.29 and Aly 1957: 165–78; Jameson 1968; Mayerson 1995.

14 Gal. 14.189; 203 Kühn 1827–33. Although there is some doubt regarding the identity of this Gallus, the allusion to Arabia as well as the connection with Augustus makes it probable that he was the Gallus of Strabo.

15 Cf. Lasserre 1984: 19–22, who contends that this campaign is an original histo-riographical part of the *Geography*, not based on any written source.

16 On this phenomenon see Crawford 1978: esp. 203–4.

17 On Calpurnius see Tac. *Ann.* 1.13; 2.43; Caes. *Bell. Afr.* 3; 18; *PIR*² 287 cf. Bowersock 1965: 133 and n. 3.

18 Cf. Aly 1957: 385.

19 On Servilius see Münzer *RE* s.v. Servilius (no. 67) col. 1798; Ormerod 1922. On the suggestion that Strabo's name derives from this relationship see chapter 1, p. 7.

20 The most notable of these are Lucullus, Crassus, Pompey, Brutus, Agrippa, the two Drusi, Tiberius' brother and his son, and Germanicus. The rest are gener-ally commanders of military campaigns.

21 Cf. Schmitt 1983: 568–9.

22 Cf. Hahn 1906: 131–4.

23 Polyb. 3.9.4–5; Dion. Hal. *AR* 1.6.2; Diod. 7.5.4–5. On Fabius see Münzer *RE* s.v. Fabius (no. 126) col. 1836; Scholz *DNP* s.v. Fabius (no. 35) col. 373.

24 Silanus was present at the destruction of Carthage and translated Mago the Carthaginian's work on agriculture into Latin. See Plin. *Nat.* 18.22–3; Münzer *RE* s.v. Iunius (no. 160) col. 1088.

25 On Coelius see Gensel *RE* s.v. Coelius (no. 7) col. 185; Kierdorf *DNP* s.v. Coelius (no. I 1) col. 56. On the manuscript tradition of Strabo's text see chapter 6, p. 145.

26 On Acilius see Klebs *RE* s.v. Acilius (no. 4) col. 251; Kierdorf *DNP* s.v. Acilius (no. I 2) col. 86. The suggestion of Biraschi 1981 that the inferred historian was Q. Aelius Tubero is indeed attractive and connects well to the social milieu in Augustan Rome, but does not seem to have a firm enough foundation.

27 Klotz 1910: 69–75.

28 Cf. Wilkens 1886: 7–22.

29 On Dellius see Wissowa *RE* s.v. Dellius col. 2447; Strothmann *DNP* s.v. Dellius col. 393.

30 On Pollio see Groebe *RE* s.v. Asinius (no. 25) col. 1589; Schmidt *DNP* s.v. Asinius (no. I 4) col. 82; Bosworth 1972.

31 Some of the manuscripts read 'Gabinius', an unknown and unidentifiable person in this context. On Tanusius see Münzer *RE* s.v. Tanusius (no. 2) col. 2231.

32 Cf. Aly 1957: 114–34. Strabo's use of Roman miles may derive from another source, probably Agrippa's *Commentaries*, on which see chapter 4, p. 128.

33 *Pace* Pais 1886: 7–9, drawing a completely different picture of a geographer who spent only a short time in Rome and remained Asian Greek in his language, culture and interests.

34 Strabo mentions another Roman cultural feature of his time, the Fabula Atellana, referring to stage poems and mimicry in the Oscan dialect performed in a certain competition: 5.3.6, C 233.

35 3.2.13, C 150; 3.4.3, C 157; 5.1.4, C 212; 12.3.8, C 544; 12.4.5–6, C 565; 13.1.27, C 595; 13.1.53, C 608.

36 5.2.2, C 220–1; 5.3.4–5, C 231–2; 5.3.7, C 234; 8.6.20, C 378.

37 *Theogony* 1008–13 and see West 1966: 432 on the tradition of Aeneas in early Greek literature and art.

38 Strabo does not mention any Roman character active in the early republic, that is, between the last king and Fabius Maximus. On his choice of Roman historical heroes see Dueck 1999b.

39 On the Greek attitude towards other cultures and particularly the Roman see Momigliano 1975: esp. 1–21.
40 See, for example, Verg. *G.* 3.16–39; 4.560–62; *A.* 1.286–96; 6.792–805; 8.722–8; Hor. *Carm.* 1.12; 1.35.21–30; 3.14.14–16; 4.5; 4.14.41–52; 4.15; *Saec.*; *Ep.* 2.1.1–3; Prop. 2.10.13–18; 3.4.1–10; 4.6.37–44; Ov. *Met.* 15.819–39; Liv. 1.19. On the literary evaluation of Augustus see Gabba 1984; Griffin 1984; Raaflaub and Samons 1992: esp. 436–47, concluding that there was no real intellectual opposition to Augustus, cf. Bowersock 1965: 108–11.
41 *LSJ* s.v. *sebastos* II.1. Mason (1974) s.v. *sebastos* does not mention Strabo.
42 On the document see Suet. *Aug.* 101.4; Tac. *Ann.* 1.11; Dio Cass. 56.33.1 and on the literary and historical significance of the text see Gagé 1950: 3–42; Ramage 1987; Nicolet 1991: 178–83.
43 Trans. F.W. Shipley (*LCL*).
44 Timagenes of Alexandria, who had some anti-Roman inclinations, regretted the fires but only because instead of the old buildings new and finer ones were set up and thus Rome became more beautiful, a cause for sorrow in Timagenes' eyes. See Sen. *Epist.* 91.13. On Timagenes and his antagonism see chapter 5, p. 135.
45 Cf. Suet. *Aug.* 25.2; Dio Cass. 55.26.4–5. And see Robinson 1977.
46 Cf. Suet. *Aug.* 89 on Augustus' Greek teachers and intellectual tendencies.
47 On the law of war concerning captives see Garlan 1975: esp. 70–1.
48 Other implications of the advantages of current monarchic rule occur in 1.1.16, C 9 and 9.4.15, C 429. According to Gabba 1984: 62; 71–6 this emphasis on the advantages of the administrative features is typical of Greek views.
49 Cf. the idea of fatherhood in Hor. *Carm.* 1.2.50; Prop. 4.6.59; Ov. *Fast.* 2.127–32; for the significance of this title, see Yavetz 1984: 6–14.
50 On their war-customs involving the kettle see 7.2.3, C 294. Mutual respect also connected Augustus and the family of Herod, including his sons, his sister Salome and her daughter Berenice (16.2.46, C 765).
51 A thorough survey of the *Imitatio Alexandri* is Weippert 1972: 56–104 (Pompey); 105–92 (Caesar); 215–59 (Augustus) and on this theme in Strabo see Engels 1998a: 152–5. Kienast 1969: esp. 432–6 focuses on Augustus' adherence to the king; and on the geographical implications of this imitation, see Dion 1973: 473–7; Nicolet 1991: 21–2; Romm 1992: esp. 140–9. See also the conscious imitation of Alexander by Mithridates VI Eupator, McGing 1986: 101–2.
52 Liv. 9.18.6 cf. Weippert 1972: 224–40 and see chapter 5, p. 135.
53 Cf. the different version in Plu. *Ant.* 71.1–2.
54 Tac. *Ann.* 4.37 and cf. Lassere 1983: 885–6 on Tiberius' conscious continuation of Augustus.

4 GEOGRAPHY, POLITICS AND EMPIRE

1 On Strabo's absorption of Augustan ideology see surveys by Mancinetti Santamaria 1978–9; Lasserre 1977; 1983; Alonso-Núñez 1984; Noé 1988; Vanotti 1992; Engels 1998a: 144–5.
2 The emendation to 'Libya' is unnecessary in this context since the idea of Italy among other influential nations is still clear. Cf. Lasserre 1967: 240 n. 2.
3 Inside Italy the northern part is the best, 5.1.12, C 218. According to Ephorus, quoted by Strabo, Boeotia also possessed natural conditions suiting an hegemony, but its leaders' neglect of training and education caused it to fall (9.2.2, C 401 partially quoted on p. 83). This passage is considered to be taken directly from Posidonius, for instance by Müller 1993: 50, though it might as well be

another expression of Strabo's being influenced by ideas current in Augustan Rome. For the advantages of Italy in other authors see Thomas 1988: 179–80 and Mynors 1990: 119.

4 Cf. Ferrary 1987: 382–94.

5 See also 2.5.8, C 115; 2.5.13, C 118; 2.5.34, C 132.

6 See also 2.5.12, C 118. On the Roman conquests and increased geographical knowledge see Dion 1977: 237–45. On the Parthians as significant rivals of the Romans see below, p. 113.

7 In 17.1.21, C 803 Strabo alludes to the desert in Arabia that limits the mobility of an advancing army, linking conquest with exploration. Hering 1970 shows that the geographical survey of Gaul reflects also the administrative situation in Augustus' time.

8 See Dion 1973. Alexander placed altars as landmarks in the territories he conquered, perhaps implying an awareness of boundaries (3.5.5–6, C 171). On the imitation of Alexander by Roman generals see chapter 3, p. 104.

9 In this context Strabo does not specifically mention the Scythians, who are the typological people of the far north; however, the picture is made whole in Augustus' *Res Gestae* where the emperor includes the Scythians (*RG* 31).

10 For possible philosophical influences on Strabo's strong objection to flattery see chapter 2, p. 65.

11 Dion 1973: 478 accuses Strabo of similar geographical distortions derived from flattery of the Romans and Augustus. On the similarity between the characters of Alexander and Augustus as Strabo presents them see chapter 3, p. 104.

12 For the political message in geography see Forte 1972: 189, 195; Dion 1977: 247–75; Nicolet 1991.

13 This is why it is especially significant that Strabo shows that these kingdoms acknowledge the power of Augustus, see chapter 3, p. 101.

14 For instance: 2.5.12, C 118; 11.9.1–3, C 514–15; 14.5.2, C 669; 15.3.3, C 728; 15.3.12, C 732; 15.3.24, C 736; 16.1.26, C 747; 17.3.24, C 839. On Strabo's information on the Parthians and his presentation of their power see Drijvers 1998. Strabo apparently discussed the customs of the Parthians in his earlier historiographical work (11.9.3, C 515), which may imply their significance.

15 Their importance is additionally manifested through their constant appearance in the monuments of the Augustan Age, for instance on the shield of Augustus in the Prima Porta sculpture, and see below, p. 123.

16 On Trogus see Klotz *RE* s.v. Pompeius (no. 142) col. 2300; Alonso-Núñez 1987; Nicolet 1991: 33–4; Syme 1995: 334.

17 Compare the situation in the time of Pompey as described in Florus 1.40.31. And see Nicolet 1991: 50 n. 25.

18 Liv. 9.18.6, trans. B.O. Foster (*LCL*) and cf. Weippert 1972: 224–40. And see another critical note about 'the Greek historians who admire only the history of Greece (*sua tantum mirantur*)', Tac. *Ann.* 2.88.4 trans. J. Jackson (*LCL*). Some scholars see this recognition of other powers as a deliberate Augustan policy meant to achieve diplomatic benefit, see Dessau 1924: 375; Syme 1995: 91, 334.

19 Wachsmuth 1891: 465–79; Alonso-Núñez 1982: 131–2; Sordi 1982: 796–7; Nicolet 1991: 33.

20 Cf. Drijvers 1998: esp. 289–92.

21 Syme 1995: 366. On political developments in Parthia and the Roman connection to it see Romer 1979; Syme 1995: 87–94; 315–34.

22 Cf. Thompson 1979; Thollard 1987: esp. 40–6.

23 On the meaning of this term in Strabo see Thompson 1979: esp. 223–5; van der Vliet 1984: 69–70.

24 See similarly 4.5.3, C 200–1 and cf. Isaac 1992: esp. 26–8; 387–9.
25 Dodds 1973: 21 points out a general tendency in Augustan literature to express scepticism of Greek cultural values and to discourage emulation of them.
26 This, of course, is very similar to the ideas of Sallust in *Cat.* 10; *Jug.* 41 and cf. McGushin 1977: 87–8 for parallels and other suggestions for the historical turning point in ancient authors.
27 On Persian style as a metaphor for exaggerated ways see Hor. *Carm.* 1.38.1 and Nisbet and Hubbard 1970 ad loc.
28 4.1.6, C 181; 5.2.5, C 222; 5.3.10–11, C 238; 8.5.7, C 367; 9.1.23, C 399; 9.5.16, C 437; 10.1.6, C 446; 12.8.14, C 577.
29 Dionysius of Halicarnassus, Strabo's contemporary, expresses similar reproof of Roman greed and extravagance. He draws a comparison between the simple triumphal procession of Romulus and the extravagant ceremony of his own times (*AR* 2.34.3); he points to greed as the driving force behind the actions of his contemporaries (2.74.5); and he compares the modesty and simplicity of the early Romans with the behaviour of the Romans of his time (10.17.6).
30 The text reads *megalophron*, which has also a positive sense of nobility and generosity and thus is translated by Jones (*LCL*) as 'magnanimous', but the spirit of the entire context and Strabo's opinion of such deeds seem to me to call for the other, negative sense of the word.
31 Cf. similar ideas in Cic. *Ver.* 2.1.11; 2.1.55; 2.4.73–4; 2.4.120–1, who also shows the moderation and humanity of Scipio Aemilianus and Marcellus, who returned some of the plundered pieces of art, or else did not take them for their own personal use.
32 Cf. *FGrH* 88 F 11.
33 Dionysius of Halicarnassus expresses the same thing, ascribing to Roman officials destruction of harmonious rule (*AR* 2.11.3); violence (4.24.4–8); and tyrannical aspirations (5.60.2). With reference to a somewhat earlier period, Timagenes ascribes to Pompey plans for profit in his military actions, a suspicion not accepted by Plutarch, who cites Timagenes' version (*FGrH* 88 F 9).
34 *Gal.* 5.12–14. On Caesar's exploitation of geography for politics see Adcock 1956: 38–9; 98–9.
35 Cf. Rawson 1985: 250–66. Augustan Latin literature abounds in geographical metaphors and details which serve to praise the age and the emperor. On this see Nicolet 1991: 29–35, who gives an extensive survey of literary precedents prior to the Augustan Age. Cf. also the criticism of his thesis by Purcell, *JRS* 80 (1990) 178–82; and Gruen, *CPh* 87 (1992) 183–5.
36 Peter 1967: xxxx–lvi; F 7–8; 10–17; 20; 25; Geiger 1985: 76–7.
37 Morel 1975: 97–8 F 14–20a.
38 Trans. Gow and Page 1968: I no. 32 cf. Dilke 1985: 144.
39 Trans. F.W. Cornish (*LCL*). Cf. poem 29 that mentions Gaul and 'furthest Britain' as new targets for Mamura's greed.
40 *Saec.* 53–6 trans. C.E. Bennett (*LCL*). Cf. *Carm.* 1.12, 53–7; 4.14, 41–52; Verg. *G.* 2.171–2. On the poem and its Augustan meaning see Armstrong 1989: 136–8.
41 *A.* 8.722–8 trans. H.R. Fairclough (*LCL*). See also the portrayal of Augustus as subduer of remote nations in *A.* 6.792–805.
42 Plin. *Nat.* 1.5. On Livy's son see Quint. *Inst.* 10.1.39.
43 Gow and Page 1968: I 41 no. 47; II 58–9.
44 Gow and Page 1968: I 214 no. 26; II 234–6.
45 Gow and Page 1968: I 214 no. 28; II 239.
46 Gow and Page 1968: I 216 no. 29; II 239–41.
47 On the connection between geographical knowledge and political aspirations see Moynihan 1985: 149–56.

48 On the practical use of geography by the Romans and on their concept of space see Bekker-Nielsen 1988.
49 For surveys see Toynbee 1934: esp. 7–23; Silberberg-Peirce 1986; Smith 1988: 70–7; Zanker 1988: esp. 297–334; Nicolet 1991: 29; 38–47.
50 Suet. *Nero* 46.1; Plin. *Nat.* 36.41.
51 Plu. *Pomp.* 45.5 trans. B. Perrin (*LCL*).
52 Plin. *Nat.* 36.39; Vell. 2.39.2; Servius ad *Aen.* 8.721. On the Forum Augusti as a whole see Zanker 1988: esp. 112–14; 194–5; 210–15; Smith 1988: 33–74; Nicolet 1991: 41–3.
53 Tac. *Ann.* 1.8.4 trans. J. Jackson (*LCL*) and cf. Dio Cass. 56.34.3; 75.4.5.
54 This monument is fully analysed by Smith 1988; cf. Nicolet 1991: 45–7.
55 For remains of an inscription probably originating in this monument see *CIL* XIII pp. 227–48 nos. 1164–725. For similar monuments in Jerusalem, Asia Minor and Athens, see, respectively, Jos. *AJ* 15.272–9; Phlegon of Tralleis *FGrH* 257 F 36 (XIII); Paus. 1.18.6. For the latter, cf. Toynbee 1934: 3. For an epigraphic indication of a similar depiction of vanquished peoples in Rome, see Gonzáles 1984: 58 line 11; cf. Smith 1988: 71 n. 50.
56 Plin. *Nat.* 3.136; *CIL* V 7817.
57 *CIL* V 7231.
58 *CIL* II 4701; 4703; 4712; 4715–16 cf. Dion 1973: 474 and n. 1.
59 Vermeule 1968: 336–50; Kleiner 1985: 25–86; Silberberg-Peirce 1986: 314–19.
60 Formige 1949; Picard 1957; Turcan 1982; Silberberg-Peirce 1986: 312–14.
61 Toynbee 1934: 9–143; Nicolet 1991: 35–8; 41.
62 The manuscripts read '*a sorore eius*' i.e. Agrippa's sister, and Dio says that the portico was built by Paula the sister of Agrippa (55.8.4). Therefore, other conjectures or emendations into '*sua*' in order to assume the involvement of Augustus' sister, Octavia, in this project are unnecessary.
63 *Nat.* 3.17 adapted from the translation by H. Rackham (*LCL*).
64 Some important studies on the 'map' and its character are Kubitschek *RE* s.v. *Karten* col. 2100; Tierney 1963; Sallmann 1971: 91–107; Roddaz 1984: 573–91; Dilke 1985: 41–53; 1987a: 207–9; Nicolet 1991: esp. 98–114.
65 Brodersen 1995: 268–85.
66 The references in Pliny are collected in Riese 1964: 1–8 and Dilke 1985: 44–52.
67 The word *pinax* also means 'map', but more commonly a list or engraved plate, cf. Brodersen 1995: 280–4.
68 On these measures in Polybius and in Strabo see Pothecary 1995.
69 Scholars who identify the chorographer with Agrippa: Klotz 1931: 45; Schnabel 1935: 417–20; Tierney 1963: 152; Riese 1964: 1–8; Nicolet 1991: 100–1. Dilke rejects this suggestion, Dilke 1985: 43–4; 52; 1987b: 209.
70 Dueck 1999a and chapter 6, p. 146.

5 GREEK SCHOLARS IN AUGUSTAN ROME

1 On this social and intellectual phenomenon from the end of the second century to the time of Tiberius see Hillscher 1891; Rhys Roberts 1900; Goold 1961: esp. 189–92; Bowersock 1965: 30–41; 122–39; Kennedy 1972: 301–77; Jocelyn 1976–7; Crawford 1978: 193–207; Rawson 1985: 66–99; Syme 1986. On Strabo's presumed contacts see Stemplinger 1894: esp. 76–9; Bowersock 1965: 126–9; van der Vliet 1977: 316–17; Engels 1999: 350–3.
2 On Dionysius see *FGrH* 251; Radermacher *RE* s.v. Dionysios (no. 113) col. 934; Fornaro and Heinze *DNP* s.v. Dionysios (no. 18) col. 635; Bonner 1939: 1–23; Gabba 1991.

3 Trans. E. Cary (*LCL*).
4 The Romans were originally Greek: 1.5.1; 1.9.2; 1.17.1; 1.31.1; 1.34.1. Rome as a Greek city: 1.60.3; 1.89.1; 4.26.5; 7.70.1–73.5. Compare Strabo's emphasis on the Greek origins of many Italian cities, chapter 6, p. 172.
5 2.11.3; 2.34.3; 2.74.5; 4.24.4–8; 5.60.2; 10.17.6.
6 On these works see Bonner 1939: 10–11 and n. 3; Kennedy 1972: 342–63; Gabba 1991: 24–34.
7 Cf. Martin 1971; Gabba 1984: 65–6.
8 *Pomp.* 3.20 (Caecilius); *Amm.* 2.1.1; *Th.* 1.1; 55.5 (Tubero); *Comp.* 1.4; 26.17 (Rufus).
9 *Pomp.* 1.1 (Pompeius and Zeno); *Amm.* 1.3.1; 2.17.2; *Orat. Vett.* 1.1; *Dem.* 58.5 (Ammaeus); *Pomp.* 3.1 (Demetrius).
10 On Nicolaus see *FGrH* 90 T 1–15; Laquer *RE* s.v. Nikolaos (no. 20) col. 362; Wacholder 1962: esp. 14–36; Bowersock 1965: 130–2; Gabba 1984: 61–4; Bellemore 1984: xv–xvii; Toher 1989: 160 and nn. 2–4.
11 Jos. *AJ* 16.299; 17.219. Other occasions on which he assisted the king: Jos. *AJ* 16.29–30; 370–2; 17.99; 315, always emphasizing Herod's personal and unconditional loyalty to Rome and to Augustus.
12 Another version of the story ascribes the naming of the fruit to Herod who said that Nicolaus, like the palm and its fruit, was 'tall, sweet and red', see Athen. 14.652a and Plu. *Mor.* 723 D (*Q. Con.* 8.4.1); cf. Bab. Tal. *Abb. Zar.* 14b.
13 Other than the two works discussed here because of their relevance to Augustan Rome, Nicolaus also composed a Peripatetic collection of customs, dedicated to Herod (*FGrH* 90 F 103–24), some remarks on Aristotle's philosophy, tragedies and comedies now lost, and an autobiography emphasizing his education (*FGrH* 90 F 131–9).
14 Jos. *AJ* 16.183–6. On the contents and style of the work see *FGrH* 90 F 1–102; Jos. *AJ* 1.94; 14.104; Athen. 249a–b; Suda s.v. *Nikolaos* N 393 (Adler); Wacholder 1962: 65–70, 73; Toher 1989: 160–71; Alonso-Núñez 1995.
15 Trans. P. Marcus (*LCL*). The entire story: Jos. *AJ* 16.27–60.
16 There is no support for the suggestion (Roller 1998: 21, 61, 64) that Nicolaus and Strabo studied together with Timagenes of Alexandria.
17 On Timagenes see Bowersock 1965: 109–10; 125–6; Bosworth 1972: esp. 445; Sordi 1982.
18 Trans. M. Winterbottom (*LCL*).
19 Sen. *De Ira* 3.23.4–8.
20 Sen. *Ep.* 91.13.
21 9.18.6 trans. B.O. Foster (*LCL*).
22 *FGrH* 88. Another work of his was *On Kings*.
23 On criticism of Augustus by his contemporaries see Raaflaub and Samons 1992, esp. 435–47, concluding that there was no real intellectual opposition in Rome at the time and cf. Bowersock 1965: 108–11.
24 Bowersock 1965: 139.
25 Cf. Rhys Roberts 1900: 442; Goold 1961: 190–2.
26 *FGrH* 188; Laquer *RE* s.v. Theophanes (no. 1) col. 2090; Anastasiadis and Souris 1992. As Strabo's source: Aly 1957: 91–101. On his son see White 1992.
27 *FGrH* 21; Bux *RE* s.v. Theopompos (no. 5) col. 2174.
28 Wißenberger *DNP* s.v. Artemidoros (no. 5) col. 50.
29 *FGrH* 190; Funaioli *RE* s.v. Hypsikrates (no. 3) còl. 434; Meister *DNP* s.v. Hypsikrates col. 821; *OCD* (1996) s.v. Hypsicrates.
30 *FGrH* 91 F 17.
31 On Potamon see *FGrH* 147; *IG* xii 2 nos. 23–34 (=*Monumentum Potamoneum*).

32 *Suas.* 2.15.

33 Suda s.v. *Potamon* P 2127 (Adler).

34 On both orators see Wißenberger *DNP* s.v. Apollodoros (no. 8) col. 860; Suda s.v. *Theodoros* Θ 151 (Adler); Kennedy 1972: 338–42.

35 Trans. H.E. Butler (*LCL*).

36 Quint. *Inst.* 2.15.12 and 21. Cf. Sen. *Con.* 2.1.36.

37 Hor. *Sat.* 1.10.82; *Carm.* 2.9.

38 Suet. *Aug.* 89.1.

39 Quint. *Inst.* 3.1.18.

40 Suet. *Tib.* 57.1.

41 Wißenberger *DNP* s.v. Hermagoras (no. 2) col. 417.

42 Wißenberger *DNP* s.v. Aischines (no. 3) col. 349.

43 Cic. *Fam.* 13.56.1.

44 Wißenberger *DNP* s.v. Hybreas col. 770.

45 Hülser *DNP* s.v. Athenodoros (no. 2) col. 203.

46 Plu. *Cat. Mi.* 4.2 and Geiger 1971 ad locum; Cic. *Off.* 2.86; Diog. Laert. 7.193; 150; 157; v. Arnim *RE* s.v. Antipatros (no. 27) col. 2516.

47 Modrze *RE* s.v. Nestor (no. 5) col. 124; Hahm 1990.

48 Runia and Heinze *DNP* s.v. Areios (no. 2) col. 1042; Göransson 1995: 208–18 and chapter 1, p. 9.

49 Gercke *RE* s.v. Athenaios (no. 19) col. 2025.

50 *OCD* (1996) s.v. Philodemus; Gigante 1990; Obbink 1994; 1996. His epigrams in Gow and Page 1968: I, 351–69.

51 Diog. Laert. 7.164; Sharples *DNP* s.v. Ariston (no. 2) col. 1116; Baltes and Lakmann *DNP* s.v. Eudoros (no. 2) col. 221.

52 Gottschalk *DNP* s.v. Andronikos (no. 4) col. 694.

53 *FGrH* 53; Cohn *RE* s.v. Aristonikos (no. 17) col. 964; Montanari and Heinze *DNP* s.v. Aristonikos (no. 5) col. 1119.

54 *FGrH* 697; Montanari and Söllner *DNP* s.v. Asklepiades (no. 8) col. 92.

55 Dion. Hal. *Din.* 8; Montanari and Söllner *DNP* s.v. Aristokles (no. 3) col. 1111.

56 Geffcken *RE* s.v. Krinagoras, col. 1859; *IG* xii 2 no. 35; Gow and Page 1968: I, 198–231; II, esp. 210–13.

57 Trans. Gow and Page 1968: I, no. 24.

58 Gow and Page 1968: I, 233–43, nos. 1 and 8 and corresponding commentaries, ibid. II, 265–6; 270–1.

59 On these physicians, see Nutton and Reppert-Bismarck *DNP* s.v. Asklepiades (no. 6) col. 89; s.v. Alexandros (no. 31) col. 484; s.v. Herakleides (no. 27) col. 378; s.v. Apollonios (no. 17) col. 888; Michel *DNP* s.v. Herophilos (no. 1) col. 484; Rawson 1985: 358–70; von Staden 1989: 529–58.

60 White 1992: 217–18.

6 THE *GEOGRAPHY* – A 'COLOSSAL WORK'

1 On Strabo's distinction between geography and chorography see below, p. 154.

2 Cf. Aly 1968: 2*–8*.

3 On the papyrological findings see *P. Oxy.* vol. 49 (1982) 47–73 no. 3447; vol. 65 (1998) 71–5 no. 4459; Krebbler 1972; Kramer and Hübner 1976: 27–32 no. 8. On the palimpsest see Diller 1975: 19–24; Baladié 1978: 44–9. For the tradition of the text, see Jones 1917: xxxiv; Diller 1954: 29–33; Aujac and Lasserre 1969: xlviii–lxxxi; Diller 1975; Baladié 1978: 40–9; Sbordone 1981; 1982; Baladié 1989: 53–61; 1996: 39–44. The *Geography* has also a ninth-century *scholia* attributed to Photius, see Diller 1954.

4 Suda s.v. *Straton* (sic) Σ 1155 (Adler); Stephanus s.v. *Abrotonon* and *passim*. The Suda reads '7 books', which seems to be a mere mistake. The division into chapters and sections originated in the 1763 Bréquingny edition, see Diller 1975: 1.

5 See survey in Radt 1991: 305–11; for editions and translations see Jones 1917: xli–xliv; Diller 1975: 167–79; Biraschi et al. 1981: 23–7; 35–9.

6 Examples illustrating the principles of this forthcoming edition are available in Radt 1991: 312–26 for 8.1.1–3, C 332–4; Radt and Drijvers 1993 for 13.1.26–42, C 593–60; Radt 1994 for excerpts from Books 8–10; Radt 1996: 183–5 for several excerpts of Book 6.

7 See a detailed discussion in Dueck 1999a.

8 J.A. Fabricius 1717: 3–4.

9 Dio Cass. 54.22.1–5 cf. *CAH* 10 (1979) 349.

10 Niese 1878: 33–6.

11 Aly 1957: 397.

12 Pais 1908: 380–409. Meyer 1890: 14–34 suggested that the text incorporates editorial comments and serious inconsistencies which indicate that the work was not completed by Strabo.

13 Syme 1995: 356–67; cf. Lindsay 1997b.

14 Pais 1908: 405.

15 Syme 1995: 367.

16 Pais 1908: 381.

17 Nicolet 1991: 19–24, esp. 21.

18 Cf. Geiger 1992: 41 n. 67.

19 Cf. Starr 1987.

20 On the diffusion of the *Geography* throughout the ages see surveys in Diller 1975: 7–19; 25–165; Salmeri 1988; Engels 1999: 383–98; cf. Aly 1968: 2*–8* nos. 12–33.

21 *GGM* II, p. 112 l. 181. The same appears also in Stephanus s.v. *Auasis*; cf. Aly 1968: 2*. Stephanus' wording seems taken directly from Strabo, whereas Dionysius' words are not identical to Strabo's.

22 Ptol. *Geogr.* 1.1.

23 Cf. Riley 1995: esp. 230–6. On Pausanias' different approach see Aly 1957: 360–7 and cf. Arafat 1996; Habicht 1998.

24 On medieval and Arab geography see J.K. Wright 1965: esp. 10; 40; Miquel 1967: esp. 28 n. 3; 267–75; Ahmad 1995: esp. 8–12.

25 Cf. Anastos 1952; Woodhouse 1986: esp. 181–6. Both Eratosthenes and Posidonius presented calculations of the circumference of the earth, but whereas Eratosthenes reached almost an accurate figure for this measure as we know it today, Posidonius produced a much smaller figure. This was in fact one of the causes for Columbus's mistaking America for India, since according to the then accepted measurement of Posidonius, the distance already traversed would suggest that the land was India. Had the correct figure of Eratosthenes prevailed, the sailors would have known that they had voyaged much less than the actual distance to the real India.

26 Cf. Beazley 1949: I, 39–40; 243–5; James and Martin 1981: 7; 93–8; 112–13.

27 Les Cases 1968: 489; 494.

28 See similar discussion in Claudius Ptolemy, *Geog.* 1.1 and cf. Nicolet 1991: 100; 107; 119 nn. 23–4; 171–2. For Polybius' attitude, see Walbank 1979: 588.

29 On this term see Brodersen 1995: 280–4 and chapter 4, p. 128.

30 On various approaches to ethnography prior to Strabo see Prontera 1984a; Oniga 1995: 11–36.

31 Strabo's fear of omission: 3.1.6, C 139; 9.1.19, C 397; 10.1.2, C 445; 13.1.51, C 657; 17.1.34, C 808; 17.2.4, C 823; 17.3.1, C 824.

NOTES

32 This is why Strabo does not extend scientific discussions, see 1.1.7, C 5; 1.1.9, C 6; 2.3.3, C 98.

33 See also 1.1.23, C 13–14 (translated below, p. 161); 1.2.13, C 23; 2.1.8, C 70; 9.5.12, C 435.

34 On the literary considerations influencing his method see Downey 1941: esp. 88–93.

35 On Strabo's style see also Honigmann *RE* s.v. Strabon (no. 3) cols. 96–7.

36 Cf. *LSJ* s.v. *kolossos*; Pais 1908: 386; Richards 1941: 88 n.1. On *Kolossoi* as large-scale statues see Dickie 1996: 237–48.

37 Aymard 1951: 483–502.

38 Intended for Roman statesmen: Aujac and Lasserre 1969: xxvi–xxix. Encouraged by Roman friends: Niese 1878: 45. Encouraged by Augustus: Sihler 1923: 138; Aly 1957. On other Greeks in Augustan Rome and their intended readers see Rawson 1985: 54–64.

39 Pais 1886: 1–26; 1908: 421–7. Stemplinger 1894, esp. 69–70 stresses the local patriotism of Strabo for Asia Minor and his focus on Asian themes and an Asian audience.

40 Dubois 1891a: 103–8. See Crinagoras' request for a *periplous* as a touring-guide, chapter 4, p. 123.

41 Cf. Polybius' openings to his first four books.

42 See also 2.5.17, C 120; 7.6.1, C 318; 9.2.21, C 408; 12.3.42, C 563.

43 Thollard 1987: 59–84.

44 Cf. Wijsman 1998.

45 Cf. Massaro 1986.

46 Cf. Baladié 1980: esp. 295–300. For a similar approach in earlier sources see Heracleides of Pontus in the fourth century BCE in Plu. *Cam.* 22.2 and Aristotle in Dion. Hal. *AR* 1.72.3–4. Aristodemus of Nysa, Strabo's teacher, did the opposite, presenting Rome as Homer's birthplace and thus as the origin of Greek culture. On Plutarch's emphasis on the Greek education of his Roman heroes see Swain 1996: 139–41.

47 Cf. Momigliano 1975: 1, 14–19; Crawford 1978: 194–7. On *Ktiseis* in Greek literature, see Fraser 1972: 513–4; 775–6. In Latin literature there is a fragmentary indication of this genre in the *Origines* of Cato the elder, based in form on Greek precedents. Composed around 168–149 BCE, this seven-book work exploited local traditions and Greek legends in order to describe the origins of the Romans. We cannot know if Strabo knew Cato's work. Strabo himself mentions elsewhere two authors interested in the genre of foundation stories. These are Dionysius of Chalkis who composed *Ktiseis* (12.4.8, C 566) and Menecrates of Elea who wrote on foundations (*peri ktiseon*) (13.3.3, C 621).

48 See maps in Chevallier 1989: 133, 135 and cf. Sitwell 1981.

49 Cf. tables in Barbour 1974: 67, 70, enumerating the number of place names from each continent: 55 per cent in Europe, 32 per cent in Asia Minor, 8 per cent in other parts of Asia and 5 per cent in Africa, a total of 4,050 place names. Barbour compares these figures to Pliny who refers to a total of 245 names, thus indicating the colossal dimension of Strabo's work.

50 Cf. Thollard 1987: 3–4.

51 Editions and translations of separate books according to region are listed in Biraschi et al. 1981: 28–9; 40.

52 See an attempt by Floratos 1972: 76.

53 Lasserre 1966: 9–11; 111–12.

54 Cf. Wijsman 1998.

55 On Strabo's use of Pytheas and the mathematical aspect see Szabó 1985.

BIBLIOGRAPHY

Adcock, F.E. (1956) *Caesar as man of letters*, Cambridge.
Ahmad, S.M. (1995) *A history of Arab-Islamic geography (9th-16th century A.D.)*, Amman.
Albert, K. (1902) *Strabo als Quelle des Josephus*, Aschaffenburg.
Alonso-Núñez, J.M. (1982) 'L'opposizione contro l'imperialismo Romano e contro il principato nella storiografia del Tempo di Augusto', *RSA* 12: 131–41.
—— (1983) 'Die Abfolge der Weltreiche bei Polybios und Dionysios von Halikarnassos', *Historia* 32: 411–26.
—— (1984) 'Die Weltreichsukzession bei Strabo', *ZRGG* 36, 1: 53–4.
—— (1987) 'An Augustan world history: The *Historiae Philippicae* of Pompeius Trogus', *Greece and Rome* 34, 1: 56–72.
—— (1992) 'El nordeste de la Península Ibérica en Estrabón', *Faventia* 14, 1: 91–5.
—— (1994) 'Die Weltgeschichte bei Poseidonios', *GB* 20: 87–108.
—— (1995) 'Die Weltgeschichte des Nikolaos von Damaskos', *Storia della Storiografia* 27: 3–15.
Aly, W. (1957) *Strabon von Amaseia*, vol. 4, Bonn.
—— (1964) 'Der Geograph Strabon als Philosoph', in *Miscellanea Critica B.G. Teubner*, Leipzig, 9–19.
—— (1968) *Strabonis Geographica*, vol. 1, Bonn.
Ambaglio, D. (1988) 'Strabone e la storiografia greca frammentaria', in *Studi di storia e storiografia antiche per Emilio Gabba*, Pavia, 73–83.
—— (1990) 'Gli Historika Hypomnemata di Strabone', *MIL* 39, 5: 377–425.
Anastasiadis, V.I. and Souris G.A. (1992) 'Theophanes of Mytilene: A new inscription relating to his early career', *Chiron* 22: 377–82.
Anastos, M.V. (1952) 'Pletho, Strabo and Columbus', *AIPHOS* 12: 1–18.
Anderson, J.G.C. (1923) 'Some questions bearing on the date and place of composition of Strabo's Geography', in *Anatolian Studies presented to Sir W.M. Ramsay*, Manchester, 1–13.
Anderson, J.G.C., Cumont, F. and Grégoire, H. (1910) *Recueil des inscriptions grecques et latines du Pont et de l'Arménie*, Bruxelles (*Studia Pontica* 3).
André, J. (1949) *La vie et l'oeuvre d'Asinius Pollion*, Paris.
Arafat, K. (1996) *Pausanias' Greece. Ancient artists and Roman rulers*, Cambridge.
Armayor, O.K. (1985) *Herodotus' autopsy of the Fayoum: Lake Moeris and the Labyrinth of Egypt*, Amsterdam.
Armstrong, D.C. (1989) *Horace*, Yale.
Aujac, G. (1966) *Strabon et la science de son temps*, Paris.
—— (1969) 'Sur une définition d'ARETH', *REG* 82: 390–403.
—— (1972) 'Les traires "Sur l'ocean" et les zones terrestres', *REA* 74: 74–85.

—— (1983) 'Strabon et le Stoicism', *Diotima* 11: 17–29.

—— (1986) 'Strabon et la musique', in G. Maddoli (ed.) *Strabone, contributi allo studio della personalità e dell'opera*, vol. 2, Perugia, 11–25.

Aujac, G. and Lasserre, F. (1969) *Strabon, Géographie* I [Book 1], Paris.

Aymard, J. (1951) *Essai sur les chasses romaines des origines à la fin du siècle des Antonins*, Paris.

Baladié, R. (1978) *Strabon, Geographie* V [Book 8], Paris.

—— (1980) *Le Péloponnèse de Strabon. Étude de géographie historique*, Paris.

—— (1989) *Strabon, Géographie* IV [Book 7], Paris.

—— (1996) *Strabon, Géographie* VI [Book 9], Paris.

Baldry, H.C. (1965) *The unity of mankind in Greek thought*, Cambridge.

Bar-Kochva, B. (1997) 'Mosaic Judaism and Judaism of the Second Temple period – the Jewish ethnography of Strabo', *Tarbiz* 66, 3: 297–336 (Hebrew), English summary: v–vi.

Barbour, K.M. (1974) 'The geographical knowledge of the Greeks and Romans', *Museum Africum* 3: 57–76.

Bassi, D. (1941–2) 'La Mitologia in Strabone', *RIL* 75, 2: 319–26.

Beazley, C.R. (1949) *The dawn of modern geography*, New York.

Bekker-Nielsen, T. (1988) 'Terra Incognita: The subjective geography of the Roman Empire', in *Studies in ancient history and numismatics presented to Rudi Thomsen*, Aarhus, 148–61.

Bellemore, J. (1984) *Nicolaus of Damascus, Life of Augustus*, Bristol.

Berger, H. (1964) *Die geographischen Fragmente des Eratosthenes*, Amsterdam.

Biffi, N. (1988) *L'Italia di Strabone. Testo, traduzione e commento dei libri V e VI della Geografia*, Genova.

Biraschi, A.M. (1981) 'Q. Elio Tuberone in Strabone V,3,3?', *Athenaeum* 59: 195–9.

—— (1984) 'Strabone e la difesa di Omero nei prolegomena', in F. Prontera (ed.), *Strabone, contributi allo studio della personalità e dell'opera*, vol. 1, Perugia, 129–53.

—— (1986) 'Strabone e gli 'onomata' omerici. A proposito di Strab. VIII,3,2', in G. Maddoli (ed.), *Strabone, contributi allo studio della personalità e dell'opera*, vol. 2, Perugia, 67–77.

—— (ed.) (1994a) *Strabone e la Grecia*, Perugia.

—— (1994b) 'Strabone e Omero. Aspetti della tradizione omerica nella descrizione del Peloponneso', in A.M. Biraschi (ed.), *Strabone e la Grecia*, Perugia, 25–57.

Biraschi, A.M. et al. (1981) *Strabone saggio di Bibliografia 1469–1978*, Perugia.

Bölte, F. (1938) 'Triphylien bei Strabon. Eine Quellenuntersuchung', *RhM* 87: 142–60.

Bonner, S.F. (1939) *The literary treatises of Dionysius of Halicarnassus*, Cambridge.

Bosworth, A.B. (1972) 'Asinius Pollio and Augustus', *Historia* 21: 441–73.

Bosworth, A.B. and Wheatley, P.V. (1998) 'The origins of the Pontic house', *JHS* 118, 155–64.

Bowersock, G.W. (1965) *Augustus and the Greek world*, Oxford.

—— (1992) 'Les Grecs 'barbarisés'', *Ktema* 17: 249–57 = 'The barbarism of the Greeks', *HSCPh* 97 (1995) 3–14.

Bradford Welles, C. (1962) 'Hellenistic Tarsus', *MUSJ* 38, 2: 43–75.

Brodersen, K. (1995) *Terra Cognita. Studien zur römischen Raumerfassung*, Hildesheim.

Calzoni, A. (1940) *Conception de la géographie d'après Strabon*, Lugano.

Capelle, W. (1932) 'Griechische Ethik und römischer Imperialismus', *Klio* 25: 86–113.

Chavallier, R. (1989) *Roman roads*, London.

Clarke, K. (1997) 'In search of the author of Strabo's Geography', *JRS* 87: 92–110.

Clavel-Lévêque, M. (1974) 'Les Gauls et les Gaulois: Pour une analyse du fonctionnement de la *Géographie* de Strabon', *DHA* 1: 75–93.

Coleman, K.M. (1990) 'Fatal Charades: Roman executions staged as mythological enactments', *JRS* 80: 44–73.

Cordano, F. (1994) 'La città cretesi in Strabone', in A.M. Biraschi (ed.) *Strabone e la Grecia*, Perugia, 187–98.

Crawford, M.H. (1978) 'Greek intellectuals and the Roman aristocracy in the first century B.C.', in P.D.A. Garnsey and C.R. Whittaker (eds), *Imperialism in the ancient world*, Cambridge, 193–207.

Cruz Andreotti, G. (1994) 'La visión de Gades en Estrabón. Elaboración de un paradigma geográfico', *DHA* 20, 1: 57–85.

—— (ed.) (1999) *Estrabón e Iberia: nuevas perspectivas de estudio*, Malaga.

Cumont F. and Cumont E. (1906) *Voyage d'exploration archéologique dans le Pont et la petite Arménie*, Bruxelles (*Studia Pontica* 2).

Däbritz, R. (1905) *De Artemidoro Strabonis auctore capita tria*, Leipzig.

De Lacy, P. (1948) 'Stoic views on poetry', *AJPh* 69, 3: 241–71.

Desideri, P. (1972) 'L'interpretazione dell'impero Romano in Posidonio', *RIL* 106, 481–93.

—— (1992) 'Eforo e Strabone sui 'popoli misti' (Str. XIV, 5.23–26)', in M. Sordi (ed.), *Autocoscienza e rappresentazione dei popoli nell'antichità*, Milan, (*Contributi dell'Istituto si storia antica*, 18. Scienze storiche 49), 19–31.

Dessau, H. (1924) *Geschichte der römischen Kaiserzeit*, vol. 1, Berlin.

Dickie, M.W. (1996) 'What is a *Kolossos* and how were *Kolossoi* made in the Hellenistic period?', *GRBS* 37, 3: 237–57.

Dicks, D.R. (1955) 'The KLIMATA in Greek geography', *CQ* 5: 248–55.

—— (1956) 'Strabo and the KLIMATA', *CQ* 6: 243–7.

—— (1960) *The geographical fragments of Hipparchus*, London.

Dilke, O.A.W. (1985) *Greek and Roman maps*, London.

—— (1987a) 'Maps in the service of the state: Roman cartography to the end of the Augustan era', in J.B. Harley and D. Woodward (eds), *History of cartography*, vol. 1, Chicago, 201–11.

—— (1987b) 'Itineraries and geographical maps in the early and late Roman empires', in J.B. Harley and D. Woodward (eds), *History of cartography*, vol. 1, Chicago, 234–57.

Diller, A. (1934) 'Geographical latitudes in Eratosthenes, Hipparchus and Posidonius', *Klio* 27: 258–69.

—— (1954) 'The scholia on Strabo', *Traditio* 10: 29–50.

—— (1975) *The textual tradition of Strabo's Geography*, Amsterdam.

—— (1986) *Tradition of the minor Greek geographers*, New York.

Dion, R. (1973) 'La géographie d'Homère inspiratrice de grand desseins impériaux', *BAGB* 4, 4: 463–85.

—— (1977) *Aspects politiques de la géographie antique*, Paris.

Dirkzwager, A. (1975) *Strabo über Gallia Narbonensis*, Leiden.

Dobson, J.F. (1914) 'Boethus of Sidon', *CQ* 8: 88–90.

Dodds, E.R. (1973) *The ancient concept of progress and other essays on Greek literature and belief*, Oxford.

Domínguez Monedero, A.J. (1988) 'Los Romanos e Iberia como tema histórico en la 'Geografía' de Estrabón', *Actas il congreso Andaluz de Estudios Clasicos*, Malaga, vol. 1, 177–83.

Downey, G. (1941) 'Strabo on Antioch: notes on his method', *TAPhA* 72: 85–95.

Drijvers, J.W. (1998) 'Strabo on Parthia and the Parthians', in J. Wiesenhöfer (ed.) *Das Partherreich und seine Zeugnisse*, Stuttgart, 279–93 (*Historia Einzelschriften* 122).

Dubois, M. (1891a) *Examen de la géographie de Strabon. Étude critique de la méthode et des sources*, Paris.

—— (1891b) 'Strabon et Polybe', *REG* 4: 343–56.

Dueck, D. (1999a) 'The date and method of composition of Strabo's *Geography*', *Hermes* 127, 4: 467–78.

—— (1999b) 'Historical *exempla* and their role in a geographical context', forthcoming in *Studies in Latin Literature and Roman History, Collection Latomus*.

Edelstein, L. and Kidd, I.G. (1972) *Posidonius: The Fragments*, Cambridge.

Engels, J. (1998a) 'Die Geschichte des Alexanderzuges und das Bild Alexanders des Großen in Strabons Geographika – Zur Interpretation der augusteischen Kulturgeographie Strabons als Quelle seiner historischen Auffassungen', in W. Will (ed.), *Alexander der Große. Eine Welteroberung und ihr Hintergrund* (Antiquitas Serie I), Bonn, 131–72.

—— (1998b) 'Die strabonische Kulturgeographie in der Tradition der antiken geographischen Schriften und ihre Bedeutung für die antike Kartographie', *Orbis Terrarum* 4: 63–114.

—— (1999) *Augusteische Oikumenegeographie und Universalhistorie im Werk Strabons von Amaseia*, Stuttgart.

Fabricius, J.A. (1717) *Bibliotheca Graeca, Liber IV*, Hamburg.

Fabricius, W. (1888) *Theophanes von Mytilene und Quintus Dellius als Quellen der Geographie des Strabon*, Strassburg.

Ferrary, J.L. (1987) *Philhellenisme et impérialisme. Aspects idéologiques de la conquête romaine du monde hellénistique*, Paris.

Floratos, C.S. (1972) *Strabon über Literatur und Poseidonios*, Athens.

Formige, C.J. (1949) *Le Trophée des Alpes (La Turbie)*, Paris.

Forte, B. (1972) *Rome and the Romans as the Greeks Saw Them*, Rome (*Papers and Monographs of the American Academy in Rome*, 24).

Fraser, P.M. (1970) 'Eratosthenes of Cyrene', *PBA* 61: 175–207.

—— (1972) *Ptolemaic Alexandria*, Oxford.

Funke, P. (1991) 'Strabone, la geografia storica e la struttura etnica della Grecia nord-occidentale', in F. Prontera (ed.), *Geografia storica della Grecia antica, Tradizioni e problemi*, Rome, 174–93.

Gabba, E. (1982) 'Political and cultural aspects of the classicistic revival in the Augustan age', *ClAnt* 1, 1: 43–65.

—— (1984) 'The historians and Augustus' in F. Millar and E. Segal (eds), *Caesar Augustus. Seven aspects*, Oxford, 61–88.

—— (1991) *Dionysius and the history of archaic Rome*, Berkeley.

Gagé, J. (1950) *Res Gestae Divi Augusti*, Paris.

García Bellido, A. (1945) *España y los Españoles hace dos mil años según la Geografía de Strabón*, Madrid.

Garlan, Y. (1975) *War in the ancient world. A social history*, London.

Geiger, J. (1971) *A Commentary on Plutarch's Cato Minor*, Oxford.

—— (1985) *Cornelius Nepos and ancient political biography*, Stuttgart (*Historia Einzelschriften* 47).

—— (1992) 'Julian of Ascalon', *JHS* 112: 31–43.

Gigante, M. (1990) *Philodemus in Italy. The books from Herculaneum*, Ann Arbor.

Glover, T.R. (1969) 'Strabo the Greek in the world of Caesar', in *Greek Byways*, New York and London, 223–59.

Gonzáles, J. (1984) 'Tabula Siarensis, Fortunales Siarensis et Municipia Ciuium Romanorum', *ZPE* 55: 55–100.

Gonzáles Ponce, F.J. (1990) 'Estrabón, Geografía III.5.1 [C 167] y la concepción hodológica del espacio geográfico', *Habis* 21: 79–92.

Goold, G.P. (1961) 'A Greek professional circle at Rome', *TAPhA* 92: 168–92.

Göransson, T. (1995) *Albinus, Alcinous, Arius Didymus*, Göteborg.

Gow, A.S.P. and Page, D.L. (1968) *The Greek Anthology. The Garland of Philip and some contemporary epigrams*, Cambridge.

BIBLIOGRAPHY

Greco, E. (1986) 'Strabone e la topografia storica della Magna Grecia', in G. Maddoli (ed.), *Strabone, contributi allo studio della personalità e dell'opera*, vol. 2, Perugia, 121–34.

Griffin, J. (1984) 'Augustus and the poets' in F. Millar and E. Segal (eds), *Caesar Augustus. Seven aspects*, Oxford, 189–218.

Grilli, A. (1979) 'Die Gebirge Tirols: Poseidonios bei Strabo', *APA* 4: 46–7.

Grimal, P. (1945) 'Auguste et Athenodore', *REA* 47: 261–73.

—— (1946) 'Auguste et Athenodore', *REA* 48: 62–79.

Güngerich, R. (1950) *Die Küstenbeschreibung in der griechischen Literatur*, Münster (*Orbis Antiquus* 4).

Haarhof, T.J. (1948) *The stranger at the gate. Aspects of exclusiveness and co-operation in ancient Greece and Rome*, Oxford.

Habicht, C. (1998) *Pausanias' guide to ancient Greece*, California.

Häbler, A. (1884) 'Hat Strabo seine Geographie in Rom verfasst?', *Hermes* 19: 235–41.

Hahm, D.E. (1990) 'The ethical doxography of Arius Didymus', *ANRW* II.36.4: 2935-3055.

Hahn, L. (1906) *Rom und Romanismus im griechisch-römischen Osten*, Leipzig.

Heeren, A.H.L. (1823) *De fontibus geographicorum Strabonis*, Göttingen.

Heidel, W. H. (1976) *The frame of the ancient Greek maps*, New York.

Heilmann, C. (1885) *Quibus auctoribus Strabo usus sit in describenda ora maris Pontici a Byzantio usque ad Tanaim*, Halle.

Hering, W. (1970) 'Geographie und römische Politik. Bemerkungen zur Beschreibung Galliens bei Strabon', *ACD* 6: 45–51.

Hillscher, A. (1891) *Hominum litteratorum Graecorum ante Tiberii mortem in urbe Roma commoratorum historia critica*, Leipzig (ex supplementis 18 Annalium Philologicorum), 355–444.

Huby, P.M. (1981) 'An excerpt from Boethus of Sidon's Commentary on the Categories?', *CQ* 31, 2: 398–409.

Hunrath, G. (1879), *Die Quellen Strabo's im sechsten Buche*, Cassel.

Isaac, B. (1992) *The limits of empire. The Roman army in the east*, Oxford.

Jacob, C. (1986) 'Cartographie et rectification. Essai de lecture des 'Prolégomènes' de la 'Géographie' de Strabon', in G. Maddoli (ed.), *Strabone, contributi allo studio della personalità e dell'opera*, vol. 2, Perugia, 29–64.

Jaeger, M. (1995) 'Reconstructing Rome: The Campus Martius and Horace ode 1.8', *Arethusa* 28: 177–91.

James, P.E. and Martin, G.J. (1981) *All possible worlds. A history of geographical ideas*, New York.

Jameson, S. (1968) 'Chronology of the campaigns of Aelius Gallus and C. Petronius', *JRS* 58: 71–84.

Janni, P. (1984) *La mappa e il periplo. Cartografia antica e spazio odologico*, Rome.

Jocelyn, H.D. (1976–7) 'The ruling class of the Roman republic and Greek philosophers', *BRL* 59: 323–66.

Jones, H.L. (1917) Introduction to the *Loeb Classical Library* translation, vol. 1, Cambridge, Mass.

Kajanto, I. (1965) *The Latin Cognomina*, Helsinki (*Commentationes Humanarum Litterarum* 36/2).

Kauchtschischwili, T. (1978) 'Strabon und das alte Georgien', *Philologus* 122: 68–87.

Kennedy, G. (1972) *The art of rhetoric in the Roman world*, Princeton.

Kidd, I.G. (1988) *Posidonius: the commentary*, Cambridge.

Kienast, D. (1969) 'Augustus und Alexander', *Gymnasium* 76: 430–56.

Kleiner, F.S. (1985) *The arch of Nero in Rome. A study of the Roman honorary arch before and under Nero*, Rome.

210

Klotz, A. (1910) *Caesarstudien, nebst einer Analyse der strabonischen Beschreibung von Gallien und Britannien*, Leipzig.

—— (1931) 'Die geographischen commentarii des Agrippa und ihre Überreste', *Klio* 24: 38–58; 386–466.

Kramer, B. and Hübner, R. (1976) *Kölner Papyri (P. Köln)*, vol. 1, Cologne.

Krebbler, B. (1972) 'Ναυστολογοι bei Strabon: ein neues Papyrusfragment', *ZPE* 9, 3: 204–21.

Kühn, D.C.G. (ed.) (1827–33) *Claudii Galeni: opera omnia*, Leipzig.

Lasserre, F. (1966) *Strabon, Géographie* II (Books 3–4), Paris.

—— (1967) *Strabon, Géographie* III (Books 5–6), Paris.

—— (1971) *Strabon, Géographie* VII (Book 10), Paris.

—— (1975) *Strabon, Géographie* VIII (Book 11), Paris.

—— (1977) 'Strabon devant l'empire romain', *REL* 55: 15–16.

—— (1981) *Strabon, Géographie* IX (Book 12), Paris.

—— (1983) 'Strabon devant l'empire romain', *ANRW* II. 30. 1: 867–96.

—— (1984) 'Histoire de première main dans la *Géographie* de Strabon', in F. Prontera (ed.) *Strabone, contributi allo studio della personalità e dell'opera*, vol. 1, Perugia, 11–26.

Law, W.J. (1846) *Some remarks on the Alpine passes of Strabo*, London.

Leaf, W. (1916) 'Strabo and Demetrios of Skepsis', *ABSA* 22: 23–47.

—— (1923) *Strabo on the Troad, Book XIII, Cap. I*, Cambridge.

Les Cases, E. (1968) *Mémorial de Sainte-Hélène*, Paris.

Lindsay, H. (1997a) 'Strabo on Apellicon's library', *RhM* 140: 290–8.

—— (1997b) 'Syme's Anatolica and the date of Strabo's Geography', *Klio* 79: 484–507.

Long, A.A. (1974) *Hellenistic philosophy. Stoics, Epicureans, Sceptics*, London.

—— (1992) 'Stoic readings of Homer'. in R. Lamberton and J.J. Keaney (eds), *Homer's ancient readers. The hermeneutics of Greek epic's earliest exegetes*, Princeton, 41–66.

Ludlam, I. (1997) 'The God of Moses according to Strabo', *Tarbiz* 66, 3: 337–49 (Hebrew), English summary: vi–vii.

Lünemann, G.H. (1803) *Descriptio Caucasi gentiumque Caucasiarum ex Strabone, comparatis scriptoribus recentioribus*, Leipzig.

Lulofs, H.J. (1929) *Strabo over Scythen. Specimen van antieke anthropo-geographie*, Utrecht.

McGing, B.C. (1986) *The foreign policy of Mithridates VI Eupator king of Pontus*, Leiden.

McGushin, P. (1977) *C. Sallustius Crispus Bellum Catilinae. A commentary*, Leiden.

Maddoli, G. (ed.) (1986) *Strabone, contributi allo studio della personalità e dell'opera*, vol. 2, Perugia.

—— (ed.) (1988) *Strabone e l'Italia antica*, Perugia.

Mancinetti Santamaria, G. (1978–9) 'Strabone e l'ideologia Augustea', *AFLPer* 16, 2: 129–42.

Marrou, H.I. (1965) *Histoire de l'éducation dans l'antiquité*, Paris.

Martin, P.M. (1971) 'La propagande Augustéenne dans les Antiquités Romaines de Denys d'Halicarnasse (Livre I)', *REL* 49: 162–79.

Mason, H.J. (1974) *Greek terms for Roman institutions. A lexicon and analysis*, Toronto.

Massaro, G.D. (1986) 'I moduli della narrazione storica nei libri di Strabone sull'Italia meridionale', in G. Maddoli (ed.), *Strabone, contributi allo studio della personalità e dell'opera*, vol. 2, Perugia, 81–117.

Mayer, R. (1994) *Horace Epistles Book I*, Cambridge.

Mayerson, P. (1995) 'Aelius Gallus at Cleopatris (Suez) and on the Red Sea', *GRBS* 36, 1: 17–24.

Meyer, P. (1890) *Straboniana*, Grimma.

Millar, F. and Segal, E. (eds) (1984) *Caesar Augustus. Seven aspects*, Oxford.

Miquel, A. (1967) *La géographie humaine du monde musulman jusqu'au milieu du 11ème siècle*, Paris.

Momigliano, A. (1975) *Alien wisdom. The limits of Hellenization*, Cambridge.

Morel, W. (1975) *Fragmenta poetarum Latinorum epicorum et lyricorum*, Stuttgart.

Morr, J. (1926) *Die Quellen von Strabons drittem Buch*, Leipzig.

Moscati Castelnuovo, L. (1987) 'Sul rapporto storiografico tra Antioco di Siracusa e Strabone (Nota a Strab. VI 1,6 C 257)', in *Studi di antichità in memoria di Clementia Gatti,* Milano, (*Quaderni di Acme* 9), 237–46.

Moynihan, R. (1985) 'Geographical mythology and Roman imperial ideology', in R. Winkes (ed.), *The age of Augustus*, Providence, RI, 149–62.

Müller, R. (1993) 'Das Barbarenbild des Poseidonios und seine Stellung in der philosophischen Tradition', *Emerita* 61, 1: 41–52.

Munz, R. (1918) *Quellenkritische Untersuchungen zu Strabo's Geographie mit besonderer Rücksicht auf die posidonianische Sprachtheorie*, Basel.

—— (1929) *Poseidonios und Strabon*, Göttingen.

Musti, D. (1988) *Strabone e la Magna Grecia. Città e popoli dell'Italia antica*, Padua.

—— (1995) 'Sul lessico coloniale di Strabone', *Kokalos* 41: 345–7.

Mynors, R.A.B. (1990) *Virgil, Georgics*, Oxford.

Neumann, K.J. (1881) *Strabons Quellen im elften Buche. I. Kaukasien*, Leipzig.

—— (1886) 'Strabons Gesammturtheil über die homerische Geographie', *Hermes* 21: 134-41.

Nicolai, R. (1984) 'Un sistema di localizzazione geografika relativa. Aorsi e Siraci in Strab. XI 5, 7–8', in F. Prontera (ed.) *Strabone, contributi allo studio della personalità e dell'opera*, vol. 1, Perugia, 101–25.

Nicolet, C. (1991) *Space, geography and politics in the early Roman empire*, Ann Arbor.

Niese, B. (1877) 'Apollodors Commentar zum Schiffskataloge als Quelle Strabo's', *RhM* 32: 267–307.

—— (1878) 'Beiträge zur Biographie Strabos', *Hermes* 13: 33–45.

—— (1883) 'Straboniana', *RhM* 38: 567–602.

—— (1887) 'Straboniana', *RhM* 42: 559–81.

Nisbet, R.G.M. and Hubbard, M. (1970) *A commentary on Horace: Odes book 1*, Oxford.

Noé, E. (1988) 'Considerazioni sull'impero Romano in Strabone e Cassio Dione', *RIL* 122: 101–24.

Obbink, D. (1994) *Philodemus and poetry*, Oxford.

—— (ed.) (1996) *Philodemus On Piety*, Oxford.

Olshausen, E. (1974) 'Zum Hellenisierungsprozess am pontischen Königshof', *AncSoc* 5: 153–70.

Oniga, R. (1995) *Sallustio e l'etnografia*, Pisa.

Ormerod, H.A. (1922) 'The campaigns of Servilius Isauricus against the pirates', *JRS* 12: 35–56.

Otto, P. (1889) 'Strabonis ΙΣΤΟΡΙΚΩΝ ΥΠΟΜΝΗΜΑΤΩΝ Fragmenta', *LS* suppl. 11: 1–224.

Pais, E. (1886) 'Straboniana. Contributo allo studio delle fonti della Storia e dell' amministrazione Romana', *RFIC* 15: 97–246 (Printed again in Bologna, 1977: 1-150).

—— (1908) 'The time and place in which Strabo composed his historical Geography', in *Ancient Italy*, Chicago, 379–428.

Pédech, P. (1956) 'La géographie de Polybe: Structure et contenu du livre XXXIV des Histoires', *LEC* 24, 1: 3–24.

—— (1971) 'La géographie urbaine chez Strabon', *AncSoc* 2: 234–53.

—— (1972) 'Strabon Historien', in *Studi classici in onore di Q. Cataudella*, Catania, vol. 2: 395–408.

—— (1974a) 'L'analyse géographique chez Posidonius', in R.Chevallier (ed.), *Littérature gréco-romaine et géographie historique. Mélanges à R. Dion*, Paris, 31–43.

—— (1974b) 'Strabon Historien d'Alexandre', *GB* 2, 129–45.

Peter, H. (1967) *Historicorum Romanorum Reliquiae*, Stuttgart (repr. of 1906).

Picard, G.C. (1957) *Les Trophées Romains. Contribution à l'histoire de la réligion et de l'art triomphal de Rome*, Paris.

Plácido Suárez, D. (1987–8) 'Estrabon III: el territorio Hispano, la geografia Griega y el imperialismo Romano', *Habis* 18–19: 243–56.

Pothecary, S. (1995) 'Strabo, Polybios, and the stade', *Phoenix* 49, 1: 49–67.

—— (1997) 'The expression 'Our Times' in Strabo's Geography', *CPh* 92, 3: 235–46.

Prandi, L. (1988a) 'La critica storica di Strabone alla geografia di Erodoto', in M. Sordi (ed.), *Geografia e storiografia nel mondo classico*, Milan (*Contributi dell'Istituto di storia antica*, 14. *Scienze storiche* 41), 52–72.

—— (1988b) 'Strabone ed Eforo; un'ipotesi sugli *Historikà Hypomnémata*', *Aevum* 62: 50-60.

Price, M.J. and Trell, B.L. (1977) *Coins and their cities. Architecture on the ancient coins of Greece, Rome and Palestine*, Detroit.

Prontera, F. (1984a) 'Prima di Strabone: Materiali per uno studio della geografia antica come genere letterario', in F. Prontera (ed.) (1984) *Strabone, contributi allo studio della personalità e dell'opera*, vol. 1, Perugia, 189–256.

—— (ed.) (1984b) *Strabone, contributi allo studio della personalità e dell'opera*, vol. 1, Perugia.

Raaflaub, K.A. and Samons, L.J. (1992) 'Opposition to Augustus' in K.A. Raaflaub and M. Toher (eds), *Between republic and empire. Interpretations of Augustus and his principate*, Berkeley, 417–54.

Radt, S.L. (1991) 'Eine neue Strabonausgabe', *Mnemosyne* 44: 305–26.

—— (1994) 'Tragikfragmente in Strabons Beschreibung Griechenlands', in A.M. Biraschi (ed.) *Strabone e la Grecia*, Perugia, 61–91.

—— (1996) 'Aus der Arbeit an der Groninger Strabonausgabe', *Philologus* 140, 1: 183–5.

Radt, S.L. and Drijvers, J.W. (1993) 'Die Groninger Neuedition von Strabons Geographika, vorgestellt anhand des Abschnittes über Troia', *Studia Troica* 3: 201–31.

Ramage, E.S. (1987) *The nature and purpose of Augustus' 'Res Gestae'*, Stuttgart (*Historia Einzelschriften* 54).

Rawson, E. (1985) *Intellectual life in the late Roman republic*, London.

Reesor, M.E. (1951) *The political theory of the old and middle Stoa*, New York.

Rhys Roberts, W. (1900) 'The literary circle of Dionysius of Halicarnassus', *CR* 14: 439–42.

Richard, J.C. (1970) '"Mausoleum": D'Halicarnasse à Rome, puis à Alexandrie', *Latomus* 29: 370–88.

Richards, G.C. (1941) 'Strabo, the Anatolian who failed of Roman recognition', *Greece and Rome* 10: 79–90.

Richardson, L. (1992) *A new topographical dictionary of ancient Rome*, Baltimore and London.

Richardson, N.J. (1992) 'Aristotle's reading of Homer and its background', in R. Lamberton and J.J. Keaney (eds), *Homer's ancient readers. The hermeneutics of Greek epic's earliest exegetes*, Princeton, 30–40.

Ridgeway, W. (1888) 'Contributions to Strabo's biography', *CR* 2: 84.

Riese, A. (1964) *Geographi Latini Minores*, Hildesheim (repr.; 1st edn, Heilbronn, 1878).

Riley, M.T. (1995) 'Ptolemy's use of his predecessors' data', *TAPhA* 125: 221–50.

Rist, J.M. (1969) *Stoic philosophy*, Cambridge.

Robert, L. (1940) 'La bibliothèque de Nysa de Carie', *Hellenica* 1: 144–8.
Robinson, O. (1977) 'Fire prevention at Rome', *RIDA* 24: 377–88.
Roddaz, J.M. (1984) *Marcus Agrippa*, Rome.
Roller, D.W. (1998) *The building program of Herod the Great*, California.
Romer, F.E. (1979) 'Gaius Caesar's military diplomacy in the east', *TAPhA* 109: 199-214.
Romm, J.S. (1992) *The edges of the earth in ancient thought*, Princeton.
Ruge, G. (1888) *Quaestiones Strabonianae*, Leipzig.
Sallmann, K.G. (1971) *Die Geographie des älteren Plinius in ihrem Verhältnis zu Varro. Versuch einer Quellenanalyse*, Berlin.
Salmeri, G. (1988) 'Tra politica e antiquaria: Letture di Strabone nel XV e XVI secolo', in G. Maddoli (ed.), *Strabone e l'Italia antica*, Perugia, 289–312.
Sandbach, F.H. (1975) *The Stoics*, London.
Sbordone, F. (1981) 'La tradizione manoscritta di Strabone, di Tolomeo e dei geografi greci minori', in E. Flores (ed.), *La critica testuale greco-latina, oggi Metodi e problemi*, Rome, 331–42.
—— (1982) 'Riconstruzione dei frammenti di Strabone, Geografia VII', *ICS* 7: 197–206.
Schenkeveld, D.M. (1976) 'Strabo on Homer', *Mnemosyne* 29: 52–64.
Schmitt, R. (1983) 'Die Sprachverhältnisse in den östlichen Provinzen des römischen Reiches', *ANRW* II. 29. 2: 554–86.
Schnabel, P. (1935) 'Die Weltkarte des Agrippa als wissenschaftliches Mittelglied zwischen Hipparch und Ptolemaeus', *Philologus* 90: 405–40.
Schulten, A. (1952) *Estrabón Geographía de Iberia*, Barcelona (*Fontes Hispaniae Antiquae* 6).
Schweighaeuser, I. (1805) *Animadversiones in Athenaei Deipnosophistas*, Strasbourg.
Shackleton-Bailey, D.R. (ed.) (1965) *Cicero's Letters to Atticus*, vol. 1, Cambridge.
Sherwin-White, A.N. (1967) 'Strabo and the Northerners', in *Racial prejudice in imperial Rome*, Cambridge, 1–13.
Sihler, E.G. (1923) 'Strabo of Amaseia: his personality and his works', *AJPh* 44: 134–44.
Silberberg-Peirce, S. (1986) 'The many faces of the Pax Augusta: Images of war and peace in Rome and Gallia Narbonensis', *Art History* 9, 3: 306–24.
Sitwell, N.H.H. (1981) *Roman roads in Europe*, London.
Smith, R.R.R. (1988) 'Simulacra gentium: the Ethne from the Sebasteion in Aphrodisias', *JRS* 78: 50–77.
Smyth, H.W. (1956) *Greek grammar*, Cambridge, Mass.
Sollima, F. (1897) *Le fonti di Strabone nella geografia della Sicilia (VI.265–274 C)*, Messina.
Sordi, M. (1982) 'Timagene di Alessandria: uno storico ellenocentrico e filobarbaro', *ANRW* II.30.1: 775–97.
von Staden, H. (1989) *Herophilus. The art of medicine in early Alexandria*, Cambridge.
Starr, R.J. (1987) 'The circulation of literary texts in the Roman world', *CQ* 37, 1: 213-23.
Steinbrück, C. (1909) *Die Quellen des Strabo im fünften Buche seiner Erdbeschreibung*, Halle.
Steinby, E.M. (1993) *Lexicon topographicum urbis Romae*, Rome.
Stemplinger, E. (1894) *Strabons literarhistorische Notizen*, Munich.
Stern, M. (1976) *Greek and Latin authors on Jews and Judaism*, Jerusalem.
von Stern, E. (1917) 'Bemerkungen zu Strabons Geographie der taurischen Chersonesos', *Hermes* 52: 1–38.
Strasburger, H. (1965) 'Poseidonios on problems of the Roman empire', *JRS* 55: 40–54.

Strenger, F. (1913) *Strabos Erdkunde von Libyen*, Berlin.

Sullivan, R.D. (1980) 'Dynasts in Pontus', *ANRW* II.7.2: 913–30.

Swain, S.C.R. (1990) 'Hellenic culture and the Roman heroes of Plutarch', *JHS* 110: 126–45.

—— (1996) *Hellenism and empire. Language, classicism, and power in the Greek world AD 50–250*, Oxford.

Syme, R. (1986) *The Augustan aristocracy*, Oxford.

—— (1995) *Anatolica. Studies in Strabo*, Oxford.

Szabó, A. (1985) 'Strabo und Pytheas – die geographische Breite von Marseille. Zur Frühgeschichte der mathematischen Geographie', *Historia Scientiarum* 29: 3–15.

Theiler, W. (1982) *Poseidonios. Die Fragmente*, vol. 1, Berlin.

Thollard, P. (1987) *Barbarie et civilisation chez Strabon. Étude critique des Livres III et IV de la Géographie*, Paris.

Thomas, R.F. (ed.) (1988) *Virgil, Georgics*, vol. 1, Cambridge.

Thompson, L.A. (1979) 'Strabo on civilization', *Platon* 31: 213–29.

Tierney, J.J. (1963) 'The map of Agrippa', *PRIA* 63 c: 151–66.

Toher, M. (1989) 'On the use of Nicolaus' historical fragments', *ClAnt* 8, 1: 159–72.

Toynbee, J.M.C. (1934) *The Hadrianic school. A chapter in the history of Greek art*, Cambridge.

Trotta, F. (1999) 'Estrabón, el libro III y la tradición geográfica', in G. Cruz Andreotti (ed.) *Estrabón e Iberia: nuevas perspectivas de estudio*, Malaga, 81–99.

Turcan, R. (1982) 'L'Autel de Rome et d'Auguste "ad confluentem"', *ANRW* II.12.1: 607–42.

Vanotti, G. (1992) 'Roma e il suo impero in Strabone', in M. Sordi (ed.), *Autocoscienza e rappresentazione dei popoli nell'antichità*, Milan (*Contributi dell'Istituto si storia antica*, 18. Scienze storiche 49), 173–94.

Vermeule, C.G. (1968) *Roman imperial art in Greece and Asia Minor*, Cambridge, Mass.

Visser, E. (1997) *Homers Katalog der Schiffe*, Stuttgart.

van der Vliet, E.C.L. (1977) *Strabo over Landen, Volken en Steden*, Amsterdam.

—— (1984) 'L'ethnographie de Strabon: Idéologie ou tradition?', in F. Prontera (ed.) *Strabone, contributi allo studio della personalità e dell'opera*, vol. 1, Perugia, 29–86.

Vogel, A. (1874) *De fontibus quibus Strabo in libro quinto decimo conscribendo usus sit*, Göttingen.

—— (1884) 'Strabons Quellen für das siebzehnte Buch', *Philologus* 43: 405–16.

Wacholder, B.Z. (1962) *Nicolaus of Damascus*, Berkeley.

Wachsmuth, C. (1891) 'Timagenes und Trogus', *RhM* 46: 465–79.

Waddy, L. (1963) 'Did Strabo visit Athens?', *AJA* 67: 296–300.

Wagner, D.L. (ed.) (1983) *The Seven Liberal Arts in the Middle Ages*, Bloomington.

Walbank, F.W. (1948) 'The geography of Polybius', *C&M* 9: 155–82.

—— (1957) *A historical commentary on Polybius*, vol. 1, Oxford.

—— (1972) *Polybius*, Berkeley.

—— (1979) *A historical commentary on Polybius*, vol. 3, Oxford.

Wallace, P.W. (1969) 'Strabo on Acrocorinth', *Hesperia* 38: 495–99.

—— (1970) Summary of P.W. Wallace, *Strabo and the catalogue of Ships* in *AJA* 74: 205.

—— (1972) 'Boiotia in the time of Strabo', *Proceedings of the First International Conference on Boiotian antiquities, Teiresias* supplement 1: 71–5.

—— (1979a) 'Did Strabo visit Boiotia?', in Wallace (1979b) 168–72.

—— (1979b) *Strabo's description of Boiotia, a commentary*, Heidelberg.

Weippert, O. (1972) *Alexander-Imitatio und römische Politik in republikanischer Zeit*, Augsburg.

215

Weiss, I. (1991) *Die Italienbücher des Strabon von Amaseia*, Frankfurt.

Weller, C.H. (1906) 'The extent of Strabo's travels in Greece', *CPh* 1: 339–56.

West, M.L. (ed.) (1966) *Hesiod, Theogony*, Oxford.

White, P. (1992) '"Pompeius Macer" and Ovid', *CQ* 42, 1: 210–18.

Wijsman, H.J.W. (1998) 'Thule applied to Britain', *Latomus* 57, 2: 318–23.

Wilkens, H. (1886) *Quaestiones de Strabonis aliorumque rerum Gallicarum auctorum fontibus*, Marburg.

Wiseman, T.P. (1979) 'Strabo on the Campus Martius: 5.3.8, C 235', *LCM* 4, 7: 129–34.

Woodhouse, C.M. (1986) *George Gemistos Plethon, the last of the Hellenes*, Oxford.

Wright, G.R.H. (1969) 'Strabo on funerary customs of Petra', *PEQ* 101: 113–16.

Wright, J.K. (1965) *The geographical lore of the time of the Crusades. A study in the history of medieval science and tradition in western Europe*, New York.

Yavetz, Z. (1984) 'The *Res Gestae* and Augustus' public image', in F. Millar and E. Segal (eds), *Caesar Augustus. Seven aspects*, Oxford, 1–36.

Zanker, P. (1988) *The power of images in the age of Augustus*, Ann Arbor.

Zimmermann, R. (1883) 'Quibus auctoribus Strabo in libro tertio Geographicorum conscribendo usus sit, quaeritur', in *Dissertationes Philologicae Halenses*, Halle, vol. 5, 329–64.

—— (1888) 'Posidonius und Strabo', *Hermes* 23: 103–30.

INDEX OF GEOGRAPHICAL
NAMES

island = is.; lake = l.; mountain = mt.; river = r.

217

INDEX OF PERSONAL NAMES

INDEX OF PERSONAL NAMES

Arius of Alexandria 9, 11, 139, 142
Arsinoe 105
Artemidorus of Cnidus 137
Artemidorus of Ephesus 19, 25, 43,
  59, 60, 93, 143, 155, 180, 181,
  182, 183, 184, 186
Artemis 19, 25, 82
Asander 137
Ascanius 95
Asclepiades of Bithynia 142
Asclepiades of Myrleia 141
Asclepius 27, 82
Asinius Pollio 70, 94, 135, 143, 180
Asinius Pollio of Tralleis 94
Athenaeus of Naucratis 10, 145, 151
Athenaeus of Seleucia 68, 140, 143
Athene 67, 100
Athenodorus of Tarsus 10, 11, 24, 65,
  68, 99, 140, 142, 143
Athenodorus Cordylion of Tarsus 139,
  143
Atticus see T. Pomponius Atticus
Augustus 3, 4, 9, 10, 11, 14, 20, 64,
  66, 70, 85, 86, 87, 88, 91, 94, 95,
  97–106, 107, 109, 110, 111, 114,
  115, 117, 119, 121, 123, 124, 125,
  126, 127, 128, 129, 130, 133, 134,
  135, 136, 137, 138, 139, 140, 141,
  142, 143, 147, 148, 149, 151, 163,
  174, 177, 178, 179, 180, 192 n.34
Aurelius, Catullus' friend 123
Autolycus 82

Balbus of Gades 136, 143
Bellerophon 174
Billarus 82
Boethus of Sidon 10, 11, 65, 68
Bogus of Mauretania 105
Borras 44
Brutus see D. Iunius Brutus

Caecilius of Calacte 133, 138, 142
C. Caesar 124
Caesar, Julius see C. Iulius Caesar
Calamis 82
Calanus 104
Cn. Calpurnius Piso 88, 142, 143, 152
L. Calpurnius Piso Caesoninus 140,
  143
Candace of Ethiopia 102, 111
Cato the elder see M. Porcius Cato
  Censorius

Cato the younger see M. Porcius Cato
  Uticensis
Catullus see C. Valerius Catullus
Ceres 86
Cicero see M. Tullius Cicero
M. Claudius Marcellus (cos. 166) 22,
  170
M. Claudius Marcellus (aed. 23) 139,
  141, 143
Claudius Ptolemy 57, 125, 152, 153
Cleanthes of Corinth 82
Cleitarchus of Alexandria 74, 186
Cleopatra VII 72, 99, 105, 121
Clüver, Philipp (Cluverius) 154
L. Coelius Antipater 93
Columbus, Christopher 153
Coponius 125
Cornelius Nepos 123
P. Cornelius Scipio Aemilianus 46, 53,
  87
L. Cornelius Sulla 7, 9, 71, 130
Cosmas Indicopleustes 152
Crassus see L. Licinius Crassus
Crates of Mallus 38, 39, 141, 169
Crinagoras of Mytilene 123, 124, 137,
  141, 143, 144
Cybele 19

Q. Dellius 94, 180
Demetrius of Scepsis 25, 36, 38, 39,
  77, 169, 179, 183, 184, 185
Democritus 64
Diodorus of Sardis 10, 11, 141, 144
Diodorus of Sicily 49, 72, 92
Diodotus (sculptor) 82
Diodotus of Sidon 10, 11, 69
Dionysius of Chalkis 205 n.47
Dionysius of Halicarnassus 88, 92, 93,
  131–3, 136, 138, 141, 142, 143, 172
Dionysius Atticus of Pergamon 138
Dionysius 'Periegetes' 152
Dionysus 35, 82, 86
Diotrephes 139
Domitius Marsus 138, 142
Dorylaus of Amisus (the general) 5, 6,
  7, 29
Dorylaus (the priest) 5, 6, 18
Drusus see Nero Drusus Claudius

Empedocles 13
Ennius 81, 96, 142
Enyo 18

224